Decolonizing Mission

Decolonizing Mission

Harvey C. Kwiyani

scm press

© 2025 Harvey Kwiyani

Published in 2025 by SCM Press

Editorial office
3rd Floor, Invicta House,
110 Golden Lane,
London EC1Y 0TG, UK
www.scmpress.co.uk

SCM Press is an imprint of Hymns Ancient & Modern Ltd
(a registered charity)

Hymns Ancient & Modern® is a registered trademark of
Hymns Ancient & Modern Ltd
13A Hellesdon Park Road, Norwich,
Norfolk NR6 5DR, UK

All rights reserved. No part of this publication may be reproduced,
stored in a retrieval system, or transmitted,
in any form or by any means, electronic, mechanical,
photocopying or otherwise, without the prior permission of
the publisher, SCM Press.

The Author has asserted their right under the Copyright, Designs and
Patents Act 1988 to be identified as the Author of this Work

British Library Cataloguing in Publication data

A catalogue record for this book is available
from the British Library

ISBN: 978-0-33-406319-3

EU GPSR Authorized Representative
LOGOS EUROPE, 9 rue Nicolas Poussin, 17000, LA ROCHELLE, France
Email: Contact@logoseurope.eu

No part of this book may be used or reproduced in any manner for the
purpose of training artificial intelligence technologies or systems.

Typeset by Regent Typesetting

To the memory of my dear friend and conversational partner, Peter Rowan (1967–2024), who went to be with the Lord as I finalized the manuscript of this book. A fellow labourer in the work of decolonizing mission who will not get to see the fruit of our conversations, he thought with me on many of the issues I have written about in this book. I am forever grateful for his friendship.

Every day is an opportunity not to be a colonizer.

Contents

Acknowledgements ix
Bible Acknowledgements xi
Preface xiii

Introduction 1

1 We Need an English Colony Here 20

2 Jesus and the Empire 41

3 Imperializing Jesus 66

4 To Dominate and Christianize 76

5 Whoever Wishes to Serve as a Soldier 108

6 Mission and Colonialism in the Nineteenth and Twentieth Centuries 128

7 Decolonizing Mission Language 143

8 Mission According to the Colonized 184

9 We Need a New Missiology 201

Bibliography 208
Index of Names and Subjects 219

Acknowledgements

The process of writing this book was a long and arduous one. I am grateful for the many friends who cheered me on. My team at Church Mission Society was very generous to let me miss some events so I could focus on writing. Jonny Baker believed in me more than I did myself. Cathy Ross and James Butler stretched my thinking in ways I could not on my own. Joseph Ola thought with me when I needed a sounding board. Nuam Hatzaw listened to me when I rumbled on about the need to decolonize mission.

My family, Nancy, Rochelle and Roxanne, allowed me to stay at the desk way into the night or to spend countless hours at The Coffeeshop so I could get some writing time. They have also been patient with me when I travelled around the world for research and to try out the argument I make in this book at conferences. Nancy held the house together when the demands of this book made me unavailable.

I owe gratitude to many people who have, in one way or another, helped me shape the argument I make in this book. Patrick Keifert, Jehu Hanciles, Zac Niringiye, Claudia Währisch-Oblau, Moritz Fischer and many others, I can never thank you enough.

David Shervington, Rachel Edge and Hannah Ward at SCM Press, I am always delighted to work with you.

Bible Acknowledgements

Scripture quotations, unless otherwise indicated, are from New Revised Standard Version Bible: Anglicized Edition, copyright © 1989, 1995 National Council of the Churches of Christ in the United States of America. Used by permission. All rights reserved worldwide.

Scripture quotations marked The Message are from are taken from The Message. Copyright 1993, 1994, 1995, 1996, 2000, 2001, 2002. Used by permission of NavPress Publishing Group.

Scripture quotations marked NRSVUE are from the New Revised Standard Version Updated Edition. Copyright © 2021 National Council of Churches of Christ in the United States of America. Used by permission. All rights reserved worldwide.

Scripture quotations marked NLT are from New Living Translation, copyright © 1996, 2004, 2015 by Tyndale House Foundation. Used by permission of Tyndale House Publishers, Inc., Carol Stream, Illinois 60188. All rights reserved.

Bible extracts marked KJV are from the Authorized Version of the Bible (The King James Bible), the rights in which are vested in the Crown, are reproduced by permission of the Crown's Patentee, Cambridge University Press.

Preface

Over the years, I have interested myself in the many lists of things that are attributed to Jesus that he never said or did, found on the internet and social media. A simple Google search for something like 'things Jesus never said' reveals numerous books, blogs and sermons dedicated to discussing why many Christians believe things about Jesus that he never said. Some of the lists are short, with as few as only two items, while others are long, containing as many as fifteen. Some of them are quite simple and straightforward – Jesus never said, 'God will never give you more than you can handle.' Others sound serious and controversial. Jesus never said, 'Women shall not preach in church.' Many of them will include such things as Jesus never said, 'I am God.' He never said, 'Follow me.' Indeed, he never said, 'Hate the sin, but love the sinner.' The intention of these lists is to disabuse the Church of its erroneous ideas about Jesus (and about things he is believed to have said) in order to have a better informed Body of Christ as his witness in the world. The prophet Hosea is correct in his assessment: '[God's] people are destroyed for lack of knowledge' (Hos. 4.6).

There is one thing that I have never seen on any of these lists that I think is critical to how we follow Jesus and bear witness to his name around the world today. Jesus never said, 'I need you to be my soldiers.' As a matter of fact, he never said, 'I need soldiers.' Nowhere in the Gospels did he ever say, 'I need an army.' Throughout his ministry, he never called upon his followers to form an army. He did not have an army when he ministered up and down in the villages of Galilee. He did not have an army when he was tried and crucified in Jerusalem. He carried no sword for, in his words, 'all who take the sword will perish by the sword' (Matt. 26.52). When he came to the end of his time on earth, he did not send the apostles to recruit or *mobilize* soldiers for him among the nations. His commandment was for the apostles to 'Go therefore and make disciples of all nations, baptizing them in the name of the Father and of the Son and of the Holy Spirit, and teaching them to obey everything that I have commanded you' (Matt. 28.19–20). He never asked his followers to give him their young men and women to join his army to go and fight for him at the frontiers of barbaric darkness in any other country or continent.

I have heard people talk about the 'Jesus Army', and I have wondered if he would tolerate such language. In first-century Palestine where Jesus lived, he knew that if he called for an army or asked his followers to be soldiers, his ministry would be cut short by the Romans who, being the dominant empire of his era, had legions of soldiers on the ready to put down anything that looked like an insurrection. He was aware, as he says in Matthew 26.31, that the Romans would effectively strike the shepherd to scatter the flock (quoting Zech. 13.7). Later on in the same Matthew 26, he did say that if he needed an army he could call upon the Father in heaven to provide him with military support: 'Do you think that I cannot appeal to my Father, and he will at once send me more than twelve legions of angels?' (Matt. 26.53). The fact that he did not do this should cause us to think carefully about how we carry on his work in the world today when it appears, because of mission's colonial legacy, that Jesus is a commander of a human army, complete with navy ships, stealth bombers and nuclear artillery.

The point of this book is that, since the conversion of Constantine, the work of witnessing for Christ and proclaiming the gospel of the kingdom of God have been unnecessarily attached to the Roman Empire, the Byzantine Empire and now the Western empires (including the British Empire in the nineteenth and twentieth centuries and the contemporary US Empire that, at the time of publishing this book, is having a Constantinian moment in Donald Trump's government). In doing so, the work of mission appears to be something that only powerful and wealthy Christians can do. This missionary imperialism is reflected in the military language that informs a great deal of our popular missiology – we 'mobilize', 'deploy' missionaries and, if you are in Africa, go on a 'crusade'. Whether we think the military connotations are real or figurative, the language we use has creative power. It shapes us as much as we shape it. Mission is often understood as war and conquest. Mission agencies recruit and mobilize missionary-soldiers to fight at the front lines of darkness.

It is no coincidence, then, that Christianity has spread around the world in the centuries of European expansionism, following the 1400s when the Portuguese managed to reach India by sea while the Spanish brought it to Europe's attention that there was a continent across the Atlantic Ocean. In the centuries that have followed, European Christians took the Christian faith along with them when they migrated to the rest of the world. The numerous overlaps between British mission history and its imperial history, especially in the nineteenth and twentieth centuries, provide undeniable evidence for this. Whether we speak of William Carey in India or David Livingstone in Central Africa, mission and colonialism influenced one another more than many current mission scholars would like to admit.

In this book you will read about an uncomfortable aspect of mission history. I do not talk about this history to make mockery of the mistakes of the old missionaries. I am actually writing to improve the global Church's ability to share the good news of Jesus in all nations in ways that are relevant in the context of the twenty-first century. I stand with all Christians who believe that Jesus must have followers in every family in the world. I live for this. However, I am also persuaded that all followers of Christ, no matter the colour of their skin or their bank balances, must join in the work of sharing the good news of the coming of the kingdom of God (and not the arrival of the empire of Rome or any other human power). I am doubly persuaded that one can only preach the gospel of the kingdom of God or that of the empires of the world, but not both. To truly embrace and embody this simple fact that all followers of Christ are called to make other followers of Christ, we must decolonize mission.

It is high time mission became a worldwide affair in all aspects – human resources, finances, language and geography, to mention a few. It is indeed time to decolonize mission.

Harvey Kwiyani
Liverpool

Introduction

This book will not attempt to convince you that every Christian missionary from the West was a colonialist. As a matter of fact, I do not believe that every missionary was a colonialist. Whatever I say in this book, I do not start from that premise. Any argument that suggests that there were no good missionaries is of no interest to me because it is untrue. It overstates and overstretches the truth and paints a whole movement of people with a broad stroke that risks burning the very bridges it seeks to mend. Indeed, if we look back at the history of European missionary work, we will find that at any point in that story there were many missionaries who refused to be involved in the expansionist projects of European empires and governments. Over the centuries, we will see many missionaries who were good people who were responding to God in obedience when they packed up their belongings and set off for unknown lands simply because they believed God had called them to share the good news of Jesus to the numerous peoples around the world who had never heard the gospel and, therefore, needed saving.

If, at any point, you hear the book saying that all missionaries were seeking to colonize the world, most likely you will have missed the point it is trying to make. The argument I am trying to make does not need a discussion that singles out individual missionaries, trying to discern whether they participated in the colonial project or not. This book is not about individual missionaries, though of course there are stories of many of them who behaved badly on the mission field. Conversations focused on individuals are often driven by the desire to justify the entire missionary enterprise and the missionaries who were involved in it while seeking to prove that whoever is saying mission and colonialism worked hand in hand is wrong. Many of those conversations have no real interest in taking an honest look back at the way the story developed, especially from Christopher Columbus' arrival in the West Indies until today. They are either too afraid to look – they know they will discover that the enterprise they take great pride in was not as dazzling as they believe – or they know mission history is messy and would rather leave it in the past. This privilege – to label something 'past' and, therefore, unchangeable – is not available to many who were on the wrong end of the colonial project: many of them feel they are still colonized.

Those who defend Western mission and missionaries must avoid any serious critical look underneath the glorious hagiographical biographies they have been given in order to keep their heroes on the pedestals they have built. They want to keep believing that David Livingstone single-handedly saved East Africa and would rather not be informed about his ideas about colonialism and the barbarism that was perpetuated at his daughter's colonial estate in Malawi, A. L. Bruce Estates, which was the scene of John Chilembwe's tragic uprising in 1915 in which William J. Livingstone and Duncan McCormick were killed. When something negative like this is unearthed, they often say that the missionaries were the children of their times and they may have behaved just like any Westerner at the time.

I have also learned that most of those who work to defend Christian mission from a critique of its colonial history do so to protect the legacy of not only their organizations but also their ancestors. I quite often hear people say, 'Behind our organization are generations of thousands of supporters and missionaries who have given their lives for people in Africa and other parts of the world to hear the good news of God's love. Are you saying they were colonizers who were up to no good?' Others come to me saying, 'You are surely not arguing that my grandparents, who gave up the comfort of the West to serve as missionaries in the remote jungles of Africa for many years, were colonialists. Or are you?'

To put your minds at ease before you get any further into this book, I am not suggesting either of these things. I understand and appreciate that this subject requires a sensitive approach. It is historical holy ground. I must take my shoes off before I enter its story of a sacred past marked by the blood of thousands of Western Christians who went overseas to evangelize the nations well aware that they might never come back to see their beloved families. I can only stand in awe when I read about the many missionaries who loaded up their belongings in coffins and shipped them to the mission field because they knew they would die there. I am deeply appreciative of the fact that in the past 500 years, for decades upon decades, numerous people have left the said 'comforts of the Western life' to share the story of God's love with the world that needed to hear of Jesus, the Jewish Messiah, who died to save them from their sins.

Some of them went to West Africa when it was known that it was called the white man's grave – the lifespan of a missionary in Africa in the nineteenth century was extremely short. There was malaria and yellow fever waiting for them on the other side of the mission trip.

INTRODUCTION

Many of them would die within months of arriving on the mission field. I am too aware of this history. Quite a few missionaries are buried in my home area in Malawi. They all died young, having served in Malawi for only a few months. Bishop Charles Mackenzie who, in 1861, led the Universities Mission to Central Africa to my home, Magomero, in what is southern Malawi today, died only six months after setting up his first mission station.[1] They arrived at Magomero in July 1861 and the honourable bishop died on 31 January 1862, at the young age of 36. Before his death, he had buried three of his team in the seven months they worked at Magomero. Two others would die soon after Mackenzie's death.

David Livingstone's 32-year mission service in Africa was rather uncharacteristic at the time. Most missionaries died within months, and the lucky ones within years of their arrival on the continent. Livingstone's wife, Mary Moffat, died in Mozambique, three months after Charles Mackenzie's death in Malawi, at 41. She had not even reached Malawi where her husband was working at the time. Another bishop, Chauncy Maples (of Malawi), died in 1895 at 42 years of age. I am also painfully aware of many other men and women who died young on the mission field. Some of their graves are marked not by their names or their ages but by the number of days they survived on the mission – three, seven, 90, 130. Many died en route to their mission stations.

I have also read about many missionaries who were killed by hostile chiefs driven by fear or superstition: 'White men are here to take our land', or, as was believed in some places, 'White men are powerful witches and ghosts that need to be killed to protect people's spiritual heritage.' Kabaka Mwanga II of the Baganda had Bishop James Hannington executed because he feared that white men would destroy the kingdom. Hannington died in 1885 at the age of 38. The mission field of the 1800s was, for many, a death trap they knowingly walked into. Their immense sacrifices are not to be trivialized.

It would not be accurate to suggest that all these missionaries were individually driven by the desire to dominate. Many of them really believed God had sent them to bring the good news to the world. This is the easy part of the work I am doing. I do not have to argue that many missionaries were good people. History proves that. However, things get a little complicated when we begin to consider the broader history of mission going back beyond the sixteenth century into the wider expansion of Christianity in Europe in the centuries that followed Constantine's conversion. We will realize that a great deal of mission was built on the foundations of Roman supremacy over its empire, both in Rome and in Constantinople, ruling over millions of people scattered around the empire's cities from York, Carthage, Alexandria and Antioch all the way to Babylon. Since the 1400s, the expansion of Christianity has depended on European supremacy over the nations (the Americas, Africa and large parts of Asia), which, they believed, gave them the mandate to dominate, civilize and Christianize the world. That system is still in operation today, and Christian mission is still shaped by and attached to it.

That said, things get even more interesting when we begin to consider that, whether we look at India or Africa or, indeed, many other parts of the world, the inception of European colonialism accelerated the establishment of Christianity in the colonies. On the one hand, it made European access to the colonies a lot easier – the numbers of missionaries working across many colonies grew rapidly after the imposition of colonialism. It was safer to go and live in the colonies knowing that the colonial armies were not too far away to provide protection. In addition, the military might of the colonizers enforced the false ideas that Europeans were superior to other ethnicities around the world, which in many places meant that the Europeans' religion was also better. I have heard old people praying to the god of the Europeans because that God made the Europeans more powerful. In the end, of course, people believed (as some still do today) that everything European or, indeed, anything that comes from the West is better than their own. The process of Christianizing and civilizing the world needed the Europeans to be in charge – to colonize peoples around the world – and Christian mission was the handmaiden that could make this happen.

Having read so far, I am sure some of you are wondering, 'If you are not saying that all missionaries were colonialists, what is the point of this book?' Others are relieved that I am not here to demonize their grandparents. Fair enough. However, I wish to suggest that the entire discourse of decolonizing mission is about the systemic legacy of European expansionism, together with its enabling ideologies of white supremacy, the doctrine of discovery, and civilizing mission. It is this attaching of the great work of sharing the good news of Jesus' finished work of Calvary with the nations to the colonizing agendas of empires that this book is trying to explore. I am doing this as an African follower of Jesus, the Christ. I am fully persuaded – I have not an ounce of doubt in me – that Jesus calls us to share with others the good news that he – *not Caesar* – is Lord. He is the Lord who has come to set the colonized free and not to lead them into another bondage. In addition, as my friend Girma Bishaw of London puts it, 'Jesus has also come to set the colonizers free from their instincts to colonize others, to help them see the image of God in those they would otherwise want to colonize.'

INTRODUCTION

It is because of this conviction that I believe that mission, if we can call it that, does not need to depend on human empires. Mission can happen without imperial backing. As a matter of fact, mission ought to happen without the help of emperors, governments and their armies.

When I read a great deal of the history of the expansion of the Christian Church from 312 CE when Constantine converted to Christianity, but more especially from the sixteenth century, it becomes quite apparent to me that Christian mission has been irredeemably tied to European expansionism. Christian theology was used to justify European expansionism – mission and missionaries were often the shock absorbers of the colonial powers. I am aware of the many scholars, almost all of them Western, prominent among them Stephen Neill and Brian Stanley, who effectively argue that colonialism did not have anything to do with mission. Neill's all-important book, *Colonialism and Christian Missions*,[2] seems overly keen to highlight the great things that some missionaries did, for instance protecting indigenous peoples from slavery. Neill had served as a Church Mission Society missionary in India for almost two decades and had thus seen the complex relationship between mission and colonialism. In the book, he does acknowledge that, in some instances, missionaries did not always speak up in defence of local populations, but his overall tone is one that downplays such mistakes. Of course, the book was published in 1966 when many African colonies were gaining their independence, and there was a great anti-colonial urgency across the continent, with some murmurings among African and Asian Christians about the moratorium to prevent Western missionaries from going to Africa and Asia for some time. Less than two decades earlier, China had expelled all Western missionaries. There was a need to explain the connection between colonialism and mission in a way that restored confidence among Western Christians about the important work that had been central to their identity as missionaries and civilizers of the world. As such, he agrees that mistakes were made on the mission field, but they were inconsequential. To paraphrase his argument, colonialism played no real role in mission. In the same manner, mission did not benefit from the colonial expansion of European imperialism. If there were any connections between colonialism and mission, they were rare, minimal and had little to no impact. Of course, I am writing this book almost 60 years after *Colonialism and Christian Missions* was published. We understand the connection between colonialism and mission better, enough to know that Neill's analysis is not entirely accurate.

Brian Stanley's book, *The Flag and the Bible: Protestant Missions and British Imperialism in the Nineteenth and Twentieth Centuries*,[3] was published in 1990. Thus, it presents to readers an understanding of the conversation on mission and colonialism more than 20 years after Neill's book was published. As a historian, Stanley approaches the subject with better objectivity but his overall tone is sympathetic to mission. He was largely interested in explaining the inevitability of the British Empire's hand in mission in its colonies. He was concerned that, 'The belief that "the Bible and the flag" went hand in hand in the history of Western imperial expansion is fast becoming established as one of the unquestioned orthodoxies of general historical knowledge.'[4] Thus, he wrote the book to submit the theme of 'the Bible and the flag' to a detailed historical investigation. This he does well. His overall conclusion is that mission and colonialism were, generally speaking, not directly connected in the colonies. He makes the same argument as Stephen Neill, only that his is more nuanced and, to some extent, more objective. However, his history of 'the Bible and the flag' is written from a Western perspective and is largely informed by Western resources – including many other Western mission history books, as well as missionary journals and other archive materials. In the end, while not necessarily inaccurate it is still a history of mission according to the empire. It does not do justice to the stories of local African, Asian and Latin American Christians in the same way those local people would tell them.

What you will find in this book is, without doubt, an African reading of the story. It is the same history that Neill and Stanley tell, only in this book it is told by those who were actually colonized. A proverb well known throughout sub-Saharan Africa says, 'Until the lions can speak and tell their story, the story of the hunt will always glorify the hunter.' In this book you will find the story of the hunt from the perspective of the hunted lion. Here, the colonized are trying to speak and their story will be different from that of the colonizers. In this sense this book is a mission history according to the colonized. It intends to shed light on some aspects of mission that are not talked about in Western historic discourses on imperialism and the expansion of Christianity from Europe to the rest of the world. Curiously, outside the world of Christian scholarship on the subject of mission (to which both Neill and Stanley belong), there is overwhelming evidence that corroborates the argument I am making here that the philosophical foundations of mission are colonial and, indeed, that many missionaries were happy to serve as the religious arm of Western imperialism. For example, Anna Johnston is quite blunt in the opening statement of her book, *Missionary Writing and Empire*:

Christian missionary activity was central to the work of European colonialism, providing British missionaries and their supporters with a sense of justice and moral authority. Throughout the history of imperial expansion, missionary proselytising offered the British public a model of 'civilised' expansionism and colonial community management, transforming imperial projects into moral allegories.[5]

It is worth mentioning Lamin Sanneh at this point. Sanneh (1942–2019) was one of the most respected scholars of world Christianity as well as Islamic studies. He has left us a great deal of material to learn from. One of his most popular books is *Translating the Message*,[6] in which he argues that translating the gospel into local languages has been instrumental to the spread of Christianity even after colonialism had ended. He has a good chapter in the book, titled 'Mission and Colonialism', which discusses the effect of translation in subverting colonial powers in the colonies.[7] In fact he goes a step further to suggest that the work of translating the message empowered local Christians in the colonies to seek their independence. '[The work of mission] is the logical opposite of colonialism, for the means and methods of mission, though perhaps not the motives, conspired together with the consequences to determine a vernacular destiny for the cause.'[8] He adds that Western colonial power was irreparably damaged by the consequences of vernacular translation – and often by other activities of the missionary.[9]

In making this statement he may seem to suggest that the works of the missionaries brought colonialism to an end. This is true, even though it is indirectly so. Yes, the gospel calls us all to freedom. Once the good news of Jesus lands among a people, it is rather difficult to keep them in bondage. Case in point: to keep enslaved Africans oppressed for longer in the USA, the white enslavers created a heavily redacted version of the Bible – the Slave Bible – which was used to promote obedience and suppress hopes of freedom among the enslaved population. Freedom, among the enslaved in the Americas and the colonized around the world, was never automatic. It had to be fought for. This explains why the decolonizing of African Christianity took much longer than that of African politics. Many missionaries did not want to leave because they did not believe that the 'young churches', as they called them, were ready to stand on their own feet. It took some African agency to liberate the continent. Many had to agitate to get their freedom. African Independent Churches, which were for the most part out of bounds for European missionaries and colonial agents, exploded to begin to shape African Christianity in an African way once political colonialism came to an end. Unfortunately, political colonialism was easier to identify and therefore bring down than the ideological (and theological) colonialism that still exists today.

While the missionaries brought the tools needed for the liberation of the African continent, and I am not sure they knew that this would be the result of bringing education and translation to Africa (in the United States, it was for a long time illegal to teach an enslaved African how to read and write), they also brought an ideology that colonized the minds of Africans – a type of colonialism that is alive and well today. I have two examples to explain this. First, I know too many middle-class Africans who live in Africa and work hard to prevent their children from learning their African languages. My friend in Malawi takes pride in his children's inability to speak Chichewa even though his parents cannot speak English. His children are taught only English, and the intention is to make their English sound as American as possible. These Africans do not think they need translation. They want to hear the gospel in a Western (colonial) language. Second, there has arisen a generation of Africans who do not want to be African at all. A student of mine, Joseph Ola, did research for a master's degree that surveyed young African Christians' identity.[10] The conclusions were quite stunning. Many young Africans cannot wait to shed their African identity. They want to be Westerners. They read Western books. They sing Western songs. They listen to Western preachers. All this, too, is the work of the missionaries.

In this book you will meet many other voices from outside the missions community who are basically saying the same thing – colonialism and mission worked hand in hand, not always and not everywhere, but enough to justify a generalization. It appears to me that Western Christians choose to ignore this history because it is uncomfortable. They would rather feign ignorance or pretend it does not exist. I write as one of them, having lived and been educated in the West for many years, hoping to draw their attention to this critical subject in the hope that we can lament and repent of what has become of the call Jesus gives to his followers to make the nations disciples. Acknowledging the troubled past of mission will help the global Body of Christ to be confident as it moves forward in the business of making disciples for Christ in all parts of the world. It will communicate a humble posture and a gesture of vulnerability, especially on the side of the Western missions community. Of course, we who have come from the formerly colonized lands will often not trust Westerners until we see them vulnerable with us. Most important for me is the possibility of sharing the gospel among the nations without exporting Western cultures – or any other cultures – alongside it. The era of Western civilizing missions when Christian mission was used as a means to civilize (by which they meant to Europeanize) people around the world should never have happened. The Body needs the variety that comes from the diversity of cultures that shapes its members. The global uniformity that we see in parts of the Evangelical community is a gross injustice to the Body and to who Jesus intends us to be.

Why does God use flawed people?

In 2022, Chris Sugden published a blog post, assisted by Vinay Samuel (from India) and Kiprotich Chelashaw (from Kenya), in which he attempted to pre-emptively discredit the argument I present in this book. Notably, he positioned himself behind voices from the Global South to advance his case in a manner that carried troubling racial undertones. He suggested that we ought not to be concerned about racism and colonialism. All we need is to celebrate the fact that God sends people, even flawed ones, to share the good news with the world. He further suggested that to critique the colonial history of mission is to be informed by the Black Lives Matter discourse with its grounding in Critical Race Theory (both these were hot topics in the USA at the time). Of course, I do wonder if they really took time to understand what both Black Lives Matter and Critical Race Theory really mean. Sugden appeared unsettled by the general observation that many missionaries behaved poorly on the mission field, prompting him to rush to their defence. They behaved badly because, for him, God sent flawed people to other parts of the world. There is no denying, though, that many missionaries were racist. For instance, it has been proved numerous times that many missionaries treated local people as second-class citizens, even those who had converted. There are many examples of this. For instance, Edward Andrews explores the narratives of missionary work in West Africa, which reveals quite a few missionary malpractices.[11]

In addition, as I will argue in this book, the entire Western missionary enterprise, right from when it started in the fifteenth century, was founded upon the belief that Europeans had the right to the world. They could dominate, civilize and Christianize the world by any means necessary. To dismiss all the historical evidence for this as Critical Race Theory is what an unsettled white man like Sugden (and the black and brown friends who want to sustain and uphold white domination in mission and in the world in general) will do. If it is Critical Race Theory, there is no need to even listen to what is being said. Furthermore, to try and explain it away as 'God using flawed people' is a questionable attempt to make us forget that this is part of the history of the missionary movement. In other ways, it comes across as an attempt to gaslight us that there were only *a few bad apples* responsible for racism and colonialism in mission when we know that the system itself was entirely suspect. Good people working in a bad system may actually only make the system worse. Essentially, Sugden and his friends want us to blame God for using flawed people. Central to their argument is the question: 'Why does God use flawed people?' This refuses to take responsibility for the fact that many missionaries, for generations, went around the world seeking to colonize it and defile other people's cultures.

'Why does God use us when he knows we are flawed?' One has to be pretty privileged to believe that being flawed absolves them of all responsibility for wrongdoing. Of course, God always uses flawed people. That is all he has – flawed people. No one among us is not flawed in one way or another. Yet we cannot blame God for our mistakes. When we refuse to take responsibility for our attitudes, motives and postures, we cannot learn from history. The history of mission, for that matter, is full of lessons that we can learn from to serve God better in our communities today. We can gain many great lessons from the work of Bishop William Colenso among the Zulus in South Africa. We can also learn how to relate with local peoples from the outstanding missionary endeavours of Bartolomé de las Casas in Latin America. Or Francis Xavier in Japan. However, we may also learn a thing or two from the not so glittery parts of William Carey's story in India. Or that of many missionaries who ran boarding schools for native boys and girls in North America. What we cannot do is to bury that history because God sent flawed men and women.

The argument for decolonizing mission that I make in this book does not depend on the flaws of a few bad apples. Neither does it depend on the great works of a few good apples. Indeed, in the end it makes little difference that some good missionaries disapproved of colonialism or that some bad missionaries served their colonial governments. Those facts are inconsequential to the work we need to decolonize mission. Again, the flaws of some individual missionaries are not central to the argument of this book. I am not talking about anyone's parents and grandparents: the bad apples are evidence of a system that could be made better.

Why decolonize mission?

In this book I have a double-edged agenda. First, I am attempting to imagine a contextually relevant missiology for a postcolonial world. In a sense, then, I am imagining a 'postcolonial missiology' that would help make our sense of mission relevant in the twenty-first century. To explore such a missiology, I am trying to answer the questions:

- What does engaging in mission in a postcolonial manner look like? How do we then get to engage in mission in a postcolonial world?
- How do the colonizers and the colonized (or former colonizers and formerly colonized) engage in God's mission together?
- Even more, how do we – Christians living in the twenty-first century – evangelize the world without depending on our empires and their imperialism?

Second, in imagining a postcolonial missiology, I am keen to explore the decolonizing of mission itself (and missiology). A decolonized mission/missiology is only possible if we can begin to listen to the voices of the non-Western others just as much as we listen to Westerners as we engage in mission. Of course, the process of decolonization is always about power dynamics. Mission, as we stand today in the twenty-first century, is still a very white field even though an overwhelming majority of Christians (and pretty soon, missionaries) are anything but white. While these events continue to unfold, and non-Western Christianity continues to explode, there is still an unjustifiable theological/missiological hegemony by the West over the world. The global context of the twenty-first century requires us to think afresh about God's mission in the world – what it is and how to participate in it. We cannot continue to depend on twentieth-century thinking to shape our twenty-first-century missiology. The world order that made the twentieth century, bracketed as it were between the rise of the European and American colonial empires on the one hand and the collapse of the Berlin Wall, the ensuing triumph and dominance of capitalism over socialism, and the emergence of multinational corporations that have become more powerful than nation-states on the other, required a missiology that could make sense in the context of colonialism and Western supremacy, but that missiology falls short in the current postcolonial post-Christendom world of the twenty-first century. Of course, when I say it made sense back then, I should add that it made sense to Westerners who were the Christians who sent their missionaries and colonial agents and traders to the unevangelized lands out there. To most of us in the colonized and oppressed world, such mission was unacceptable.

The reason I believe we need to wrestle with the subject of Western imperialism in mission is because, first and foremost, the evangelization of the world in the twenty-first century depends on it. If the gospel will be preached in the nations in the decades to come, it is very likely that black and brown people will play a key role. Many of them will not be (professional) missionaries. They will not be sent by a mission agency. To a great extent they will lack all the accolades that come with being a missionary in some remote part of the world. As a matter of fact, many will be young Christian migrants, in their twenties and thirties, migrating for employment or education. Their missionary work, identity and posture will have to be different. Essentially, their missiology must also be different. However, herein is the challenge we have with mission, and why we need to decolonize it. First, it is impossible to truthfully tell the history of the expansion of the Church in the past 500 years without acknowledging the European conviction that the world was theirs to civilize by means of Christianization. Yet, of course, when we study mission history, we generally hear a whitewashed history in which self-sacrificing saints went overseas to share the good news of Jesus and had nothing to do with European imperialism. We now know that in many places, this was not the case.

Second, with the era of European imperialism gone, the injustice of colonialism is becoming difficult to ignore or justify. The violence of colonialism – physical, economic, intellectual and its many other forms – needs to be named and, hopefully, abolished. The violence of colonialism in Christian mission also needs to be acknowledged. Some people need to repent of their role in making it happen (even if it is on behalf of their ancestors). We all need to lament its impact on both the Body of Christ and Christian witness among the nations. After this, we need a 'never again' commitment. Only when this happens can world Christians be confidently involved in global witness. Indeed, the colonial legacy of Christian mission that I am concerned about here does not only affect Western missionary work in the world. Even those Christians who have come from other parts of the world are affected. We also hear it often, especially among young black and brown people: 'Christianity is the religion of the colonizer ... Christian missionaries were the religious foot soldiers of the colonial empires.'

Some find it difficult to evangelize because those they want to reach are still affected by the old imperial ways of doing mission. I have had to explain to many European Christians why an African can be a missionary in Europe. Others find that the old imperial mission model is the only one they know, and yet it does not always work in many parts of the world. For example, several of my African friends believe that *mission* is what the Europeans did in Africa in the 1800s and 1900s, including condemning other people's cultures, establishing themselves as superior and setting the moral standards by which a person may be a follower of Christ. I hear them ask British Christians: 'How can you be a Christian and be going to the pub?' The best of these happened in Switzerland when a Malawian pastor told Swiss Christians that revival would only come to their land when they stopped calling their pastors by their first names. Needless to say, numerous questions followed.

My concerns about colonialism and mission are further shaped by another set of deeper questions. Undergirding those questions is the historical fact that for the past 600 years, Africa's relationship with Europe has been based on abuse and exploitation (in the name of civilization). From the mid-1400s when the Portuguese brought the first African enslaved boys to work for the king and the Church in Lisbon, to 1891 when the last slave ship left Benin for Brazil, European Christians kidnapped and enslaved millions of Africans, forcing them to provide free labour in the plantations of the Americas. After the 450 years of slave trade came colonialism. Once the transatlantic slave trade was successfully stopped, and Europeans could no longer capture and sell Africans into slavery, they came and colonized them right in Africa. This political colonization of the continent (by European Christian governments) lasted from the 1880s to the 1960s, even though some countries had to wait longer – Zimbabwe got her independence in 1980. However, that was not the end of the West's exploitation of African peoples and resources. Economic colonialism is still running to this day. African minerals are still enriching Western economies while millions of Africans die of poverty-related causes every year. Exorbitant debts given at the onset of independence still weigh down the economies of many African countries. Inhumane trading conditions established in the 1950s and 60s sustain an imbalance that is nothing short of a critical social justice issue for our generation.

Until the mid-1900s, Europe was Christianity and Christianity was Europe. Of course, Europe was the Christian-dom, or Christendom – *Christianity on the map.* European migrants to the Americas brought Christianity and, using unchristian methods of evangelism, managed to establish Christianity among Native Americans (and I use this term to include those Americans who lived in South America). Yet the United States continues to identify itself as a 'city of Zion on a hill' and a beacon of Christian hope in the world. Both the transatlantic slave trade and colonialism are systemic sins committed by Christians, generation after generation, for a good 600 years. To make this possible, there must always be an ideology that informs the Western reading of Scriptures that allows for such sins to continue. Whether it was 'Blacks are two-thirds of a human and God created them to work for white people' or 'Africans cannot govern themselves and must be colonized and civilized by Europeans' or even, as we see today, 'All we are interested in is the minerals, as long as the Africans do not come to Europe or America', we recognize that it is largely Western Christian thinking and must, as such, shape and be shaped by some theology. During slavery many Westerners adjusted their theologies to justify both the selling and using of enslaved Africans and the colonization of the continent. They said it was God-ordained. During colonialism they said once again that God designed it that way – *that colonialism was for the good of the Africans.* Today, in Europe, the God story is on mute, but the United States still believes that its military might is God-given to fight God's wars against other faiths. It is this understanding of God that should cause us in the twenty-first century to imagine again what God calls us to do and to be in the world. African American scholars have stated clearly that God and Christian theology were often invoked to justify the enslavement of their ancestors while South Africans have also shown us that theology was used to justify apartheid. I wonder here how these slavery-colonialism-apartheid-justifying theologies were used also to argue for mission and evangelism among those who were colonized, oppressed and marginalized in Latin America, Africa and Asia. Indeed, if theology was used to explain colonialism, how could it also be used to justify evangelism? I am not convinced that Western theology has properly corrected itself. What things are we, knowingly or unknowingly, theologically justifying today that are questionable? For example, neocolonialism in the form of continued economic exploitation of Africa is still wreaking havoc across the continent. Will future generations look at us and wonder why we were all right with it?

More important for me is the question: How has the Western understanding of God, God's mission and the Church defined mission for the rest of the world?[12] Indeed, if Latin Americans, Africans or Asians were to think about mission using their own understanding of God and not through resources transmitted to them via Western thought, what would it look like? What would a missiology that is not rooted in Western thought – individualism, capitalism and racism – look like? Or a missiology that refuses to bow down to modernity and the Enlightenment, one that is shaped by spirit-centred world views of the Africans, Native Americans or, as I have come to learn, the Asians? Essentially, I am wondering if mission itself has been taken captive and colonized by Western thought and theology. Of course, the Western captivity of theology is well documented. Could missiology be just as colonized?

INTRODUCTION

Calling fishermen to disciple the world

Decolonizing mission is about the system, its historical grounding, theological foundations, as well as its social location. When Jesus said to the disciples, 'Go and make disciples among the nations' he was speaking to a group of Galilean fishermen and their fellow lower-class followers. They lived in a colonized land that would be crashed by the Roman Empire barely four decades later. They had no means and, most probably, no need to colonize the nations for Christ. This book calls all followers of Jesus to imagine themselves as those colonized Galileans, with everything going against them, yet taking the gospel to the nations. What would this look like today? Many things. Most pertinent for me is the possibility of a missionary movement running on the power of the Holy Spirit and not that of an empire. It is my hope that as you read this book, you will notice that the history of mission since the fifteenth century has been shaped mainly by European expansionism – in many cases this makes mission and colonialism seem as if they are the same thing. Again, I hear many young Africans say, 'Colonialism and mission are two sides of the same coin – and that coin is Western imperialism.' The Gikuyu of Kenya have an old saying that goes, *gũtirĩ mũthũngũ na mũbĩa*, which loosely translates to 'There is no difference between a colonizer and a missionary.' When I asked some of my Gikuyu friends, they told me this saying has been around for generations; it came into being in the early decades of the nineteenth century and meant that mission and colonialism were one thing. The whole affair of converting people and colonizing them was the work of one entity. There was no difference between them. In their minds, one cannot be a missionary without being a colonizer, and vice versa one cannot be a colonizer without being a missionary. Indeed, in numerous cases the same people were involved in both. Of course, like many other communities in Africa, and possibly in Asia and Latin America, most local peoples viewed colonizers and missionaries as equally exploitative and oppressive, with no distinction between the two. This history should cause us to lament together, repent and turn from our wicked ways.

Every empire needs a theology

I also argue in this book that the problem of colonialism in mission is not only a historical problem but also a theological one. Yes, colonialism made practical sense for the work of civilizing and Christianizing a people. In many cases it was the easiest way to claim converts and disciple people. Forced mass conversions had been part of the European mission strategy in Europe a few centuries earlier. Something similar, only a little softer, was to play a key role in the nineteenth- and twentieth-century evangelization of Africa, parts of Asia, and Latin America. With Europeans firmly in charge at the end of the nineteenth century in Africa, the slave trade was quickly abolished in East Africa, Western hospitals were introduced and mission schools made Western education accessible to many Africans. The success of the missionary movement would have taken longer if the Europeans had not colonized Africa. We also know that the colonization of the continent of Africa could have taken longer if the missionaries had not been there. As such, colonialism had a practical use for mission just as much as mission had a practical use for colonialism. The civilization of a people through Western forms of education made upward mobility possible for many (which, in some places around the world, was *and still is* a mark of true discipleship, God's blessings and prosperity and, indeed, being civilized) and meant that people's lives were practically made better. In addition, the colonial governments and their people had a steady supply of labour: clerks, cooks, gardeners, houseboys and housegirls. However, these practical implications of mission are not all that is there.

Colonialism is founded on a premise that God has given some people rights over other peoples' lives, land and property. Of course, colonialism goes totally against a belief that all humans are *imago Dei*, made in the image of God. When we begin to behave as if some of us are first-class humans and others are second class, colonialism is inevitable. Yet there is no such thing as a second-class image of God. If any humans are made in the image of God, we are all made in the same image – equal in our humanity before God. Referencing George Orwell's famous phrase from *Animal Farm*, a US friend likes to say, 'All men are created equal, but some are more equal than others.'[13] This intentionally messes up both the grammar and mathematics to make a point – there are indeed in the world some people who believe themselves to be superior to others because God made them so. This belief is central to imperialism. Without a doubt, Christian theology was invoked to justify European imperial expansionism. A very vivid example is the South African system of apartheid, which was based on a theology of the Dutch Reformed Church.[14] While having faulty social anthropology as its justifying philosophy, apartheid was, above everything else, a theological problem. God was spoken of as the author of the racial hierarchies and segregation through a misreading of the stories about the curse of Ham and the tower of Babel. Theologies such as these have no place in the kingdom of God. We need to emancipate ourselves from their captivity if we will see the fullness of what God has for all of us.

INTRODUCTION

The purposes of God are to decolonize us

I am writing this book after more than two decades of working in mission in Europe (Germany, Switzerland, Austria and the UK) and in the United States. In those years I have learned quite a few things about mission – even though God calls the whole of the Church to bear witness for Christ among the nations, mission is firmly a Western project. Since 2014, I have been in constant contact with leaders of British mission organizations. I have had numerous chances to listen in on some of the conversations that shape British practice of mission around the world. Most of those conversations reflect the broader missiological discourses taking place among Westerners. One of the key issues that I have found fascinating is that many European mission agencies have not adapted to the current reality that Christianity now exists in every country. They continue to behave as they did many decades ago without regard to the fact that God is at work among the nations in many ways that have nothing to do with them. They do not know how to engage world Christians as equals. They do not say it in the open, but their behaviours communicate an attitude that says, 'What can black and brown people teach us? We brought them Christianity and taught them everything they know.' The imperialism and white supremacy that have shaped our human existence since the 1400s is alive and well in many mission organizations. This, I think, is quite critical for twenty-first-century missiology. In a generation or two, it will be black and brown Christians taking the gospel to the ends of the earth.

In other words, God's mission decolonizes. The Messiah came to set the captives free. It is for this reason that, for me, decolonizing mission only makes sense when God's work in our lives leads to our liberation. The word 'decolonizing' in the title of this book is not only a verb that calls us to action – to decolonize our mission theology and practice – it is also an adjective that describes (or qualifies) mission. In a nutshell, it says that mission decolonizes. I am not only interested in decolonizing our missiological thought and practice – a dichotomy that needs to be abolished – I also want to highlight the fact that God intends us to decolonize the contexts where he places us. As I read Luke 4, connecting it to Isaiah 61, it becomes evident that our work in God's mission is about decolonizing those who have been colonized by oppressive powers. The Spirit of Jesus working in us calls us to work with him to set the captives free. This is important. Mission in the twenty-first-century global context of world Christianity must be different from what it was 200 years ago. It needs to be freed from its Western captivity, decolonized and set free so that all followers of Christ, no matter what passport they hold or the colour of their skin, can take part in the world of sharing the good news around the world. If there is anything we need in mission in this century, it is to decentre whiteness to make space for all followers of Christ – the whole Body of Christ – to engage in the whole of God's mission in the whole of God's world. As long as we keep attaching this beautiful and life-giving *good news of Jesus* to empires, it will always be used to marginalize, dominate and colonize others. It will also rise and fall with our empires.

Notes

1 I was born and raised at Magomero. My family has lived at Magomero for several generations. It was home to my great-great-grandfather, Mtimawanzako Nacho, the first Malawian Christian to lead a mission station without the leadership of white missionaries (at Chiradzulu Mission, which was a substation of Blantyre Mission). He travelled to Edinburgh in 1885 for education at Stewarts Melville College and became a leader at the Blantyre Mission before being handed leadership at Chiradzulu Mission in the 1890s. His life at Magomero was marked by colonial violence from David Livingstone's descendants who owned the A. L. Bruce Estates. His experience of mission and colonialism – the violence that was done to his family (which is *my* family) – continues to animate the people at Magomero. If he had a chance to speak to the world today, he would say a combination of mission and colonialism is a deadly one, even for the converted. In his case, even though he was a respected leader in the Church, the colonial violence at Magomero pushed him to take his life at a ripe old age of 76.

2 Stephen Neill, *Colonialism and Christian Missions* (New York: McGraw Hill, 1966).

3 Brian Stanley, *The Bible and the Flag: Protestant Missions and British Imperialism in the Nineteenth and Twentieth Centuries* (Leicester: Apollos, 1990), p. 12.

4 Stanley, *The Bible and the Flag*, p. 12.

5 Anna Johnston, *Missionary Writing and Empire, 1800–1860* (Cambridge: Cambridge University Press, 2003), p. 13.

6 Lamin O. Sanneh, *Translating the Message: The Missionary Impact on Culture*, American Society of Missiology Series (Maryknoll, NY: Orbis Books, 1989).

7 See Sanneh, *Translating the Message*, ch. 3.

8 Sanneh, *Translating the Message*, p. 105.

9 Lamin O. Sanneh, 'Christian Missions and the Western Guilt Complex', *Christian Century* 104, no. 11 (April 1987), p. 330.

10 Joseph Ola, 'African, Millennial, and Christian: Exploring the Question of Identity among Young Nigerian Christians in the 21st Century', MA dissertation, Liverpool Hope University, 2021.

11 Edward E. Andrews, *Native Apostles: Black and Indian Missionaries in the British Atlantic World* (London: Harvard University Press, 2013).

12 By 'Western' I am talking about *white* Europeans and their descendants in other continents such as America, Australia and New Zealand. I know that not every Westerner is involved in this, but on a generalized scale, to the eyes of a

watching world, the Western hegemony makes it look as if all Westerners are in agreement. I was greatly shocked when I heard one of my professors saying, 'The Irish were, for a long time, the negroes of the white race.' And then I moved to the UK where I heard more than a few times that some Eastern Europeans were the undesirables of the white race. The hierarchies in the white Western world, with all the distinctions it brings, are not common knowledge beyond that world. To many of us outside the West, the Italians, the Belgians and the Canadians only differ in the languages they use. Otherwise, they are culturally the same, and they share whatever history Westerners have in the world.

  13 George Orwell, *Animal Farm* (London: Constable, 2021), p. 93.

  14 For example, see Johannes Albertus Loubser, *The Apartheid Bible: A Critical Review of Racial Theology in South Africa* (Cape Town: Maskew Miller Longman, 1987).

I

We Need an English Colony Here

This book seeks to make sense of the coloniality of mission. It is a book about the colonial legacy of mission. For me, this is the first step on a long journey of imagination seeking to explore a missiology that will be fit for purpose in the twenty-first century. I was born in Malawi, in south-east Africa. Our popular history of Malawi – as I learned it in school – starts with David Livingstone's chance visit to what we now call the Shire Highlands and Lake Malawi in 1859.[1] As a matter of fact, those well informed on Malawi's history tend to divide it into two eras: 'Before Livingstone' and 'After Livingstone'. Of course, oral historical traditions suggest that there were people around this body of water that local people called *Nyanja ya Nyenyezi* (meaning 'Lake of Stars', for the numerous stars that reflect on the surface of its clear waters at night) for centuries. The land of Malawi has been inhabited continuously since the first century of the Common Era. The Chewa people who form a majority of Malawi's population migrated to the area around Lake Malawi from Congo in the sixteenth century, with some of them having settled as far west as north-western Zambia and spreading out through Mozambique to the Indian Ocean. Following them, a few other smaller Bantu nations – Tumbuka, Ngoni, Yao, Lhomwe, Sena and others – arrived and settled to the north, south and east of the lake. Some Europeans, especially the Portuguese, had been aware of the Lake of Stars since the early 1600s when Gaspar Boccaro, a Portuguese trader, recorded his visit to the lake in 1616, almost 250 years before Livingstone. Yet it was Livingstone's visit to the lake (and the land to its south, divided by the Shire River that flows from Lake Malawi to the Zambezi River in Mozambique) that opened a new chapter in the telling of the story of what would be called Central Africa and that of its many peoples. Thus 1859 is, to many people, the watershed moment in Malawian historiography. It marked the end of the pre-Livingstone era, of which little has been written, and the beginning of a new chapter that was precipitated by the arrival of British missionaries, explorers and traders, many of whom kept journals and wrote books about the land of the lake. The first British missionaries arrived in Malawi in 1861. Thirty years later, in 1891, Malawi became a British Protectorate. It was declared a full British colony in 1893 and adopted Nyasaland as its official name in 1907.

From the time of Livingstone's visit to southern Malawi in 1859, a great deal has been written. We glean of it in Livingstone's own journals and books, as well as those of others who were with him on parts of his long journeys, for instance David Livingstone's brother Charles and long-term partner John Kirk left considerable notes, journals and letters about their expeditions in southern Africa. Many other missionaries, traders and colonial agents have had their own stories published about life in Malawi since the 1860s.[2] Thus, even though there exist centuries of oral histories of Malawi that precede Livingstone, it is fair to admit that Malawi's written history started with his 1859 trip. In this sense, then, 1859 marks the end of Malawi's pre-historic era and inaugurates a new era of what has come to be accepted as Malawi's history. This is not to say that Malawi has no history before 1859. However, Livingstone's trip marks a critical point in Malawi's historiography – many Malawians know a lot more about Malawi's post-1859 history than they do about the centuries before it.

To make sense of why this incomplete and therefore erroneous telling of the history of Malawi is accepted – it ignores centuries of human existence in the area – we must look at the broader context that shapes Livingstone's narrative. To do this well, we ought to explore the significance of his trips, especially in southern Malawi and, later, his travels around Lake Tanganyika and his famous meeting with Henry Morton Stanley at Ujiji in 1871. These travels, beginning in 1859, set up for us a perfect demonstration of how mission and colonialism have often been, for centuries, two sides of the same coin. We must understand, as far as that is possible, how his visit to Lake Malawi in 1859 serves as a beginning point of a great deal of Central African history – a history created by the British, the Belgians, the Germans and the Portuguese. Let us take a step back in history to have a panoramic view of Livingstone's life and work in Africa.

The smoke of a thousand villages

By the time he visited Lake Malawi in September of 1859, Livingstone had lived in Africa continuously from 1841 to 1856 – long enough for him to claim authoritative knowledge of parts of southern Africa, especially the areas around the Zambezi River which he had become familiar with in 1854–55.[3] He came to South Africa in 1841, but his journey towards becoming a missionary in Africa started two years earlier, in 1839. After completing his theological and medical training and while waiting for the Opium War to end so he could go to China as a medical missionary, his mission organization, the London Missionary Society, suggested that he go to the West Indies instead. He turned this offer down, responding that it would feel like being a missionary at home.[4] He moved to London on 2 January 1840 and stayed at a boarding house in Aldersgate. It was while living in this house that he met a fellow Scottish missionary, Robert Moffat (1795–1883) who, in Moffat's own words, had 'braved the wilds of Africa and wrought civilization out of savagery'[5] since 1817 (when Livingstone was only four years old). Moffat had come back with his family (including his daughter Mary, whom David would marry a few years later) on a furlough in 1839 and was spending some time at the hostel in Aldersgate. During his time at the hostel, Livingstone heard Moffat talk about his work in Africa several times. Moffat was, of course, intentionally looking to encourage some people to join him in mission in Africa. Slowly, the message of Moffat got to Livingstone, and he started to explore what he could do if he went to Africa. He got a chance to ask Mr Moffat if he really thought that he (Livingstone) could make it as a missionary for Africa.

> 'Yes,' came the answer in no uncertain tones, 'particularly if you will not go to an old station but will push on into unoccupied fields.' ... 'In the north,' continued the missionary, his eyes blazing with the vividness of recollection, 'I have seen in the morning sun the smoke of a thousand villages where no missionary has ever been.'[6]

Finally, instead of going to the West Indies, he chose the 'more taxing field of labour and suggested South Africa'.[7] *The smoke of a thousand villages!* He ruminated on those words for a long time. In the end, with characteristic directness he said, 'What is the use of my waiting here for the abominable Opium War? I will go at once to Africa.'[8] Livingstone came to Africa in 1841. At first he went to Kuruman in South Africa but, following Moffat's counsel back in London, he immediately began to explore – with another LMS missionary, Roger Edwards – the possibility of a new mission station at Mabotsa in Botswana. That mission station was established in 1843 while the Moffats were still on their furlough in England. Robert Moffat and his family returned to South Africa in 1844. Livingstone met them at Vaal River and used the long trek to Kuruman to further acquaint himself with them. He also got to know Moffat's daughter, Mary (1821–62), whom he married a few months later, on 9 January 1845.[9]

In the years that Livingstone stayed at Mabotsa in Botswana where he served as missionary, teacher and doctor, a burning desire grew inside him to explore Africa, to see and map out the 'the thousand villages where no missionary had been before' that Moffat spoke about.[10] His real explorer journeys started in 1849 when he crossed the Kalahari Desert twice in two years, before 1851, and in the process mapped out Lake Ngami in northern Botswana. His key objective in his explorations was to make possible a missionary road into the continent – 'God's Highway', as he would later call it – that ran northward from Kuruman to the interior, to what we call Botswana, Zambia and Zimbabwe today, to bring Christianity and civilization to the numerous smoking villages that Moffat only saw from a distance. He later reached a place called Linyanti, on the borders between Botswana and Namibia's Caprivi Strip, not too far from both Zambia and Zimbabwe and, of course, the Zambezi River.

After dispatching his family to England in April 1852, Livingstone went back to Linyanti and on 11 November 1853, with a group of workers, left Linyanti, turned westwards and proceeded all the way to Luanda, the current capital city of Angola, arriving in Port Town in May 1854. A great deal of this trek was in territory that the Portuguese and, to some extent, Arabs had mapped out. After a short four-month rest, he turned around and went back to Linyanti, which he reached in September 1855. Once again, he left Linyanti on 3 November 1855, this time following the Zambezi River to the Indian Ocean, on the eastern coast of Africa. It is during this leg of the trip that he came to the mighty waterfalls called *Mosi-Oa-Tunya* by locals (which translates 'thundering smoke') on 17 November 1855. Livingstone took the liberty of renaming them Victoria Falls (after Queen Victoria). He arrived at Quelimane on the Indian Ocean on 25 May 1856, being the first European recorded to make a trip overland from the west to the east. For various reasons, this long trip from the Cape Colony in South Africa to Kurumun, Linyanti, Luanda and then to Quelimane is easily recognized as the most important trip he ever made. In his earliest almost exhaustive biography, published in 1874 – soon after his burial at Westminster Abbey in London – this trip is described in this manner (in a language that would most certainly not be appropriate today):

When Dr Livingstone reached the delta of the Zambesi, he had shown by his own explorations that journeys could be made to central South Africa *from the east, the west, and the south*. He had become acquainted with large numbers of tribes, about all of whom were addicted to polygamy, some to repulsive customs and superstitions, idolatrous rites and degrading beliefs. He found many of these people who had large herds of cattle and who, in a rude way, gave considerable attention to agriculture. Many were little inclined either to superstition or true religion. Few had any notion of trade until he himself taught them by precept and example what it was. He had discovered several lakes and beautiful rivers, immense level plains of great fertility, many lovely valleys capable of producing heavy crops of grain. He had discovered several deposits of coal, and had visited gold washings which might again be made profitable. Portions of the country are without forest, others are covered with trees, some of which are the largest and most majestic in the world.[11]

Above all this, it was because it had exposed Livingstone to the problem of the slave trade that was still rampant in the region that this trip left a lasting impression on him and effectively changed his understanding of his mission in Africa and, therefore, shifted the trajectory of his work for the rest of his time in the continent.[12] So far he had understood his missionary work to focus on the setting up of a mission station, which he did at Mabotsa, and now exploration – the Zambezi River could become God's highway into Central Africa – but from then on, his mission included doing something about the slave trade.

From Mozambique he took a break and travelled back to England to see his family, arriving in December 1856. While in England he published his most famous book, *Missionary Travels and Research in South Africa*,[13] to tell the stories of his long trip from South Africa to Botswana, Zimbabwe, Angola and Mozambique. The book was an instant bestseller, with its first run of 12,000 fully pre-ordered before it was published. Both the second and the third print runs also sold out in a similar manner. Within two years, *Missionary Travels* had sold over 70,000 copies. Livingstone himself immediately became an international celebrity. In 1857, he delivered a series of lectures at several universities and public halls in various cities: Dublin, Manchester, Glasgow, Oxford, Leeds, Liverpool, Dundee, Halifax, Birmingham and, of course, his home, Blantyre. That series reached its crescendo at Cambridge University on 4 December 1857 where Livingstone, at only 44 years old, but having traversed thousands of miles across Africa, mustered all the energy he could to persuade the young students that they could serve God where the ravages of the transatlantic and the Arabic slave trade were still going on in Central Africa. He finished the talk with a climactic shout:

I beg to direct your attention to Africa. I know that in a few years I shall be cut off in that country, which is now open. Do not let it be shut again! I go back to Africa to try to make an open path for commerce and Christianity. Do you carry on the work which I have begun. I leave it with you![14]

He believed that his trip from South Africa to Angola and Mozambique had started the work of opening a highway for both trade and missionary work in Central Africa and pleaded with his audience of young university students to take up his mantle and continue the work in Africa. His audience, the young students at the universities of Oxford and Cambridge, responded by forming a new mission organization, the Oxford and Cambridge Mission to Central Africa, with its objective stated as:

to provide funds for sending out at least six missionaries, under a head who should, if possible, be a Bishop; while the field for the mission was left entirely to the choice of Livingstone, with the sanction of the Metropolitan under whose care it was at first advisable to place the mission.[15]

Later, when students from Durham and Dublin Universities joined, the mission organization was renamed the Universities' Mission to Central Africa, in short, UMCA. Its first group of UMCA missionaries were commissioned by the Bishop of Oxford in 1860. They packed up and left for South Africa, where their leader Charles Frederick Frazier Mackenzie (1825–62) was ordained 'Bishop of the Mission to the Tribes Dwelling in the Neighbourhood of the Lake Nyasa and River Shire'.[16] They arrived in Malawi in July 1861.

Magomero: mission station and colonial estate

Livingstone travelled back to Africa in 1858. He came back to Central Africa via Mozambique and the Zambezi River. He hoped to continue back to Zimbabwe, beyond Tete and the Cabora Bassa Dam to reach Victoria Falls again but was prevented by the conflicts mostly between locals and the Portuguese going on in the Tete area (largely to do with the Portuguese slave trade in Mozambique). He decided to wait it out by going up north on the Shire River into what is now known as Malawi. He made the first trip into the Shire Highlands in March 1859, and this led to the sight of Lake Chirwa on 16 April that year. Having gone back to Tete, he embarked on another trip into Malawi. It is this second trip that led him to see big *nyasa* (*nyasa* being the vernacular Yao word for 'lake'), which was known as the *Nyanja ya Nyenyezi* (to be translated 'Lake of Stars', now called Lake Malawi) for the first time on 16 September 1859.[17] He was aware that the Portuguese had already written about the lake and, though he eagerly awaited seeing the lake, when it finally happened Livingstone was not excited. In his journal entries of the autumn of 1859, he does not show any excitement about seeing Lake Malawi. He just reports the facts of getting to the lake with the help of the local people.

Livingstone took it upon himself, as he was in the habit of doing, to name the lake. He had heard people talk about this big *nyasa* for months, and so when he had the chance to record it, he called it Lake Nyasa, which literally translates to 'Lake Lake'. In the end the naming error did not matter. It would be called Lake Nyasa until 1964 when Malawi gained its independence from the British. In Tanzania and Mozambique, countries that share its waters, it is still today known as Lake Nyasa and Lago Niassa respectively. The British renamed the country *Nyasaland* (literally meaning Lakeland) in 1907, having colonized it in 1891.[18]

A vision from the Shire Highlands

The first Universities' Mission to Central Africa (UMCA) team arrived in Malawi in 1861. They were led by the 36-year-old missionary bishop of Central Africa, Charles Mackenzie.[19] Livingstone himself met them on the Shire River in Southern Malawi and took them up the highlands to the east of the river, to find a good place for a mission station. After much travel, through an area later to be called Kabula (later, again, renamed Blantyre after the Blantyre in South Lanarkshire, Scotland, where David Livingstone was born), made difficult by the frequent encounters with caravans of raiders and kidnappers of people to be sold and enslaved at the ports on the Indian Ocean in Mozambique, Livingstone chose Magomero to be their station.[20] Their mission at Magomero was short-lived. It was rather difficult for the missionaries to focus on their work when their station was situated right on a slave trade route. They spent a great deal of their effort saving people from raiders and kidnappers. In addition, a river passes through the area, and with it come mosquitoes and malaria. Many of the missionaries died only a few months after arrival. Mackenzie himself died on 31 January 1862, having been in Malawi for six months. By 1863, after some more missionary deaths, the mission was withdrawn to Zanzibar.[21] Needless to say, Livingstone was not happy about this.

All in all, Magomero had been home to the mission for less than three years. Its mission station story, important as it is, remains very short-lived. It was the first British mission station in Central Africa, but the missionaries only stayed for a short time. As far as I can tell, the few people they converted mainly did so because of the fear of slave raids. Fast-forward to 1891 when the British government made the land of Malawi its Protectorate (largely to defend the British missionary legacy in the area),[22] David Livingstone's eldest daughter, Agnes, and her husband, Alexander Low Bruce (of Edinburgh), acquired two large pieces of land totalling 170,000 acres in Malawi, one at Magomero (which included the plot given to the missionaries in 1861 as the nucleus of the new A. L. Bruce Estates) and the other at Likulezi in the Mulanje-Phalombe area. Alexander Low Bruce had married Agnes Livingstone in 1875, and they had two sons and two daughters. The sons were David Livingstone Bruce (1877–1915) and Alexander Livingstone (1881–1954). The older boy, David, had health challenges. As a result, it is the younger boy, Alexander, who was sent to Malawi to manage the Magomero estate. Between 1893 and 1908, it was a cousin of the family, William J. Livingstone, who was in charge. William was the worst kind of colonial master there could ever be. He unleashed on Africans the kind of violence that was seen in the slave plantations in the Americas. Local oral histories tell of the many instances when the colonial government threatened him with deportation if he did not stop brutalizing his workers. Alexander arrived in 1908 and stayed in the area until the late 1940s when he returned to Edinburgh. Even with Alexander there, the violence continued. The estate was liquidated in 1959, having made no real profit in its entire existence.

This short story of a mission station that became a colonial estate is the backdrop against which this book marks its argument. What happened at Magomero was not a coincidence. It was rather an outcome of what mission was expected to do at the time. David Livingstone himself had not only anticipated this. He argued for it to happen. The only way to ensure missionary success in Africa was to convince European governments to colonize Africa. Magomero was a perfect example. Mission led directly to domination and colonization. In the A. L. Bruce Estates' early years, neither Christianity nor education were allowed on the estates. Alexander L. Bruce believed that having converted Africans and educated Africans around the estate would not be good for the estates' commercial enterprise.

Healing the open sore

Back in the 1860s, Livingstone spent quite some time in Malawi, moving up and down the Shire River, and in Mozambique, up and down the Zambezi as far as Tete, before eventually taking another trip to England. By this time he had spent a great deal of his time exploring and mapping the area that would become southern Malawi. For instance, in March 1862 he left Malawi and went to Quelimane, on the coast in Mozambique, to welcome Mary, his wife. Unfortunately, she died of malaria only a few days after they met. She was buried at Chupanga close to the ocean, long before they could reach Malawi. Unfazed, Livingstone continued his exploration of not only the Shire River, the Shire Highlands and Lake Nyasa but also the Ruvuma River in Mozambique, to the east of the Big Nyasa. This time was marked largely by the overwhelming grief over the slave trade – something he had become acutely aware of in the early 1850s when he went north of Mabotsa to Linyanti and beyond. As he travelled up and down the land, he witnessed the cruelty of the Portuguese and Arab slave traders who carried out their business with the help of many local chiefs and agents. On his journeys, he encountered numerous slave caravans. His very group of African helpers included many who had been saved and freed from such caravans, most notable of them Jacob Wainwright, Wakatani and James Chuma, who, with Susi, brought Livingstone's body back to England in 1874. Thus, he personally witnessed the deadly effects of the slave trade upon the entire region of Central Africa, from the Tanzania–Mozambique region in eastern Africa all the way to Congo–Angola on the other side of the continent. The journals of his final trip, from 1865 to 1873, are filled with entries about dead men and women left on the slave train by angry traders not wanting to be slowed down:

> 19 June 1866: We passed a woman tied by the neck to a tree, and dead. The people of the country explained that she had been unable to keep up with the other slaves in a gang, and her master had determined that she should not become the property of anyone else if she recovered after resting for a time. I may mention here that we saw others tied up in a similar manner, and one lying in the path shot or stabbed, for she was in a pool of blood. The explanation we got invariably was that the Arab who owned these victims was enraged at losing his money by the slaves becoming unable to march, and vented his spleen by murdering them but I have nothing more than common report in support of attributing this enormity to the Arabs.[23]

26 June 1866: We passed a slave woman shot or stabbed through the body, and lying on the path. A group of men stood about a hundred yards off on one side, and another of women on the other side, looking on; they said an Arab who passed early that morning had done it, in anger at losing the price he had given for her, because she was unable to walk any longer.[24]

Livingstone wrote in his journal:

At present, let me give a glimpse of the slave trade, to which the search and discovery of most of the Nile fountains have brought me face to face. The whole traffic, whether by land or ocean, is a gross outrage on the common law of mankind. It is carried on from age to age and, in addition to the evils it inflicts, presents almost insurmountable obstacles to intercourse between different portions of the human family. This *open sore* in the world is partly owing to human cupidity, partly to the ignorance of the more civilized of mankind of the blight which lights chiefly on more degraded piracy on the high seas.[25]

Later on he said, 'All I can add in my loneliness is, may Heaven's rich blessing come down on everyone, American, English, or Turk, who will help to heal *the open sore of the world*.'[26] He had a vision for Africa as a whole, though he focused his work on the eastern and central parts of the continent, from Mozambique and Tanzania to the coast and as far inland as Zimbabwe, Zambia, Lake Tanganyika and Lake Victoria.

Christianity, commerce and civilization

Livingstone wanted to do everything in his power to heal this *open sore of the world* – he wanted to bring slave trade to an absolute end.[27] Seeing the complex nature of the systems and networks of this inglorious trade, he developed a two-pronged approach to ending the slave trade. He believed that the only way to bring it to an end was to establish a British colony in Central Africa. (He often spoke of an English colony, but we understand he meant a British one.) Such a colony would serve several purposes in addition to stopping the slave trade. As he travelled in the area around the Shire River and Lake Malawi, he became convinced that it could make a good British colony. Indeed, it had always been Livingstone's desire for Britain to have a colony in Central Africa, and the Shire Highlands would be his Ground Zero. Consequently, he made a sustained effort to convince the British government to consider having a colony in Central Africa. Between 1859 and 1860, he wrote extensively to his dear friends Sir Thomas Maclear and Sir Roderick Murchison:

> It is that the interior of this country ought to be colonised by our countrymen ... I see more in that for the benefit of England & Africa than in any other plan ... I am becoming everyday more convinced that we must have an English colony in the cotton-producing districts of Africa ... Colonization from a country such as ours ought to be one of hope, and not despair ... the performance of an imperative duty to our blood, our country, our religion, and to humankind.[28]

He later added:

> If large numbers of the British urban poor emigrated to Africa they could begin new lives, no longer 'crowded together in cities ... in close ill-ventilated narrow lanes' ... white men to compete in manual labour of 'any kind' with the Africans: 'But they [English colonists] can take a leading part in managing the land, improving the quality, increasing the quantity and extending the varieties of the production of the soil; and by taking a lead too in trade and in all public matters, the Englishman would be an unmixed advantage to every one below and around him, for he would fill a place which is now practically vacant.'[29]

Strangely, Tim Jeal suggests that Livingstone's ideas of colonialism are quite different from what we understand to be colonialism today. He says:

> His contemporaries, when they heard the words 'The British Empire', did not think of multiracial subject nations bowing to a central imperial power. Their pride in Empire was not the late-Victorian love of prestige and power, but more a pride in the idea that British men and women had settled in distant and previously thinly populated parts of the world, and were there reproducing all that was best in the British way of life – a free press, trial by jury and government by representative institutions. Most of Livingstone's fellow-countrymen during the 1850s saw Empire as the link of common nationality that bound together, more by voluntary union than by power, a mother country and her white settled, and soon to be self-governing, colonies overseas. In this family, the West Indies and, above all, India were seen as strange anomalies simply because they, unlike for example Canada, Australia and New Zealand, had large 'native' populations and were not predominantly 'British' and white.[30]

For Livingstone, colonization was the Crown's moral duty. He believed it was an essential part of a missionary's job to promote the penetration of Africa by civilized and Christian society as a whole. This, he was persuaded, would lead to the development of a civilized African 'middle-class', which would regenerate Africa by means of 'legitimate' commerce. Such a commerce would undermine the economics of the slave trade. In the end Africans drawn by agriculture would be easy to convert to Christianity. Colonial settlements could follow.

From then on, Livingstone's sense of mission in Africa was built on what he called the 'Three Cs: Christianity, Civilization and Commerce'. He believed that Britain would have to Christianize, civilize and bring a new form of commerce (to replace the slave trade) to Africa. In a letter to one friend of his, Professor Sedgwick, he had stated, 'All this [expedition's] ostensible machinery has for its ostensible object the development of African trade and the promotion of civilisation, [but] I hope may result in an English colony in the healthy highlands of Central Africa.'[31] The outworking of these three Cs would be another 'C' – colonialism, the fourth 'C' that overshadowed the first three Cs. He was convinced that: 'It is the mission of England to colonize and to plant her Christianity with her sons on the broad earth which the Lord has given to the children of men.'[32] He was absolutely convinced that Africans would benefit from sharing in European culture, from legitimate trade which would take the place of the slave trade, and from the spread of Christianity, its broad principles rather than its dogma.[33] There is enough evidence in the stories of the growth of Christianity in Africa that suggests that the Church began to explode during the era of the Scramble for Africa, especially in the 1890s. We have a record that the Livingstonia Mission (of the Free Church of Scotland) that worked in Malawi from 1875, led by the capable Robert Laws (1851–1934), could only point to 15 converts in 1890. The next year, British rule was extended over northern Malawi. By 1964, when British rule came to an end, 49 new missionaries and 9,500 communicants had been added and 900 schools established, having 1,600 teachers and 57,000 students.[34] Colonialism made a huge difference to the work of the missionaries.

From mission station to colonial farm

Looking back at the era of mission when Livingstone made the proposal for an English colony in southern Africa, it is unlikely that Jeal's explanation of what Livingstone meant is correct. As said above, Livingstone's daughter Agnes was right at the forefront of colonial farming in Malawi when she purchased the land around the mission station and established the A. L. Bruce Estates at Magomero. William J. Livingstone's time at Magomero, where he was manager from 1893 to 1915, is *still* notorious for his extremely harsh treatment of the locals. He was brutal in his lordship over his servants. He often engaged in physical fights with locals, including employees of his estate who were also his tenants. He banned the presence of any schools around the estate. He did not want the locals around the area to waste time on education. Educated Africans were quite challenging to manage. In addition, he burned down several churches built by local Malawians around Magomero. Some of those churches belonged to an African independent Church, the Providence Industrial Mission, led by a Malawian known as John Chilembwe (1871–1915), a Baptist minister. In the 1890s, Chilembwe was mentored by Joseph Booth (1851–1932), another English missionary who is popular among Africans because of his anti-colonial stance expressed in his 1897 essay, *Africa for the African*.[35] It was Booth who brought Chilembwe to the United States in 1897.

On 23 January 1915, Chilembwe sent a militia to Magomero to kill William J. Livingstone in a protest at the three-pronged evils of colonialism, forced free labour and the involvement of local Malawians in the First World War – all of which affected the people at Magomero significantly. On that fateful night, William J. Livingstone and a Scottish colleague, Duncan McCormick, were killed, while the women and children were not harmed – they were escorted to other white farmers nearby.[36] As the people gathered for their usual worship that Sunday at Chilembwe's church at Nguludi, everybody was aware that the service would not be business as usual. There was both a great sense of excitement and a heavy cloud of fear in the people's hearts. They were excited because their greatest enemy, William J. Livingstone, was dead. They were, however, paralysed with fear because they knew that the colonial British government that sat in Zomba, 50 miles from Mbombwe, would retaliate with full force. They were fully aware that many people would die, and that many more would be jailed for a very long time because of the angry yet joyful transgressions of their leader John Chilembwe and his militia. They celebrated – Chilembwe was their Moses, their Messiah, the liberator who broke the yoke of the Livingstones at Magomero. If successful, he could break the yoke of British colonialism before it really took root in Malawi. However, before long, the British government in Zomba reacted. Or should I say, *overreacted*.

Strike a blow and die

Chilembwe's people understood the risk. They knew that what they did in killing a Livingstone was tantamount to declaring war on the colonial government. This was, for them, essentially a suicide mission – there was no way they could win. They understood that their mission was simply to 'strike a blow and die, saying, "for our blood will surely mean something at last"'.[37] They expected that the British government would respond with full force, and it did not disappoint. Many people were killed as the British government tried to supress the uprising. Many others were condemned to the hangman's gallows by a quick judicial ruling in Zomba. Yet many more were arrested for a very long time. Chilembwe himself was killed a few days after the uprising as he tried to flee to Mozambique. While his uprising failed to change anything for the people of Malawi – in a sense, it made British colonialism in Malawi extra harsh – he is celebrated to today for his courage to stand up to the colonial bullies. His uprising was the start of a Christian-based anti-colonial uprising wanting to free Nyasaland from British colonialism.[38] Similar Christian insurrections against colonialism would eventually help bring the entire colonial project to an end some 50 years after Chilembwe.

Chilembwe's 1915 uprising was made necessary by several factors. Chief among those was that Chilembwe's church was located just outside the A. L. Bruce Estates where William J. Livingstone was a menace and a nightmare to the people in his community. Unfortunately, many of Chilembwe's followers were tenants on Bruce's estate. Livingstone not only displaced and moved people around the estate, he also constantly terrorized them. He loved beating up any locals who did not meet his job requirements. Second, after the First World War broke out in 1914, the colonial British government rounded up young men in Malawi and its other colonies, just as they and all the other European colonizers did in their colonies, and drafted them as porters to the British Army fighting against the Germans in northern Malawi. Sadly, 95,000 of the one million Africans conscripted to be porters in East Africa died during the First World War.[39] Most of those conscripted – almost one million young men – did not return home. As a result, many young women and children were left vulnerable and without care. Chilembwe found this disturbing. Third, the issue of taxes was a huge pain as it forced Malawians to work at the colonial farms that they generally despised. In Malawi, just as in many other colonies, the European taxation system was introduced to force Africans to work on colonial farms and thus to have colonies pay for their own colonization (and civilization), saving

European governments money in the process. Africans had to pay taxes for their wives, huts, livestock, land and almost everything they had to keep the government running.[40] Thus, they had to work the colonial farms to earn enough to afford these taxes to keep the British government happy. As if this was not enough, the British colonial government required Malawians to work *for free* at the colonial estates as help to the farmers, to save them some money.

The British government responded with full force, especially as the seat of the colonial government was only 18 miles from Magomero, at Zomba. In addition, a local British Battalion, the King's African Rifles, was already in a state of war – the First World War. There was a state of emergency at Magomero for a long time. It looked as if Chilembwe had given the British government an opportunity to assert itself in Malawi. Many people were killed. Hundreds were arrested for many months without trial. Those convicted spent upwards of 15 years in jail as a warning to everyone – the British will not tolerate insurrections in their colonies. Even missionaries, like those of the Churches of Christ who were active in the area, were interned and deported. Chilembwe was killed only a few weeks later.

Joseph Booth and *Africa for the African*

A British missionary from Derbyshire, known by the name Joseph Booth (1851–1932), arrived in Malawi in 1892, just a year after the country had been formally adopted as a Protectorate of Britain. Since Southern Malawi was the land of Livingstone's memory, where British missionaries had been present since the mid-1870s, the British wanted to prevent the Portuguese from incorporating it into their colony in Mozambique. He had spent several years farming in New Zealand and training in Australia for missionary work in Africa. Upon arrival, he settled just a few miles from the Blantyre Mission established by the Scottish missionaries in 1876 at Kabula (which, as stated earlier, would later be renamed Blantyre in honour of David Livingstone's birthplace in Scotland). Booth started his own Zambezi Industrial Mission. It was called 'industrial' because, unlike his counterparts at Blantyre Mission, Booth placed a great emphasis on economic empowerment and independence for the Africans.[41]

His operational principle was to 'train and cultivate native converts' spiritual gifts and lead to *self-reliant action* in preaching and planting industrial missions in the "regions beyond"'.[42] He arrived right at the beginning of the British colonial conquest in Malawi – the *pacification* of Malawi – but immediately realized that the colonial project was evil and that the missionaries already in the country were helping make it happen. Booth, however, tended to identify more with Africans and not with fellow Europeans, possibly because he was an independent and lone (and single) missionary of a small network of budding churches (he came to Malawi with only his two children, Edward and Emily). For the rest of his time in Malawi, he was always in the bad books of both other missionaries and the colonial government, especially the first colonial governor of Malawi, a ruthless man in his early thirties at the time, Harry Hamilton Johnstone (1858–1927), who was tasked to eliminate all anti-colonial resistance to the British crown in Nyasaland.

In 1896, Booth went to South Africa to promote his vision for an African Christian Union, especially among the Zulu Christians who had some connections with the other missionaries in Malawi. As a white man, though, he was met with extreme suspicion. In the 1890s, the Zulus had a reminder for anyone wanting to deal with white people: 'Bishop Colenso is dead.'[43] That was to say, since the only white man they could trust was dead, it was no use trusting any other white man because white men – both missionaries and colonial farmers – were all violent 'men of guns'. The Zulus challenged Mataka, Booth's Malawian companion on the trip:

> there was no white man living who was a safe guide for native African people. Bishop Colenso of Natal, Sobantu, adviser of Cetewayo, was the last of the race of true white man friends, and ... no matter what Mataka thought, no living white man, whether carrying guns or not, would in the end, when war came, be friends of black men. Indeed he himself (Mataka) was only a puppet in the hands of the white man who brought him (Booth): and ... if he asked to go back home he would find no way back, but ... he was even then in a prison whilst thinking he was free.[44]

Learning about Colenso helped Booth galvanize his thoughts into a fiery anti-colonialist manifesto entitled *Africa for the African*, which he published during his 1897 trip to the United States.[45] It was immediately banned in Malawi, but Booth was unfazed. Back in Malawi in 1899, Booth led a group of Malawians to petition Queen Victoria for education, political participation and justice on behalf of all Africans. The petition, delivered to Alfred Sharpe, second governor of the Protectorate, demanded that (1) the entire amount of the hut tax in the Protectorate should be spent on African education 'to the point of equality with the average British education', (2) 'a pledge be given from your Government that this Protectorate shall never pass from the direct control of your Home Government unless it be to restore the Territory to an approved Government', (3) free higher education should be provided for not less than 5 per cent of the African population to qualify it for 'Government, professional, mechanical, or mercantile operations', (4) the whole Protectorate should revert to native ownership after 21 years, and (5) Africans from British Central Africa should not be forced to bear arms against neighbouring tribes or elsewhere in Africa.[46]

Naturally, these views did not go over well with the colonial administration. Booth escaped to Mozambique before he could be arrested. He remained there until 1900 when he was allowed to return, subject to a promise that he would not take part in any political activities. Of course, he could not keep the promise, and he was finally deported from Malawi in 1902. He would end up being officially barred from ever returning to Malawi in 1907. By the time he was finally deported from South Africa back to Britain in 1915, he had been deported by the British government from its colonies at least five other times.

Looking at Booth's work today, 130 years after his initial work in Malawi, it seems rather too ambitious of him to criticize European colonialism when it was just starting. In the 1890s, colonial euphoria was still on the rise. Colonial agents were still busy running up and down the continent seeking to sign treaties with kings and chiefs. He wrote *Africa for the African* after living in Africa for only four years – and this was only during the pacification era, before colonial cruelty was unleashed on the continent. Cecil John Rhodes was still alive and his dream of the British Highway from the Cape to Cairo was still being pursued.[47] If anything, in 1896, Rhodes was still bankrolling British Colonial efforts in southern Africa. He ran Zimbabwe (whose colonial name was Rhodesia after himself) as his personal property. Johnstone's governorship in Malawi in the 1890s was largely funded by Rhodes as he desired to take Malawi, especially the lake, as part of his mini-empire. And, of course, both Henry Morton Stanley and Leopold II, the chief architects of European colonization of the Congo – a process marked by bloodshed enough to be called a genocide – were also still alive.[48] The British were still plotting how to take down the Benin Empire – they would eventually burn its capital in 1897.

Booth was way ahead of his time. He must be commended for speaking against colonialism even before it took root. He paid heavily for it – those deportations were for a reason. His theological persuasions were all over the place – he was a Seventh Day Adventist for a while and later he became a Watch Tower missionary – and this did not help. However, his anti-colonial stance was the trademark of his ministry. *Africa for the African* is a missional manifesto that should continue to critique our mission theologies and strategies. His condemnation of colonialism must still be heard today. He rightly spoke of:

> the ingenious heartlessness to which the modern spirit of greed can descend in the exploitation of African ignorance and helplessness. Whether we look at the government, mining capitalists or the planter class the spirit is the same ... *even missionaries need teaching that the African is inferior in opportunity only.*[49]

I know the story of the complex relationship between mission and colonialism from my people at Magomero. For some time in the early decades of the twentieth century, my grandfathers were required to work on a colonial estate at Magomero that belonged to David Livingstone's family. For those who were colonized, especially in Africa, it is usually impossible to separate mission from colonialism. Colonization and Christendom are interrelated phenomena that have shared the history of Christianity for the past 1,700 years. The impulses to expand and to rule have reinforced each other through hegemonic cultural consensus that has defined the boundaries and content of Christian theological reflection. A key feature of this complex phenomenon has been the confusion of Christianity with European and North American white culture. Magomero is just one example of what happens when mission and colonialism become one. Unfortunately, the story of what happened at Magomero is the general history of the spread of Christianity throughout the past 600 years – I am intentionally leaving out the centuries of the Crusades. The story of John Chilembwe, a significant part of which took place in my village, touching five generations of my family on the one hand, and touching David Livingstone and his grandsons on the other, with Joseph Booth, another British missionary, somewhere in the web of connections, reveals the problematic theology and praxis of European missionary work in Africa. That David Livingstone's mission station became his daughter's colonial estate whose managers persecuted local Christians, burning their houses and schools, and forcing them to work on the estate for free, shows the challenges of attaching the mission of God to the mission of empires.

Notes

1 David Livingstone lived and worked in Africa for 32 years, first as a missionary and later as an explorer (though he considered his explorations in Africa part of his missionary work). He has many biographies written about him. One of the best of those is Tim Jeal, *Livingstone* (New York: Dell, 1973). The 'revised and

expanded' edition was published in 2013. A fictionalized reconstruction of the journey that brought his body from Chitambo to England for his burial at Westminster Abbey on 18 April 1874 can be found in Petina Gappah, *Out of Darkness, Shining Light: A Novel* (New York: Simon & Schuster, 2019).

2 William Robertson, *The Martyrs of Blantyre: Henry Henderson, Dr. John Bowie [and] Robert Cleland: A Chapter from the Story of Missions in Central Africa* (London: James Nisbet & Co., 1892).

3 David Livingstone and Charles Livingstone, *Narrative of an Expedition to the Zambesi and Its Tributaries: And the Discovery of the Lakes Shirwa and Nyassa, 1858–1864* (New York: Harper & Brothers, 1865). Also see the same book republished in 2005, David Livingstone and Charles Livingstone, *Narrative of an Expedition to the Zambesi and Its Tributaries: And of the Discovery of the Lakes Shirwa and Nyassa, 1858–1864* (Stroud: Nonsuch, 2005).

4 Tim Jeal, *Livingstone* (New Haven, CT: Yale University Press, 2013), p. 21.

5 Ethel Daniels Hubbard, *The Moffats* (New York: Missionary Education Movement of the United States and Canada, 1917), p. 249.

6 Hubbard, *The Moffats*, p. 250. See also Hermann Karl Wilhelm Kumm and Karl Kumm, *African Missionary Heroes and Heroines* (New York: The Macmillan Company, 1917), p. 173.

7 Jeal, *Livingstone* (2013), p. 21.

8 Jeal, *Livingstone* (2013), p. 21.

9 Together, they had six children born between 1845 and 1858. Mary died in 1862 at Chupanga in Mozambique not long after meeting Livingstone, en route to Southern Malawi. There are many biographies written about her. For instance, see Julie Davidson, *Looking for Mrs. Livingstone* (Edinburgh: Saint Andrew Press, 2012), p. 173.

10 Kumm and Kumm, *African Missionary Heroes and Heroines*, p. 173.

11 I maintain the colonial language of the time as this is a book about colonialism and mission. David Livingstone, *The Life and Explorations of Dr. David Livingstone: Comprising All His Extensive Travels and Discoveries: As Detailed in His Diary, Reports, and Letters, Including His Famous Last Journals* (Philadelphia, PA: John E. Potter & Company, 1857), p. 145 (my emphasis).

12 In the second half of the nineteenth century the slave trade was still very much a problem in Africa. The Portuguese, having depleted the Congo-Angola part of Africa, had established new slave trading stations in the east of Africa, mostly in the Mozambique area and, together with the Arabs who sent slave raids from Zanzibar and the wider Tanzanian coast, sponsored slave raids inland, as far as current Zimbabwe, Zambia and the Democratic Republic of Congo. Scholars of slave trade history suggest that more Africans were kidnapped and enslaved in the nineteenth century than in the previous centuries put together.

13 David Livingstone, *Missionary Travels and Research in South Africa* (London: John Murray, 1857).

14 Meriel Buxton, *David Livingstone* (Basingstoke: Palgrave, 2001), p. 106.

15 Anne E. M. Anderson-Morshead, *The History of the Universities' Mission to Central Africa, 1859–1896*, 2nd edn (London: Office of the Universities' Mission to Central Africa, 1899), p. 5.

16 Mackenzie had served as archdeacon to Bishop John William Colenso in South Africa beginning in 1855.

17 He was aware that two Portuguese men, Gaspar Bocarro and Candido José

da Costa Cardoso, had seen the lake before him. Bocarro is arguably the first European to record seeing the lake in 1616. Cardoso visited it in 1846.

18 This was a shift away from the usual way of naming land after the people who lived on it. For instance, Bechuanaland, Xhosaland or Zululand. After gaining independence in 1964, Nyasaland was immediately renamed Malawi (a variation of *maravi*, which means 'flames of fire' – a nod to the iron smelters who had occupied the land for many centuries before Livingstone arrived).

19 Bishop Mackenzie died of Blackwater Fever on 31 January 1862 on the Shire River in southern Malawi after only six months of work at Magomero.

20 This Magomero is my home. I was born and raised on the outskirts of the Alexander Bruce Estate. It is also at Magomero on the Bruce Estates where William Jervis Livingstone was killed during the Chilembwe Uprising in 1915.

21 The UMCA returned to Likoma Island on Lake Malawi in 1875. The rest of the story of the UMCA is not important for our discourse at the moment. Readers interested in that history are encouraged to look at Landeg White's book, *Magomero*, which has a detailed account of the story of my community, and discusses in great depth the time when the UMCA was there, between 1861 and 1863–64. See Landeg White, *Magomero: Portrait of an African Village* (New York: Cambridge University Press, 1987). Another important book in this discourse is Owen Chadwick, *Mackenzie's Grave* (London: Hodder & Stoughton, 1959). There is also the official history of the UMCA quoted above: Anderson-Morshead, *The History of the Universities' Mission to Central Africa, 1859–1896*. In addition, readers may also consult James Tengatenga, *The UMCA in Malawi: A History of the Anglican Church 1861–2010* (Zomba, Malawi: Kachere Series, 2010).

22 The British were not keen to take Malawi but could not let this small country fall into the hands of the Portuguese, because there had been too much British history already in the country. Many British missionaries were already at work in all regions of Malawi, especially at Blantyre Mission in the south and at Livingstonia Mission in the north.

23 Horace Waller, *The Last Journals of David Livingstone in Central Africa* (New York: Harper & Brothers, 1875), p. 59.

24 Waller, *The Last Journals*, p. 63.

25 Livingstone, *The Life and Explorations*, pp. 346–7 (my emphasis).

26 Livingstone, *The Life and Explorations*, p. 492 (my emphasis).

27 The British Government had outlawed slave trade through the Slave Trade Act of 1807 and passed the Slavery Abolition Act in 1833, gradually abolishing the holding of slaves in most parts of the empire. However, more Africans were captured and enslaved in the nineteenth century, after the abolition of the slave trade in the British Empire.

28 Oliver Ransford, *David Livingstone: The Dark Interior* (London: J. Murray, 1978), p. 160.

29 Jeal, *Livingstone* (2013), p. 224.

30 Jeal, *Livingstone* (2013), p. 188.

31 Ransford, *David Livingstone*, p. 159.

32 Ransford, *David Livingstone*, p. 159.

33 Buxton, *David Livingstone*, p. 105.

34 Peter Falk, *The Growth of the Church in Africa* (Grand Rapids, MI: Zondervan, 1979), pp. 181–2.

35 Joseph Booth and Laura Perry (eds), *Africa for the African* (Zomba: Kachere Series, 2008).

36 White, *Magomero*, p. 78.

37 This was the actual title of George Mwase's book on the events surrounding John Chilembwe's uprising in 1915, based on accounts of people who spoke to George Mwase while in jail in Zomba 15 years after the uprising. See George Simeon Mwase and Robert I. Rotberg, *Strike a Blow and Die: The Classic Story of the Chilembwe Rising* (Cambridge, MA: Harvard University Press, 1975, my emphasis).

38 John Chilembwe himself is mentioned in the American Lothrop Stoddard's racist and notorious 1920 book, *The Rising Tide of Color: The Threat Against White World Supremacy*, where he is described as an Ethiopian preacher with a bitterly anti-white propaganda, who asserted that Africa belonged to the Black man, that the white man was an intruder. Of Chilembwe's uprising, Stoddard first celebrates that 'The Whites acted with great vigor, the poorly armed insurgents were quickly scattered, and Chilembwe himself was soon hunted and killed.' He continues, 'In itself, the incident was of slight importance, but, taken in connection with much else, it does not augur well for the future.' See Lothrop Stoddard, *The Rising Tide of Color Against White World Supremacy*, Liberty Bell's Politically Incorrect Classics (York, SC: Liberty Bell, 2006), p. 99.

39 Geoffrey W. T. Hodges, 'African Manpower Statistics for the British Forces in East Africa, 1914–1918', *The Journal of African History* 19, no. 1 (1978), p. 116.

40 See Leigh Gardner, *Taxing Colonial Africa: The Political Economy of British Imperialism* (Oxford: Oxford University Press, 2012).

41 Harry W. Langworthy, 'Joseph Booth, Prophet of Radical Change in Central and South Africa, 1891–1915', *Journal of Religion in Africa* 16, no. 1 (1986). Also, Harry W. Langworthy, *'Africa for the African': The Life of Joseph Booth* (Blantyre, Malawi: CLAIM, 1996).

42 George Shepperson and Thomas Price, *Independent African: John Chilembwe and the Origins, Setting, and Significance of the Nyasaland Native Rising of 1915* (Edinburgh: Edinburgh University Press, 1958), p. 26 (my emphasis).

43 Bishop John William Colenso was born in Cornwall in 1814 and died in Durban in 1883. He was the first Bishop of Natal and, as his biographers say, a fervent defender of the Zulu against both the Boer and British aggressions, including during the Anglo–Zulu War of 1879. He also defended other African tribes, gaining a title of *Sobantu* in the process – the father of the people. He was widely regarded as the last honest white man. See George William Cox, *The Life of John William Colenso, D.D., Bishop of Natal* (London: W. Ridgway, 1888).

44 Shepperson and Price, *Independent African*, p. 71. In the end Mataka could not trust Booth any more and left him in South Africa, finding his way back home alone.

45 Langworthy, *'Africa for the African'*.

46 Langworthy, 'Joseph Booth', pp. 31–2.

47 Cecil John Rhodes was Prime Minister of the Cape Colony from 1890 to 1896, and he died in 1902. For his biography, see Robert I. Rotberg, *The Founder: Cecil Rhodes and the Pursuit of Power* (Oxford: Oxford University Press, 1988). Also, Antony Thomas, *Rhodes: Race for Africa* (New York: Martin's Press, 1997).

48 Henry Morton Stanley died in 1904, while King Leopold II died in 1909. See John Bierman, *Dark Safari: The Life Behind the Legend of Henry Morton Stanley* (London: Lume Books, 1990).

49 Shepperson and Price, *Independent African*, p. 110 (my emphasis).

2

Jesus and the Empire

> The early church had to negotiate empire, resist empire, flee from empire, suffer under empire, offer apologies for itself to empire ... until the church became one with empire.[1]

> Robbers of the world, having by their universal plunder exhausted the land, they rifle the deep. If the enemy be rich, they are rapacious; if he be poor, they lust for dominion; neither the east nor the west has been able to satisfy them. Alone among men they covet with equal eagerness poverty and riches. To robbery, slaughter, plunder, they give the lying name of empire; they make a solitude and call it peace.[2]

During the first century CE the Roman Empire was the dominating power in the region around the Mediterranean Sea. The empire itself extended from north-western England, through the countries of France and Spain, across all southern and central Europe, all the way to Turkey and Syria, reaching a great deal of North Africa, through modern Tunisia and Egypt. At that time the Roman Empire included an estimated 60 to 65 million people of different ethnicities and cultures scattered around the Mediterranean and beyond. At its peak in 117 CE the empire covered land between York in Britain and Babylon in Iraq.

The political situation at the time was such that, even though Judea was an independent kingdom – at least until 6 CE – Rome was in charge. Rome had been in command over the region since 63 BCE when Pompey besieged Jerusalem and brought the civil conflict between Hyrcanus and Aristobulus, the two sons of Alexander Jannaeus and Alexandra Salome (who was also known as Shlomtzion), to an end.[3] After Alex's death in 76 BCE, Salome became queen of the kingdom and ruled for nine years until she died in 67 BCE. It was after her death that Hyrcanus ascended to the throne to continue in the Hasmonean Dynasty. However, only three months into his reign, Aristobulus, his younger brother with whom he had been in conflict since 67 BCE when Salome made Hyrcanus the high priest, challenged his kingship and a civil war broke out.

The civil wars between Hyrcanus and Aristobulus went on until 63 BCE when Pompey was invited to Jerusalem to settle the matter. He was invited by both Hyrcanus and Aristobulus as well as a third party of some people interested in bringing the entire kingdom to an end. Pompey ended up siding with the older brother, Hyrcanus, for he was thought to be weaker and easier to manipulate than Aristobulus. In the end Pompey restored to Hyrcanus the high priesthood, though he stripped him of his royal title. Hyrcanus would be recognized as an ethnarch in 47 BCE. Aristobulus was brought to Rome for Pompey's triumphal procession. Thus, from 63 BCE, when Pompey overran Jerusalem, to 37 BCE, when Herod usurped the throne and brought the Hasmonean Dynasty to an end, the rule of Judea would happen from Rome.

Thus, the region that we know as Israel and Palestine today was a vassal state under the indirect rule of Rome when Jesus was born. It had its own king, Herod the Great – also known as Herod I – who lived between 72 BCE and 4 BCE. Herod ruled over Judea, Samaria and Idumea from around 37 BCE until his death. Though he was raised as a Jew, Herod was an Idumean (of the Kingdom of Edom, to the southeast of Judea). He was born in Idumea and his father, Antipater, was a high-ranking Idumean official in the Hasmonean Dynasty, while his mother, Cypros, was a Nabatean Arab princess from Petra. Antipater became a client of Rome after Pompey defeated Jerusalem in 63 BCE. He switched his allegiance to Julius Caesar after Pompey was defeated at Pharsalus in 48 BCE. With the blessing of Hyrcanus, the high priest, and leading a battalion of 3,000 troops, Antipater joined Mithridates of Pergamon as he marched to support Julius Caesar during the Siege of Alexandria in 47 BCE. As a result, Caesar made him the chief minister of Judea. Eventually, Caesar made Antipater's sons, Phasaelus and Herod, governors of Jerusalem and Galilee respectively. Six years after the death of Antipater (by poison), Herod claimed the throne and became king of the Jews.

Herod was only a vassal king. It was Caesar Augustus who, as the emperor of Rome from 27 BCE to 14 CE, was really in charge and ruled the empire for most of Herod's reign. They did not start as friends. Herod was a close friend of Mark Antony's and had sided with him against Augustus in the conflict that led to the deaths of Mark Antony and Cleopatra in Egypt in 30 BCE. After losing these two friends, Herod rebuilt his relationship with Augustus and in the end had a long working relationship with him that lasted until Herod's death.

Herod ascended to the throne after being officially made king of the Jews by the Roman Senate in 37 BCE, and he consolidated his power by intentionally aligning himself with and serving the Romans. He did the best he could to be in Rome's good books. He knew he would be weak without the help of the Romans. Essentially, then, Herod was a puppet king of Rome who carried out Caesar's agenda throughout his kingdom. He effectively ruled with Augustus' permission and sought to promote Rome's interests. For this reason he was exceedingly unpopular among his people. His kingdom maintained for Rome open access to Egypt and Syria. He ruled until his death, which the Gospel of Matthew uses to date the birth of Jesus Christ. When Herod died, around 4 BCE, his son Archelaus went to Augustus to claim the throne. His brother, Antipas, who had for a long time been favoured to succeed Herod, followed him to Rome to claim the same throne with a delegate of Jewish leaders saying that the people did not want Archelaus to be their leader. In the end Archelaus was given the throne, not as king but as ethnarch. Interestingly, when the nobleman of Jesus' parable came back (Luke 19.11–27), having been crowned as king, he rewarded his loyal subjects by making them governors of cities. This is yet another reflection of Roman language in Jesus' ministry. The Jews did not have governors.

Locating the Messiah in a colonized land

The historical location of Jesus' life on earth – his birth in Bethlehem, the years spent in exile in Egypt, his return to Nazareth (and not to Bethlehem where he was born), the very fact that he grew up in Nazareth in the Galilee of the Gentiles (and not in any other more important place in Israel, like Jerusalem, or in the Jewish diaspora, like Alexandria or Rome), the many interactions with both political and religious authorities, the death of his relation, John the Baptist, at the hands of the evil tetrarch, Herod Antipas, all the way to his capture by Roman soldiers in Gethsemane, his trial before the Roman prefect, Pontius Pilate, and his death by a Roman way of execution by crucifixion (which Pilate ordered with the blessing of the people)[4] – is critical to our understanding of his mission and strategy if, indeed, we can speak of such a thing. His entire life, from birth to death, happened under the heavy hand of the Romans. Augustus was emperor during the first half of his life, while Tiberius ruled during the second half. Throughout his life, the empire was the air he breathed and the water in which he swam.

We have today the advantage of history and hindsight that allows us to look at the events of the wider Mediterranean world and its key players of the time. We can appreciate that the historical events of the first century BCE quite significantly shaped the world into which Jesus was born. Pompey's siege of Jerusalem in 63 BCE, the death and deification of Julius Caesar in 44 BCE, the rise of Herod as king of the Jews in 37 BCE, and the collapse of the Roman Republic, the emergence of the Roman Empire and the rise of Augustus Caesar all shape the world of the first century CE in which Christ lived. Yet that world itself was also a result of centuries of geopolitical jostling in the Mediterranean basin and beyond – the emergence of the Roman Empire (after centuries of being a republic), the fall of the Greek Empire that preceded it by at least 200 years, which was also foreshadowed by the Persian Empire, the Median Empire, the Babylonian Empire, as well as the Assyrian Empire that preceded them, all of which had direct impact on the land of Judea. Of course, tucked away in Nazareth in the first century CE, Jesus and his people heard about and were almost directly affected by the developments in the empire's centres of power – Rome, Antioch, Alexandria, Jerusalem and many others – but they were powerless to influence anything significant. Later, as the empire asserted itself deep into the first century CE, the geopolitical manoeuvrings continued. Jerusalem itself would be destroyed and ransacked in 70 CE.

This historical hindsight allows us to begin to comprehend the ways that the Roman Empire dominated the world of the New Testament and, with this, to see how Jesus positioned himself, his mission and his ministry in the context of the Roman colonization of Galilee and Judea. Every time we see Jesus Christ in the Gospels, from his birth in Bethlehem all the way to his death at Golgotha and his ascension from the Mount of Olives, the imposing tentacles of the empire are present. Jesus was born during the reign of Augustus (who was the first emperor of Rome, in power between 27 BCE and 14 CE when he died). Jesus' ministry and death took place when Tiberius, Augustus' adopted son, was emperor. His reign started after the death of Augustus and went on until his own death in 37 CE. Both Augustus and Tiberius are mentioned in the Gospels. Augustus is acknowledged as the emperor who called for the census that caused Joseph and Mary to travel to Bethlehem where Jesus would be born:

> In those days a decree went out from Emperor Augustus that all the world should be registered. This was the first registration and was taken while Quirinius was governor of Syria. All went to their own towns to be registered. Joseph also went from the town of Nazareth in Galilee to Judea, to the city of David called Bethlehem, because he was descended from the house and family of David. He went to be registered with Mary, to whom he was engaged and who was expecting a child. While they were there, the time came for her to deliver her child. And she gave birth to her firstborn son and wrapped him in bands of

cloth, and laid him in a manger, because there was no room for them in the inn. (Luke 2.1–7)[5]

Tiberius, however, is mentioned to mark the beginning of the ministry of John. Luke's dating of the beginning of the ministry of John the Baptist depends entirely on the events and characters of Roman figures. He did this by mentioning seven key people who were in various imperial offices – including that of the high priest who often served as a religious as well as political leader – at the time John launched out to baptize people: Tiberius, Pilate, Herod Antipas, Philip, Lysanius, Ananias and Caiaphas:

> In the fifteenth year of the reign of Emperor Tiberius, when Pontius Pilate was governor of Judea, and Herod was ruler of Galilee, and his brother Philip ruler of the region of Iturea and Trachonitis, and Lysanias ruler of Abilene, during the high-priesthood of Annas and Caiaphas, the word of God came to John son of Zachariah in the wilderness. (Luke 3.1–2)

Jesus' ministry started only a few months after John's, and therefore these same names may be used to date his ministry. For Luke and for many people at the time, Rome was the ultimate reference point for everything important happening in Judea and Galilee. In addition, the circles of the powerful people in Jerusalem were dominated by Roman names. Those who were not Roman were most likely appointees of Roman power. The four main players in this piece of history (Tiberius, Pilate, Quirinius and Valerius Gratus) are all Roman. Everyone else, both the two Herods (Antipas and Philip) and the two high priests (Ananias and Caiaphas), were placed in their positions by Rome.

The coming of a Jewish king

We cannot understand the message of Jesus without paying attention to the world that shaped his earthly life, that of the people he interacted with and the politicians who made the rules that his community followed. The Gospel of John tells of how Jesus came and made a dwelling among us, all humanity, in the immediate context of first-century Israel. 'The Word became flesh and blood and moved into the neighborhood. We saw the glory with our own eyes, the one-of-a-kind glory, like Father, like Son, generous inside and out, true from start to finish' (John 1.14, *The Message*). In pitching his tent in the neighbourhood, Jesus had to live with the reality of our political situation and be subject to whatever government ruled Judea and Samaria at the time. He was born in Bethlehem, in a colonized nation, among a people who lived under the oppressive rule of the cruel Romans who governed Palestine with a strong hand. While it is plausible that Jesus was born long before the census of Quirinius, there is no doubt that he was born in Bethlehem. If Joseph and Mary had been living in Nazareth, or indeed around the northern shore of the Sea of Galilee, then they made the long trip to Bethlehem in time for Jesus to be born in the city of his ancestor David.

The fact that Jesus was born in the early days of the Roman Empire, when Augustus Caesar, Rome's first emperor, was in power, and that his life coincided with that of the Herodian Dynasty that paved the way for the full Roman colonization of Judea and Samaria, has direct implications for his birth, ministry, death and mission. He was born 60 years after Pompey's siege of Jerusalem. Thus, Rome's influence in Judea had been in play for a good 60 years before he was born. It was Augustus' puppet king, Herod, who was responsible for the Massacre of the Innocents, in which young boys in Bethlehem were killed. His history shows that he was ruthless in killing anyone who could threaten his throne. Indeed, he killed his own family members, including three of his sons, in fear that they could seek to dethrone him. When he heard from the magi that a king had been born in Bethlehem, he had to act. After realizing that the magi would not bring him the information he needed to pinpoint where Jesus was, he ordered the death of all male children under two years in Bethlehem. All this happened with the blessing of Rome. Such a massacre could not have happened without the knowledge or permission of the emperor.

> When Herod saw that he had been tricked by the wise men, he was infuriated, and he sent and killed all the children in and around Bethlehem who were two years old or under, according to the time that he had learned from the wise men. (Matt. 2.16)

> But when he heard that Archelaus was ruling over Judea in place of his father Herod, he was afraid to go there. And after being warned in a dream, he went away to the district of Galilee. (Matt. 2.22)

Matthew then recognizes the ascendancy of Archelaus to the throne after the death of Herod I. Archelaus took over the throne in 4 BCE. He was made ethnarch by Augustus over against Antipas, another one of Herod's sons. His reign was short, lasting only until 6 CE. He was incompetent in his leadership and, just like his father, extremely cruel to his people. As such, Augustus ended his ethnarchy and exiled him to Vienne in Gaul where he died in 16 CE.

Luke, however, places the birth of Christ during the census of Quirinius, which only took place in 6 CE when Augustus deposed Herod Archelaus. Luke is erroneous in this case, as the census took place when Jesus was about ten years old.

The census was needed because Augustus had decided to remove Archelaus from power and to create the Province of Judea and annex it to Syria. It was at this point that Augustus established colonial rule in Judea in 6 CE, with Publius Sulpicius Quirinius, located in Syria, as the legate or governor. Quirinius' first order of business was to call for the census that Luke records. Luke actually mentions Quirinius as governor in Syria (Luke 2.1–5).

Jesus was aptly named Yehoshua (or, in short, Yeshua, which is a derivative of Joshua, meaning 'save' or 'salvation'). He was to save God's people. His other name, Emmanuel, means 'God with us'. In the Jewish tradition, saying 'God is with us' is a powerful statement of faith. Their God had finally, after many centuries of afflictions, come down to be with them. God had come down to share their humanity, with everything that being human in a colonized country entailed. Having God with them on their side was a great assurance that everything would be well, no matter how bad things may look. God comes through for God's people.

Jesus grew up in a world of pervasive Roman presence. Tiberius Caesar was the Roman emperor while Valerius Gratus was the prefect of Judea from 15 to 26 CE and Pontius Pilate was governor from 26 to 36 CE. Pilate was responsible for the crucifixion of Jesus. Herod Antipas was the tetrarch of Galilee from 4 BCE to 39 CE.[6] Annas ben Seth (commonly known as Ananias) was the high priest from 6 CE, when he was appointed by Quirinius, and remained in that role until 15 CE. After his deposition, Ananias stayed on as a powerful political leader in Jerusalem and continued to exert a great deal of influence, especially when his son-in-law, Joseph Caiaphas, was made high priest by Valerius Gratus in 18 CE.[7] It was Caiaphas who was the high priest during the three and a half years of Jesus' ministry. He presided over the trial of Jesus before the Sanhedrin.

What is the Messiah good for?

By the time Jesus showed up, the Jewish people had been oppressed by one bondage or another for most of the centuries since Moses led them out of Egypt. Squashed between Egypt and the Mediterranean on one side and Assyria, Babylon and many more Eastern powers on the other side, the two tiny kingdoms of Israel and Judah occupied a small piece of land that happened to be almost always on a warpath. At one point it was the Egyptians against the Assyrians. At another time it was the Babylonians going down to Egypt. Later it would be the Greeks, having conquered Egypt and now going towards Persia. Or the Romans, having conquered the Greeks, seeking to assert their authority over the Holy Land, something they did until the rise of Islam. It was in this context of wider geopolitical conflicts between the Babylonians and the Egyptians that Judah found itself caught up around 600 BCE, which would lead to the siege against Jerusalem in 597 BCE that saw thousands of Jews taken to Babylon. Their refusal to cooperate with the Babylonians resulted in thousands of Jews being exiled for many decades.

The Romans had conquered Palestine 60 years before Jesus. However, before the Romans took control of Palestine, it was the Greeks who dominated the land from the era of Alexander the Great, around 330 BCE. In his quest to conquer the Persians, Alexander conquered Palestine in 332 BCE and made its population part of the Hellenistic world. After his death, the Ptolemies and later the Seleucids ruled Palestine. The Greeks were preceded by the Persians and Medians, who took over control from the Babylonians and the Assyrians. Thus, when Jesus showed up, almost 600 years after Nebuchadnezzar's ransacking of Jerusalem, the yoke of oppression was still on their minds. Memories of the scattering of the ten tribes and the captivity in Babylon were still alive. By the rivers of Babylon, they sat down and wept when they remembered Jerusalem (Ps. 137). The Promised Land that was supposed to be full of milk and honey had not really known peace in a long time, and had not been a safe home for them for centuries. Several messianic figures had emerged over the centuries but none had liberated them. They were desperate for the real Messiah to come and set them free. John tells of Andrew's excitement in the first chapter of his Gospel when he met Jesus and sought out his brother Simon to announce that 'We have found the Messiah' (John 1.41).

The Roman Empire so permeates the New Testament that it is plausible that the writers of the Gospels took it for granted and presumed that their readers did not need them to mention it all the time. Rome was felt in the daily lives of many. The sight of a tax collector, a Roman soldier or even a milestone, as well as the mention of a governor, a prefect or indeed a vassal king like Herod, kept Rome in sight. Yes, Jesus lived in Galilee and died in Judea, but both Galilee and Judea were part of a large Roman province that stretched from Syria to Egypt, ruled by Roman governors or non-Roman puppet kings. Egypt, where he spent some time as a child, was also a Roman colony at that time.

The language that was spoken around Jesus in the first third of the first century CE, which shaped his word, was peppered with Roman terms. Philip was the 'tetrarch' – a Roman term for a leader who shares responsibility with three others (Luke 3.1). The coin he used to pay taxes was a *denarius* – a Roman silver coin that Matthew tells us was the wage for a day's work (Matt. 20.2). Jesus cast out a 'legion' of demons from the Gerasene man (Matt. 8.28–34; Mark 5.1–20; Luke 8.26–39). 'Legion', of course, is a Roman word for a principal unit of the army, comprising between 3,000 and 6,000 soldiers. His teaching often reflects an awareness of the developments in the political circles in Jerusalem, Galilee and Rome. It is possible that he spoke of the Roman Empire when he said, 'no one can enter a strong man's house and plunder his property without first tying up the strong man; then indeed the house can be plundered' (Mark 3.27). He may have had Archelaus in mind when he told of a young man of noble birth who went away to claim his kingdom only to be followed by a delegation from his people saying they did not want him:

> So he said, 'A nobleman went to a distant country to get royal power for himself and then return. He summoned ten of his slaves, and gave them ten pounds, and said to them, "Do business with these until I come back." But the citizens of his country hated him and sent a delegation after him, saying, "We do not want this man to rule over us."' (Luke 19.12–14)

Even the geography of the entire ministry of Jesus and that of many of his followers is filled with Roman names. For instance, in one of the major events in the Gospel of Matthew, on the one occasion when Jesus took his disciples on a long trip across the Jordan river, it was to the town Caesarea Philippi, the capital of Philip's reign, named after both Caesar and Philip (Philip was the son of Herod who inherited the rule over the Roman province of Iturea).[8] It was at Caesarea Philippi, a village that had originally been called Paneas, after the Greek goat-footed god Pan, and was home to the centuries-old shrine dedicated to Pan's worship, that Peter confessed Jesus to be the Messiah, the Son of the living God.

It is either impossible or, indeed, irresponsible to try to think of Jesus without attending to the pervasive dominance of the Roman Empire in his world and day. We cannot effectively begin to understand Jesus or appreciate the movement that he started without paying attention to the overbearing image of the Roman Empire that was the backdrop to everything he did. The empire not only formed a backdrop to Jesus' work and ministry, it was also the foreground that coloured everything we see Jesus do, even in those chapters of the Gospels where the empire seems absent. Although he lived in a peasant community in a somewhat obscure corner of the empire, the smell of Roman absolute authority filled the air that he breathed. The rules of Roman living shaped the community that heard him preach. The beginning of the Pax Romana – which started with the rise of Augustus in 27 BCE, after the final wars of the Roman Republic, and lasted a good 200 years until the death of Marcus Aurelius in 180 CE – testified to the brutality of the Roman legions that could crush any resistance to the empire. The relative peace that started with Augustus and went on with Tiberius was won by violent conquest. It is this peace that Tacitus calls a lie: 'They [the Romans] make a desolation and they call it peace.'[9] The Pax Romana was good for the spread of the Christian message as trade routes were safe and people could move from one part of the empire with relative ease.

Within the imperial territory, all enemies of Rome had been brought to their knees. Many of those who were unlucky enough to survive the conquest were usually taken to Rome for the triumphal parade, to be crucified afterwards. The Roman military machinery was unprecedented in its might. Its legions were extremely violent. It was almost always a mistake, at least during this era, to go against Rome. Many living at the time of Jesus would remember, at least through oral history, the siege of Pompey against Jerusalem a few decades earlier, in 63 BCE. Some would remember the double suicide of Mark Antony and Cleopatra in 30 BCE that was a result of Augustus' military prowess. There were several messianic figures and insurrections after the death of Herod and the deposition of Archelaus, and these too were summarily resolved with violent ease. At the beginning of the reign of Tiberius, there was one legion, the XII Fulminata, stationed at Raphanae in Syria. The XII Fulminata had probably been used to respond to the messianic rebellions of Simon of Peraea, Judas son of Hezekiah, and Athronges, which took place after the death of Herod in 4 BCE. The XII Fulminata was definitely used in the first Jewish–Roman War in 66 CE. There were many other legions, such as the III Cyrenaica, III Gallica, IV Scythia, X Fretensis and XVI Flavia Firma, which could be deployed to Judea at any time. All this military might could have caused enough terror among the people in Judea and surrounding provinces to keep the region quiet for some time. Jesus had to be extremely careful in his subversion of the empire. The Romans could easily ride in on their horses to destroy the land, as they did in 70 CE.

Jesus and Antipas

Herod Antipas was the king of Galilee and Perea from 4 BCE to 39 CE. He was thus ruler of the land in which Jesus grew up and ministered for almost all his life. He ascended to the throne after the death of his father when Jesus was either an infant or a toddler. If we go by the Gospels, Antipas met Jesus only once, on the night of his trial, after several years of waiting, and was 'exceedingly glad'.

> When Herod [Antipas] saw Jesus, he was very glad, for he had been wanting to see him for a long time, because he had heard about him and was hoping to see him perform some sign. He questioned him at some length, but Jesus gave him no answer. The chief priests and the scribes stood by, vehemently accusing him. Even Herod with his soldiers treated him with contempt and mocked him; then he put an elegant robe on him, and sent him back to Pilate. That same day Herod and Pilate became friends with each other; before this they had been enemies. (Luke 23.8–12)[10]

In the course of the night, Pontius Pilate, being prefect of Judea, had realized that Jesus was from Galilee and was, therefore, under the jurisdiction of Antipas. Fortunately, Antipas happened to be in Jerusalem on that night. As a result, Pilate sent Jesus to be judged by him. By this time, Antipas had been in power for a long time. His authority had been central to the Galilean peace. Matters of his private life had political ramifications in the region. When he divorced Phasa'el, his first wife, to marry Herodias, the wife of his half-brother Philip (not the tetrarch of Iturea), John the Baptist publicly rebuked him, saying, 'It is not lawful for you to have her.' In response, on the occasion of his birthday, at the request of Salome, Herodias' daughter, Antipas had ordered the beheading of John. Later, when he heard about the miracles of Jesus, he believed it was John the Baptist who had come back to life (Matt. 14.1–2). Jesus was deeply moved by John's death – Luke tells us that their mothers were related (Luke 1.36). When he heard that John had been killed, 'he withdrew from there in a boat to a deserted place', perhaps because he was afraid Antipas could try to harm him too (Matt. 14.13). Overall, Jesus was cautious of Herod's family. Most likely, he knew of the Massacre of the Innocents. Later, in Mark 8.15, Jesus warns his disciples to beware of the yeast of the Pharisees and the leaven of Herod.

Fishers of people

Earlier in his ministry, while gathering the group of men who would become his disciples, Jesus called Andrew and his brother Peter to leave their fishing business to follow him so he could make them 'fishers of people' (Mark 1.14–20; Matt. 4.18–22, NRSVUE). Taken literally, this statement looks pretty straightforward. Jesus wanted Andrew and Peter to do something similar to what they had been doing for a long time – something that would have been totally familiar to them – but apply it in a different context. From the time he called them, Andrew and Peter – and the other disciples – would catch people instead of fish. This is a problematic analogy. Fish are caught to be sold and eaten. But Jesus was not talking about Andrew and Peter catching people for gain and consumption. He was focused on the effort and care put into the exercise of catching fish. The two brothers and their friends would have to work hard to save people.

In a great deal of mission and evangelism conversations in the past century, to be 'fishers of people' has been understood to imply being involved in proclaiming the gospel to save souls. It is very likely that Jesus had something more in mind. His ministry, according to Luke 4, would involve more than just the saving of souls. It would have to do with bringing the good news to the poor, setting the captives free, recovering sight to the blind, letting the oppressed go free and, finally, proclaiming the year of the Lord's favour. This is a lot more than fishing for people and saving souls. On their own, all these aspects of Jesus' ministry have the effect of overturning the oppression that the Galileans were suffering under the heavy hand of the Romans. Much like today, for the empire to be, there must have been millions of non-elite Romans who were exploited for the welfare of the rich few at the top of society.

When Jesus called Andrew and Peter to leave their boats and follow him, he was subverting the empire in a subtle yet big way. Fishing was a profitable activity for the empire because, of course, the emperor was sovereign over land and seas. Whatever lived in Roman waters belonged to Rome. As a result, fishermen, usually located at the bottom of the social hierarchy, were taxed quite significantly. By taking Andrew and Peter, and later James and John, from their fishing business, Jesus was showing them the need for an alternative allegiance. They would not be taxed by the empire for fishing any more. Thus, their money would not be funnelled from Galilee to Jerusalem and Rome any more. In addition, by shifting their energy from a service of imperial significance to one of God's work, Jesus was communicating to them that he, not the emperor, was powerful. The service of religion, of fishing for people, was more important than that which benefited the empire.

The Son of God

The same subversion happens when Jesus begins to claim to be the Son of God. In the Roman Empire of the first century CE, it was Augustus, the emperor, who claimed to be the son of God. By the time Augustus became emperor, his adoptive father, Julius Caesar, had been deified (42 BCE) and was worshipped as Jupiter. Once deified, Caesar was believed to have become the lord of lords and king of kings. Augustus was thus the son of god. He dropped his name, Octavian, and became *Augustus* (Latin for 'the Divine One') and *Sebastos* (Greek for 'Venerable one' or 'One-to-be-Worshipped'). As a son of god and emperor, Augustus could also claim to be king of kings and lord of lords. Indeed, his titles included 'Divine', 'Son of God', 'God' and 'God from God', whose titles were 'Lord', 'Redeemer', 'Liberator' and 'Saviour of the World'.[11]

When his followers popularized Jesus' identity as the Son of God, they were basically taking the titles that had belonged to the most powerful man in the Roman world at the time, the emperor, and ascribing them to a lowly Jewish peasant carpenter from Nazareth. One would have to be out of one's mind to take the emperor's titles upon oneself. Yet Jesus does just that. His claim that he was the Son of God meant that Caesar was not. Indeed, to say 'Jesus is Lord' back then meant that Augustus was not. Even today, when we say Jesus is Lord, we mean that he alone is Lord; no one else is. In the Roman world, to say 'Jesus is Lord' would have been a dangerous poking of the empire, and looking at Jesus' circumstances it would have been considered a joke. When Pilate handed Jesus over to be crucified, he had a sign made calling him the 'King of the Jews'. Those who wanted him crucified understood the irony and refused to acknowledge him as their king. They would rather be ruled by Caesar:

> Now it was the day of Preparation for the Passover; and it was about noon. He said to the Jews, 'Here is your King!' They cried out, 'Away with him! Away with him! Crucify him!' Pilate asked them, 'Shall I crucify your King?' The chief priests answered, '*We have no king but the emperor.*' Then he handed him over to them to be crucified.
>
> So they took Jesus; and carrying the cross by himself, he went out to what is called The Place of the Skull, which in Hebrew is called Golgotha. There they crucified him and with him two others, one on either

side, with Jesus between them. Pilate also had an inscription written and put on the cross. It read, 'Jesus of Nazareth, the King of the Jews.' Many of the Jews read this inscription because the place where Jesus was crucified was near the city; and it was written in Hebrew, in Latin, and in Greek. Then the chief priests of the Jews said to Pilate, 'Do not write, "The King of the Jews", but, "This man said, I am King of the Jews."' (John 19.14–21)

Go the extra mile

Jesus, growing up in Nazareth and the areas surrounding the northern end of the Sea of Galilee, would have been exposed to the presence of many Roman soldiers. Around the time he was born, Roman soldiers came into Galilee to maintain peace after Herod's death. Later, in 6 CE, when the entire region became a province of Rome, the presence of imperial soldiers in Galilee and Judea was somewhat normalized. The governor needed some soldiers around to maintain peace in the region. In the many years that Jesus lived in Galilee, he saw Roman soldiers on many occasions. As such, it is highly likely that he had Roman soldiers in mind when he preached in his Sermon on the Mount: 'if anyone forces you to go one mile, go also the second mile' (Matt. 5.41). Some translations, like the New Living Translation, are pretty straightforward: 'If *a soldier* demands that you carry *his gear* for a mile, carry it two miles.' This was normal in the Roman world. Roman soldiers (and sometimes citizens too) could legally require others (foreigners and people from their colonies or the lands they had conquered) or their property (such as animals, carts and wagons) to carry their load for them for one mile and one mile only. This was called 'impressment'. To resist would be interpreted as rebellion against the emperor and could be punished accordingly. Many complied and carried the load for the required one mile, and no more.

Give to Caesar what belongs to Caesar

As a Roman subject living in Nazareth, Jesus probably knew of the death of Augustus in 14 CE and that his adoptive son, Tiberius, had become emperor in his place. The death of an emperor, especially of an emperor of Augustus' calibre, could not go unnoticed anywhere in the empire. Ceremonial mourning would have been proclaimed in all colonies, including Galilee. So Jesus would have known of the changes in

Rome. He was also aware of the imperial tax system that was imposed on all its subjects. Without a doubt, taxes were the lifeline of the empire. To keep the imperial machine working, with its army, roads, temples and other buildings, the imperial powers taxed their subjects quite heavily. Refusal to pay taxes could be interpreted as rebellion against the emperor. Once, the Pharisees and the Herodians tried to trick Jesus by asking whether it was lawful for Jews to pay taxes to Caesar:

> [Jesus said,] 'Show me the coin used for the tax.' And they brought him a denarius. Then he said to them, 'Whose head is this, and whose title?' They answered, 'The emperor's.' Then he said to them, 'Give therefore to the emperor the things that are the emperor's, and to God the things that are God's.' (Matt. 22.19–21)

It's a tricky exchange. What did this self-proclaimed Messiah from Nazareth think about Jewish people paying taxes to Rome? Of course, beneath the trickery of the question is an honest desire to know if Jesus was indeed a Messiah worth following and, eventually, dying for. Whatever way he answered the question, there would be great implications. The Jewish Messiah, in the context of the first century CE, would have to liberate the Jews from the yoke of Rome, the powerful oppressor of the era. That was the Messiah's primary job – to set the oppressed Jewish population in Palestine free from the Roman overlords. How, then, could the Messiah think it was all right for Jews to pay taxes to Caesar? Was it acceptable to him for Jewish people to be colonized by the Romans? If indeed it was lawful for them to pay taxes to Caesar, then he was not the Messiah. He had failed the ultimate test. However, if he said that it was not lawful for Jews to pay taxes to Caesar, he could be charged with treason and possibly die a premature death.

Knowing the trap laid before him, Jesus needed a clever answer. This was, to a very considerable extent, a matter of life or death for him and his mission on earth. In the end his response did not disappoint: give to Caesar what belongs to Caesar and to God what belongs to God. Answering them in this manner, Jesus showed that the Jews could indeed pay taxes to Caesar while at the same time giving themselves – and their lives – to God. Those two things were not mutually exclusive. It was not one or the other: it was both, held together in a constant tension, throughout the life of the colonized. This was possible. They were to give to Caesar what belonged to Caesar and to God what belonged to God. After all, the denarius bore Caesar's face, not God's. The emperor was in charge; he owned everything that existed within its boundaries. The entire economy of the empire was at his disposal; he could do whatever he needed with it. The empire needed the taxes and Jesus knew this. In the era of the Pax Romana the army needed to be cared for very well if it were to be effective in its job of protecting the empire. The trade that thrived as the empire expanded, from York to Babylon, needed roads to transport goods. These too needed to be funded by taxpayers across the empire. In addition, the emperor's power was seen in the infrastructure he constructed around the empire. Often this included temples for various religious traditions, stadiums and other imperial buildings. In a nutshell, it was extremely risky for Jesus to even suggest that it was not lawful for Jews to pay taxes to Caesar. The money belonged to Caesar. They themselves were God's image on earth. They belonged to God. They had to give themselves to God.

Jesus clearly demonstrates an awareness of the detrimental effects of any appearance of rebelling against the emperor. If his movement encouraged non-compliance against Roman rule, not only would he endanger his own life and mission but he would also put thousands of people (including many who were not his followers) in harm's way. Jewish history of the first century CE has more than a handful of false messiahs who died at the hands of the Romans. Reza Aslan, in the semi-fictional account of the life and times of Jesus (largely based on the works of Josephus), mentions some of the false messiahs:

> The prophet Theudas, according to the book of Acts, had four hundred disciples before Rome captured him and cut off his head. A mysterious charismatic figure known only as 'the Egyptian' raised an army of followers in the desert, nearly all of whom were massacred by Roman troops. In 4 BCE, the year in which most scholars believe Jesus of Nazareth was born, a poor shepherd named Athronges put a diadem on his head and crowned himself 'King of the Jews'; he and his followers were brutally cut down by a legion of soldiers. Another messianic aspirant, called simply 'the Samaritan,' was crucified by Pontius Pilate even though he raised no army and in no way challenged Rome – an indication that the authorities, sensing the apocalyptic fever in the air, had become extremely sensitive to any hint of sedition. There was Hezekiah the bandit chief, Simon of Peraea, Judas the Galilean, his grandson Menahem, Simon son of Giora, and Simon son of Kochba – all of whom declared messianic ambitions and all of whom were executed by Rome for doing so.[12]

As a Jewish subject of Rome, Jesus paid taxes to the imperial government. However, the Scriptures also show him paying religious taxes for the sustenance of the Temple. In Matthew 17.24–27, Jesus miraculously paid the double-drachma tax that was instituted in Exodus 30.11–16: 'This is what each one who is registered shall give: half a shekel according to the shekel of the sanctuary (the shekel is twenty gerahs), half a shekel as an offering to the LORD.' Matthew says:

> When they reached Capernaum, the collectors of the temple tax came to Peter and said, 'Does your teacher not pay the temple tax?' He said, 'Yes, he does.' And when he came home, Jesus spoke of it first, asking, 'What do you think, Simon? From whom do kings of the earth take toll or tribute? From their children or from others?' When Peter said, 'From others', Jesus said to him, 'Then the children are free. However, so that we do not give offence to them, go to the lake and cast a hook; take the first fish that comes up; and when you open its mouth, you will find a coin; take that and give it to them for you and me.' (Matt. 17.24–27)

Jesus is clear about why he did this. He paid taxes to authorities, whether Roman or Jewish, to avoid causing offence. These two tax conversations show some aspects of Jesus' posture towards authority. Among his disciples was a tax collector, Levi, whom he renamed Matthew. Having a tax collector among a messianic rabbi's key followers could signal to the oppressors a recognition of their authority and a willingness to engage if necessary. It could also show the wider Jewish population not only that a tax collector (or anyone working with and for the oppressors) could be reformed but also an openness to keeping peace with the oppressors by having their interests represented.

Later on, when he was crucified, it was not for treason – Pontius found nothing for which to charge him. When the people shouted, 'Crucify him!' it was not for challenging Rome or raising an army to liberate Palestine. It was for disrupting the Jewish religious system. He was crucified not with any of his disciples but with two men who are called *lestai*, a Greek word often translated as 'thieves' in English even though it also means 'bandits'. The Romans used *lestai* for insurrectionists or rebels. Historically, Roman sieges, whether it was Pompey in 63 BCE or Titus in 66 CE, killed thousands. Would Jesus risk that for his followers? It is, without a doubt, a very significant development that when the time came for Jesus to be tried and judged (by the Romans), it was he and he alone who went on trial. Generally speaking, revolutionaries and insurrectionists do not die alone. Success for many Jewish messianic figures included being killed with their followers. The more people were willing to die for a revolutionary, the more successful that revolutionary was. But it was not so with Jesus. First, he looked just like his followers. The Romans needed one of his close allies to help them identify him and Judas did the job for them. One wonders how they did not know him if he was a bother to the empire. The fact that in the end Pilate acquitted him demonstrates that Jesus' subversion of the empire was so subtle that the empire did not mind him. Pilate found no fault with Jesus. Pilate himself said, 'Take him yourselves and crucify him; for I find no case against him.' If Pilate found no fault in him, we can safely conclude that Jesus followed the Roman law like any good subject of the empire. One of his closest disciples, Peter, denied him, probably afraid that he too would be put on trial. In the end, that was it. Jesus was crucified alone, so to speak. None of his followers were crucified with him. They would all later die their own deaths in various circumstances at the hands of the empire. Even Paul and Peter did not die for causing an insurrection. Both of them were killed by Roman soldiers more than 30 years after the crucifixion of Jesus, in Rome, right at the heart of the Roman Empire.

Choose ye between Nazareth and Rome

Throughout the Gospels, Jesus does not mention Rome. Of course, he mentions Caesar and is evidently aware of the Romans and their ever-expanding empire. However, he never mentions Rome as a focal point for the spread of the gospel of the kingdom. He tells his disciples to bear witness for him in Jerusalem, Judea, Samaria, unto the ends of the earth. In these verses that we have now called the Great Commission, there is no mention of Alexandria (which was the city closest to Jerusalem, the second largest city in the empire and very multicultural – home to a large Jewish population in addition to many other peoples from around the Mediterranean and beyond). Certainly Jesus does not mention Antioch (third largest city of the empire at the time and, as home to many foreigners from the wider empire and beyond, as multicultural as a city on a trade route of the empire could be). Most importantly for my argument, Jesus never mentioned Rome (the empire's capital). While we can argue that all these cities were included in the uttermost parts of the earth, the fact that Jesus did not mention them when he left his disciples ought to catch our attention.

In his plans there was no need to start by reaching Rome. If it were so, he no doubt could have found a way there. It is here where the central argument of this book is located. The entire ministry of Jesus took place at the margins of the Roman Empire, without ever needing him to befriend the empire to use its power to his advantage. He started his short-lived ministry among his people in Nazareth – they knew him to be the son of Joseph (Luke 4.22) – and finished it in Jerusalem, being executed by soldiers of the empire on behalf of his own people (Luke 23.26–56). As far as we can see in the Gospels, he did not consider it necessary or strategic to focus on evangelizing the heart of the empire to make disciples among the nations. He did not need to locate his headquarters in Alexandria, Antioch or Rome. Nazareth, with all its limitations, could do just fine. It was exactly what he needed. Galilee, with the many Gentiles who lived there, and its geography – the lake, the villages that dotted its northern shoreline, and the communities of fishermen – made a good starting point, far away from the powerful societies in Jerusalem or Rome.

As the one who initiated the movement that would become Christianity and touch billions of people in the centuries that followed, Jesus' life and death at the margins of the empire is a statement that should cause modern evangelists to rethink a great deal of what passes for mission today. In choosing this life of a commoner on the outskirts of a marginalized and colonized land and the death of an outcast by crucifixion outside the city, Jesus really shows us that his reign is not like any of the kingdoms of this world (John 18.36). His original impact was almost entirely localized in what were then Roman colonies of Judea and Galilee. During his ministry he did minimal travel beyond Galilee and Judea. In his entire three and a half years of ministry, he totally ignored Rome. He also did not attend to any other major cities of the empire. It appears he did not wish to serve anywhere but home – Nazareth, Capernaum, Galilee and Judea. In the face of Roman imperialism his strategy was to make disciples among the colonized, right at the margins of the empire. He would trust them to continue to make disciples who would make other disciples until the whole earth would be filled with his followers.

Jesus did not seek to convert any influential and powerful figures. Nicodemus was a Pharisee who sought Jesus out at night to have his questions answered (John 3.1–12). Jesus did not go out of his way to find Nicodemus. After his experience, we know that Nicodemus became a secret disciple of Jesus. He advocated for Jesus when the chief priests and the Pharisees sought to have him judged (John 7.50–51). He also brought a mixture of myrrh and aloes – about 100 Roman pounds in weight – to prepare Jesus' body for burial. Curiously, though, we do not hear that he brought Jesus any more Pharisees to convert.

The rich young ruler walked away grieving, without giving his life to Christ (Mark 10.17–27). Zacchaeus was the one rich and influential person who followed Jesus. Like Levi he was a tax collector. Luke mentions the fact that he was hated by his people (Luke 19.1–10). After the encounter with Jesus he gave away a lot of his riches. He did not have the social capital that could move Jesus' ministry forward. He was just an ordinary follower, among many others, of the peasant carpenter rabbi from Nazareth. In the end we note that Jesus never sought favours from political rulers (Antipas, Philip or Pilate) or religious leaders (Pharisees or the priests). Unlike Paul, Jesus never appeals to a higher Roman authority to delay his death. He totally ignored those systems, except when he called Antipas a fox (Luke 13.32). Yet he hoped that his disciples would make more disciples until the whole earth is filled with his followers. Paul explains in Philippians 2 that Jesus emptied himself, became human and took the form of a slave – a *doulos* who broke his or her back in the Mediterranean sun so that his or her master could safely belong and participate in the *ekklesia* without worrying about such matters as food on the table.

Reading the stories of how he did this in the Gospels, one may be forgiven for thinking that Jesus got all his strategy wrong. Indeed, Jesus' strategy makes very little sense to people working in mission in the twenty-first century. It seems to many of us rather careless to start a world-changing ministry in a place like Nazareth. Given a chance, we would most certainly choose to begin in Rome, not in Galilee. From there we would look for strategic cities of the empire – something akin to what has been called the 'Gateway Cities' of the world – to plant our churches. We would start in London, Paris, Seoul, Cape Town, New York or Rio. Such cities assure us access to the world – something that emerges in the book of Acts when the diaspora community evangelized Gentiles in the multicultural city of Antioch. This strategy deprioritizes places that do not show any immediate strategic significance. All this happens because we tend to need to operate from a position of strength and power. A missionary from New York carries more weight than a counterpart from somewhere in Latin America, Africa or Asia. In addition, our mission strategies cause us to seek to reach centres of power first, hoping to diffuse the gospel from imperial cities down to the rural areas and heaths that surround them. Once the centre is converted, we believe that it will be easier to convert its periphery. This is often done in the belief that these urban cities have the financial power to move the gospel around, diffusing it to smaller centres around them in the hope that these too will spread it further to even smaller centres.

Subvert. Subvert. Subvert

It is my suggestion that as he ministered in the villages of Galilee and Judea, Jesus intentionally ignored the imperial centres of the Roman Empire while he sought to subvert its colonization and the oppression of his audience. Indeed, if it were not for Peter and Paul, Rome would be absent from the books of the New Testament. With the Roman Empire shaping every aspect of his life, whether in Galilee or in Jerusalem, and indeed from birth to death, Jesus understood the power of the empire. Dealing with empire was a normal part of his life. However, he was all about subverting the empire as much as possible. This was part of his human experience. He understood that empires are a permanent part of life. Human hierarchies are a hallmark of every civilization. If it were not the Roman Empire, it would be another empire. He was not necessarily untouched by the yoke of Rome. From beginning to end his entire ministry was a subtle subversion of the empire's chokehold of God's people. Jesus alluded to this yoke when he invited his hearers to take his yoke – the yoke of following him as the Messiah with everything that was involved in it. It was easier and lighter than that of Rome:

> Come to me, all you who are weary and are carrying heavy burdens, and I will give you rest. Take my yoke upon you, and learn from me; for I am gentle and humble in heart, and you will find rest for your souls. For my yoke is easy, and my burden is light. (Matt. 11.28–30)

This is the good news. Jesus – *not* the emperor – is lord, and his lordship comes with a yoke. However, his yoke is easier and lighter than that of the empire. Being a messiah really works in times of oppression. It is broken and oppressed people who need saving. The current global political situation makes this abundantly clear. The rising waves of populism and nationalism characterize a society looking for its messiahs. People need their messiahs when life is difficult. They need someone strong enough to mobilize them to challenge the oppressing force so that they can be free. When life is all good, the messiah has nothing to offer. Yet he was a messiah without an army which, of course, does not make sense. How could he face Rome with only a group of Galilean fishermen? He did not allow Peter to defend him:

> Suddenly, one of those with Jesus put his hand on his sword, drew it, and struck the slave of the high priest, cutting off his ear. Then Jesus said to him, 'Put your sword back into its place; for all who take the sword will perish by the sword. Do you think that I cannot appeal

to my Father, and he will at once send more than twelve legions of angels?' (Matt. 26.51–53)

This is an odd thing for a messiah to say. 'I have an army of more than twelve legions. I do not need your help. Thank you.' He goes on to heal the Roman soldier who was wounded. He was definitely a different kind of messiah. He had to liberate his people without triggering a total destruction of the community. As such, he had to be subversive. Any attempt to raise an army to take on the Romans for the liberation of his people would be both futile and dangerous. (The Roman Empire was still on the rise in the 20s and 30s of the first century CE. Jesus was crucified when the empire was in its fifth decade. Tiberius was only the second emperor. It would exist for another 450 years and be ruled by around 70 emperors.) There was no way Jesus could start an armed revolution – not from Galilee and certainly not from Nazareth. His messiahship would be one of subversion.

When Jesus told his disciples to go and make disciples among the nations, he was talking to a group of powerless followers led by Galilean fishermen. This does not look like a winning strategy. They would have an uphill struggle even to be believable in Israel, not to mention in the Jewish diaspora. In their tradition, over the centuries no prophet had come out of Galilee. Yet it was to these people that Jesus left his work. These unlikely people would have to make the nations of the world disciples of Christ. Again, in trusting these powerless people Jesus may have been subverting the empire. A grass-roots movement of followers of the Messiah, led by unlikely people, would be harder to stop. He did not send any missionary heroes. Neither did he send rich missionaries. He sent unassuming, ordinary people who stuck to the task, reaching other ordinary people from generation to generation, often enduring persecutions, until Christianity conquered the empire.

After three centuries of Christian existence in the empire, a lot of it happening at the margins of the structures of power, Christianity triumphed over Rome itself. When Constantine became a Christian and made Christianity the preferred religion of the empire, he showed that, indeed, Jesus was the Lord and therefore greater than the emperor. Of course, it took 300 years and several persecutions for the empire to reach a tipping point and to convert to Christianity. Yet when converted, the change was permanent. Once subsumed into the Roman Empire, Christianity was not only propelled to a new era of expansion but it was also changed to align itself with the reality of the empire. It had to adapt to the newly found power it had in society. With this, it had to serve the empire's needs. For instance, Christians were coopted into the legions of the empire – every empire needs its soldiers. Consequently the Christian soldiers became a thing. The idea of a Just War entered into Christianity in this era. Augustine would later say:

> If, therefore, a just man is perhaps serving as a soldier under a godless human king, he can correctly fight at his command so as to preserve the order of civil peace. This is certain when what is commanded is not against the commandment of God, or when it is not certain whether it is or is not. In the latter case, the injustice in commanding perhaps makes the king guilty, but his order in obeying proves the soldier innocent. How much more is he who wages war at God's command completely innocent in the conduct of wars! For no one who serves him can fail to know that he cannot command anything unjustly.[13]

Jesus' triumph over Rome happened in a way that only makes spiritual sense, for the spiritual realm is where the real problem is. Throughout the Gospels, and in the wider New Testament, the liberation of the Jews from Roman domination was symbolic of the redemption of humanity from the devastating effects of sin. As a Jewish Messiah, Jesus was expected to deliver God's people from oppression, both local and foreign. Rome happened to be the oppressing empire when Jesus walked in Palestine. However, as the lamb that came to wash away the sins of the entire world, Jesus' agenda was on a different plane. What the Jews wanted him to do for them, he was to do for all humanity and all creation. However, in saving all humanity, he would not wrestle with the military might of Rome. His kingdom is spiritual. He would wrestle with the spiritual ruler of the age and liberate all of creation from the chokehold of the evil one. When the Roman soldiers killed him they did not realize that his death would seal his victory not only against the very spiritual powers that colonize God's creation but also over Roman imperialism itself. They crucified a Galilean rabbi, and Jesus was resurrected to be the saviour of all humanity, taking over the very titles that were used for Caesar, 'Lord of Lords', 'King of Kings' and 'Son of God'. It was only a matter of time before even the emperor himself – Constantine, in this case – became a follower of Christ. Because of the shedding of his blood, Jesus achieved something much higher than the liberation of the Jews. He also purchased the freedom of the Gentiles. He triumphed over death and in so doing redeemed all humans from eternal damnation and gave the gift of eternal life to humanity. In his resurrection, Jesus rose up to be exalted to the highest place, much higher than that of Caesar, and to receive a name that is above every name.

Therefore God also highly exalted him and gave him the name that is above every name, so that at the name of Jesus every knee should bend, in heaven and on earth and under the earth, and every tongue should confess that Jesus Christ is Lord, to the glory of God the Father. (Phil. 2.9–11)

Paul adds that he 'disarmed the rulers and authorities and made a public example of them, triumphing over them in it' (Col. 2.15). In a vision towards the end of the first century CE, Jesus said to John the Revelator, 'Do not be afraid; I am the first and the last, and the living one. I was dead, and see, I am alive for ever and ever; and I have the keys of Death and of Hades' (Rev. 1.17b–18). All this is to say that what Jesus did may not look like what the Messiah was expected to do – to liberate the Jews from Roman oppression. However, what he achieved for us all is much higher.

Notes

1 N. T. Wright and Michael F. Bird, *Jesus and the Powers: Christian Political Witness in an Age of Totalitarian Terror and Dysfunctional Democracies* (London: SPCK, 2024), p. 25.

2 Tacitus, *Agricola*, vol. 1, par. 30, in Cornelius Tacitus, *The Complete Works of Tacitus*, ed. Moses Hadas, trans. Alfred John Church and William Jackson Brodribb (New York: McGraw-Hill Education, 1942), p. 695.

3 Alexander Jannaeus (c.127–76 BCE) was the second king of the Hasmonean Dynasty. His reign over the kingdom of Judea started in 103 BCE, and he ruled until 76 BCE when he died. He had married Salome Alexandra, the wife of his brother Aristobulus I.

4 Crucifixion was a Roman way of punishing wrongdoers, especially slaves and non-Romans. The Jews did not crucify people, though in the case of Jesus they begged the Romans to crucify him for them.

5 I have argued later in this chapter that by using the census to date the birth of Christ, Luke makes an error that is quite difficult to explain. The census took place in 6 CE when Augustus finally made Judea a province of Rome. Jesus would have been a boy by then, aged between six and ten.

6 Philip, the tetrarch of Iturea, was a brother to Herod Antipas.

7 Eventually the five sons of Ananias would each serve their term as high priests, with the last one, Ananus ben Ananus, being deposed in 63 CE.

8 Caesarea Philippi was for centuries the centre of worship for both Baal (associated with the spring of Banias) and Pan, the Arcadian goat-footed god. There was a temple and a cave dedicated to Pan in the town. Philip the tetrarch made it his capital. Today the town is called Banias (a variation of 'Panaeas' after the god Pan) and is located in the Golan Heights. It was continuously inhabited until the Six-Day War in 1967.

9 Tacitus, *Agricola*, 1, 30.

10 The elegant robe would have been understood by Pilate as a sign of acquittal.

11 John Dominic Crossan, *God and Empire: Jesus Against Rome, Then and Now* (San Francisco, CA: HarperCollins, 2007), p. 10.

12 Reza Aslan, *Zealot: The Life and Times of Jesus of Nazareth* (New York: Random House, 2013), p. 11. The timing of this Theudas mentioned by Gamaliel in Acts 5 may be a different person from the Theudas who had led an insurrection before that of Judas of Galilee, for we know that the census of Quirinius took place almost 40 years prior to the one of whom Josephus writes, whose revolt took place in 45/46 CE.

13 St Augustine, *Answer to Faustus, a Manichean*, trans. Roland Teske, The Works of Saint Augustine: A Translation for the 21st Century (Hyde Park, NY: New City Press, 2007), p. 352.

3

Imperializing Jesus

The Gospels record for us the story of Jesus' life and ministry on earth. They start at different stages of his life. Matthew starts with a lineage that introduces Jesus as the son of David, the son of Abraham, before locating his birth in Bethlehem in the final years of King Herod. Mark's Jesus appears as an already grown-up man embarking on his ministry. Luke begins with the story of aged Zechariah and Elizabeth and their miraculous conception of John and then connects it with Mary's conceiving and giving birth to Jesus. John starts with the pre-incarnate Jesus who as the *Logos* was God – and was with God – in the beginning. The *Logos* became a human being, was born in Bethlehem, of the Virgin Mary, and lived with us in our human world, in Nazareth. Before going up to Nazareth to settle, he lived for some years in Egypt. His birth, as a future king of the Jews, was a threat to the Herodian Dynasty's grip on power and so he had to seek refuge in a country outside his homeland. At that time, Egypt was a colony of Rome. Egypt was quite a mixed society with many Romans, Greeks, Persians and other peoples from around the Mediterranean Sea. It was also home to many Jews. The Egyptian city of Alexandria had the largest Jewish population of all cities around the Mediterranean basin. There were more Jews in Alexandria than in Jerusalem. The reality of the Jewish diaspora in Egypt was quite pronounced. If anyone wanted to see Jews in the diaspora, Egypt was the best place. Many of them had lived there for generations. Israel had been born as a nation in Egypt more than a millennium earlier. This time around, Jewish communities had been present in Egypt from the first dispersion that scattered the ten tribes in the eighth century BCE. Consequently, it is not unlikely that while in Egypt, Joseph, Mary and Jesus lived among relatives, many of whom would have lived in the diaspora for years or probably decades. Alexandria, that beautiful city on the Mediterranean coast at the mouth of the Nile, founded by Alexander the Great himself in 331 BCE, was a melting pot of cultures, reflecting the various historical influences that had existed in the country – the Assyrians, Babylonians, Greeks, Romans and, of course, Jews. Its library, the largest in the world at the time, also reflected Alexandria's influence around the Mediterranean and beyond. It was a city of extreme importance to the Jews. Alexandria was where the Hebrew Bible – which we today know as the Old Testament – was translated into Greek at the beginning of the third century BCE. Alexandria was also home to the great Jewish historian Philo (20 BCE–50 CE).

By the time Jesus arrived in Egypt, fleeing Herod's jealous wrath, the Jews in Egypt had everything it takes to build a vibrant Jewish community away from home. Central to that was the synagogue, and Alexandria had at least three of them. We cannot tell how long Jesus lived in Egypt but we can be fairly sure that he lived with relatives. (Mark was born to Jewish parents in the diaspora – in Cyrene, close to modern-day Shahaat, in Libya.) It is also likely that wherever they stayed in Egypt, Jesus learned a few local words from the children with whom he played. Essentially, his long and winding journey from Bethlehem, where he was born, to Nazareth, where he grew up, involved some extended international travel to the foreign land of Egypt. Before he arrived and settled down in his homeland of Galilee, he had to taste diaspora life. As far as the Gospels are concerned, the only other times that Jesus would travel outside his native land of Galilee and Judea was to the 'region of Tyre and Sidon', where he met a believing Syrophoenician woman and healed her daughter (Matt. 15.21–28; Mark 7.24–30) and to Caesarea Philippi (Matt. 16.13–20; Mark 8.27–30; Luke 9.18–21). There must be a reason for this diversion that caused him to be introduced to both the Jewish diaspora and the reality of the existence of other nations beyond Judea and Galilee before he got to his home in Nazareth. The very fact that he grew up in Galilee implies that he lived with and among the nations (or Gentiles). Galilee was also called 'Galilee of the Gentiles' (Matt. 4.15) or, in Isaiah, 'Galilee of the Nations' (Isa. 9.1).

Galilee of the nations

Isaiah says a righteous king would come out of Galilee who would cause the 'people who walked in darkness' to see 'a great light' and those who 'lived in a land of deep darkness' have light shone on them (Isa. 9.1–2). This righteous king may have been Josiah, who ruled from 640 to 609 BCE, many years after Isaiah gave his prophecy though his connection with the land of Naphtali and Zebulun is not clear. Or, indeed, as Matthew seems to intimate, it is Christ whom Isaiah prophesied about. Galilee was part of the land taken by Israel when they entered Canaan under the leadership of Joshua. It was given to the tribes of Zebulun and Naphtali. In the eighth century BCE the land was invaded by the Assyrians, many of the inhabitants were taken into exile and the region was repopulated with Gentiles. Despite an attempt in the second century BCE to forcibly circumcise and convert the populace, it remained a religiously and ethnically mixed province. It was here that Jesus chose to concentrate the beginning of his public ministry. Galilee was a place, both in Isaiah's time and in the time of Jesus' ministry, where the Jewish people were a minority – the Gentiles (or the nations) predominated. It was an especially fertile land and a crossroads of international travel. Not too many years ago, archaeologists discovered the ruins of a large city in Galilee from the time of Jesus' life and ministry. From that, many have begun to think that Jesus and his neighbours spoke several languages – at least Aramaic and Greek, and possibly more.

While this journey from Bethlehem to Nazareth via Egypt may look straightforward to us who are reading the Gospels 2,000 years after they were written, those places were worlds apart. Bethlehem was in Judea, a part of the country that was quite socially Jewish. It occupied a special place in the history of the Jewish people. It was home to their most favoured king, David. It was for this reason that Joseph and Mary, both of them being descendants of David, travelled back to Bethlehem for the census. Nazareth was a village in Galilee that had seen its glory days and was now on the decline. It was one of the places with a large Gentile presence (possibly, there had been a Roman garrison nearby), and for this reason devout Jews avoided it. Certainly, Nathaniel echoes a generally known proverb when he asks, 'Can anything good come out of Nazareth?' (John 1.46). Galilee was a place, both in Isaiah's time and in the time of Jesus' ministry, where the Jewish people were a minority – Gentiles predominated.

The Galileans meet the diaspora

Acts 2 presents to us the story of the crescendo of Jesus' ministry when the Holy Spirit is given to the community of the 120 disciples, hiding in the Upper Room in Jerusalem. This pouring out of the Holy Spirit happens on a day when Jews from around the world – Luke believes there were Jews from every nation on earth in Jerusalem on that day – connect the Galilean community with the diaspora. Of the 3,000 believers who were added to the church on that day, many had come from the broader context of the Jewish diaspora – Parthians, Medes, Elamites and residents of Mesopotamia, Judea and Cappadocia, Pontus and Asia, Phrygia and Pamphylia, Egypt and the parts of Libya belonging to Cyrene, and visitors from Rome, both Jews and proselytes, Cretans and Arabs (Acts 2.9–11). The good news of the Nazarene would immediately get an international audience. When these people returned to their homes, they all bore witness to the strange thing that happened at Pentecost, saying something like:

> We found the Messiah. He is a man from Nazareth who was crucified and rose again after three days. He is the lamb that washes away the sins of the world and he lives in us through his Spirit. We heard all this from a group of Galileans who spoke in our language without knowing it.

Before the missionaries were sent from Antioch to begin to evangelize the nations in Asia Minor, even before the persecution that scattered the Christians from Jerusalem, the witness of Christ was already happening in the empire's cities and beyond. The empire is responsible for the decades of peace and quiet – Pax Romana – and the extensive travel system of roads and ships that would be helpful for the missionaries as they went to evangelize the empire. The Galileans needed to work with the diaspora Jews – most of them were economic migrants – if they were to manage the task of making the nations disciples of Christ.

Paul's fixation on Rome

I have stated earlier that Jesus himself never visited Rome. However, within a few decades following his crucifixion and the giving of the Holy Spirit at Pentecost, his disciples – Peter and Paul – slowly took the gospel westwards from Jerusalem to Rome, the heart of the empire. It is very likely that there was a group of Christians in Rome before Paul arrived. Luke mentions that there were 'visitors from Rome, both Jews and proselytes' in Jerusalem at Pentecost (Acts 2.10). Some of them may have repented, been baptized and added to the church on that day, to be counted among the 3,000. Many of these would bring with them to Rome the news about the strange phenomenon that happened at Pentecost in that year. Of course, Paul's epistle to the saints in Rome was written in Corinth, long before Paul would make it to Rome. As such, it addresses a Christian community that he did not found and had never visited.

Right from Acts 16 where the Spirit of God invited Paul to cross over from Asia Minor to Macedonia, Paul seems fixated on preaching in Rome and possibly going as far as Spain (Rom. 15.23–24). As he went on his evangelistic campaigns (which we now call missionary trips), he seemed to be setting up for a day when he would preach in Rome. His first trip was rather short (Acts 13—15). He went from Antioch, through Cyprus, to Derbe (in Asia Minor) and returned to Antioch. He continued to Jerusalem, where the Elders sat down to resolve the Gentile Question: 'What shall we do with the Gentiles who choose to follow Christ?' They agreed to let them do so without needing to be circumcised and advised them not to bring food to the table that had been offered to idols. Once that was resolved, Paul had clearance to evangelize many more Gentiles.

It was during the second preaching campaign that Paul crossed into Europe through Macedonia and went as far as Athens and Corinth, where he stayed for 18 months (Acts 16—18). During this trip, Paul met two fellow diasporan tent-making Jews, Aquila and Priscilla, who had come from Rome. He stayed with them while preaching in the synagogues on the Sabbath, seeking to evangelize both Jews and Greeks (Acts 18.1–4). It was during the third trip (Acts 18.23—21.16) that Paul sent a letter to the Christians who lived in Rome, stating, 'So, as much as in me is, I am ready to preach the gospel to you that are at Rome also' (Acts 20.1–3; Rom. 1.15, KJV). He had been eager to get to Rome for a long time (possibly for the previous ten years when he had been on two evangelistic trips). He would later, in the letter to the Romans, say that he had been hindered:

> This is the reason that I have so often been hindered from coming to you. But now, with no further place for me in these regions, I desire, as I have for many years, to come to you when I go to Spain. For I do hope to see you on my journey and to be sent on by you, once I have enjoyed your company for a little while. (Rom. 15.22–24)

At the end of the third trip he thought his time in Asia Minor and Greece had come to an end. He wanted to go westwards, towards Rome and Spain. From Corinth, Paul's mind was made up. He would go to Rome, whatever it takes. He needed to go to Jerusalem so he did one tour through Macedonia, coming through Troas, Assos, Miletus, Patara and then connecting to Tyre and Caesarea. While in Tyre, the disciples begged Paul not to go to Jerusalem:

> We looked up the disciples and stayed there for seven days. Through the Spirit they told Paul not to go on to Jerusalem. When our days there were ended, we left and proceeded on our journey; and all of them, with wives and children, escorted us outside the city. There we knelt

down on the beach and prayed and said farewell to one another. Then we went on board the ship, and they returned home. (Acts 21.4–6)

After Tyre he went to Ptolemais, where he stayed for one day. When he got to Caesarea on the following day a prophet called Agabus warned him that the Jews would arrest him in Jerusalem and hand him over to the Romans:

> While we were staying there for several days, a prophet named Agabus came down from Judea. He came to us and took Paul's belt, bound his own feet and hands with it, and said, 'Thus says the Holy Spirit, "This is the way the Jews in Jerusalem will bind the man who owns this belt and will hand him over to the Gentiles."' When we heard this, we and the people there urged him not to go up to Jerusalem. Then Paul answered, 'What are you doing, weeping and breaking my heart? For I am ready not only to be bound but even to die in Jerusalem for the name of the Lord Jesus.' Since he would not be persuaded, we remained silent except to say, 'The Lord's will be done.' (Acts 21.10–14)

Against all these warnings, Paul's desire to go to Rome was so strong that he kept on his journey towards Jerusalem, well aware that he would be jailed and sent to Rome. True to the warnings, Paul was arrested later in Acts 21:

> When the seven days were almost completed, the Jews from Asia, who had seen him in the temple, stirred up the whole crowd. They seized him, shouting, 'Fellow Israelites, help! This is the man who is teaching everyone everywhere against our people, our law, and this place; more than that, he has actually brought Greeks into the temple and has defiled this holy place.' For they had previously seen Trophimus the Ephesian with him in the city, and they supposed that Paul had brought him into the temple. Then all the city was aroused, and the people rushed together. They seized Paul and dragged him out of the temple, and immediately the doors were shut. While they were trying to kill him, word came to the tribune of the cohort that all Jerusalem was in an uproar. (Acts 21.27–31)

Eventually Paul was brought before the council. At his request he was granted an audience to address those who accused him but, of course, he tried to evangelize them. He may have made up his mind to provoke them further, knowing that he was a citizen of Rome and would, therefore, be protected. It was only after this that Jesus stood near him at night and said, 'Keep up your courage! For just as you have testified for me in Jerusalem, so you must bear witness also in Rome' (Acts 23.11). A plot to kill him allowed Paul to get the protection he needed, but also started his journey towards Rome. He would be transported by an army of 'two hundred soldiers, seventy horsemen, and two hundred spearmen' from Jerusalem to Caesarea under the cover of the night. He ended up being imprisoned in Caesarea for two years. A whole two years! All this because he wanted to go to Rome. In those two years he could have achieved a great deal of ministry work. Yet, of course, his heart was set on preaching in Rome.

After two years of imprisonment, when Festus had replaced Felix as governor of Judea, Paul was brought back to trial. Some Jews came again from Jerusalem to bring charges against him, but they failed to prove any of the charges (Acts 25.1–12). Later, Agrippa came to Caesarea to welcome Festus. Taking advantage, Festus asked Agrippa to hear Paul's case. Paul was called in to defend himself. It is at this time that he gave one of his most famous defences of the gospel. He even encouraged Agrippa to believe in Jesus (Acts 26.1–29), to which Agrippa famously responded, 'Are you so quickly persuading me to become a Christian?' Paul replied, 'Whether quickly or not, I pray to God that not only you but also all who are listening to me today might become such as I am – except for these chains' (Acts 26.28–29).

In his assessment, Festus concluded that Paul was crazy: 'You are out of your mind, Paul! Too much learning is driving you insane!' (Acts 26.24). Both Festus and Agrippa agreed that Paul had not done anything that might 'deserve death or imprisonment' (Acts 26.31). Paul could have simply 'been set free if he had not appealed to the emperor' (Acts 26.32). Paul had appealed to Caesar under his rights as a Roman citizen (Acts 25.11). This set into motion the plans for Paul to be transported from Palestine to Rome to face trial in Caesar's court.

In Acts 27, with other prisoners, Paul set sail for Rome. The trip was tumultuous; they faced many difficulties, including a shipwreck that caused him to be deserted on the island of Malta for three months. Later, he eventually arrived in Rome. He would be placed under house arrest for another two years, living in a rented house where he could receive visitors and preach the gospel to them. It was during this time that Paul wrote some of his letters, including the epistles to the Philippians, Ephesians, Colossians and Philemon. This is where the book of Acts ends. Paul has fulfilled his dream. Regardless of the circumstances, he was finally preaching in Rome. The desire to preach Christ in Rome seems to have overcome Paul to the extent that he ignored several prophetic warnings against it. In the end he took matters into his own hands by appealing to Caesar to make a trip to Rome happen. Of course, one wonders what could have happened if Paul had not forced his way to Rome. Would he have preached in many other places? Would he have planted more churches? Would he have discipled many more leaders?

Counterpoint: the mission of the Desert Fathers and Mothers

About 200 years after Paul, there arose another man bearing the same name but going in the opposite direction – Paul of Thebes (227–341).[1] He is quite a towering figure in the history of the Christian Church, especially the history of the African Christian Church. He is known by several names, including Paul the First Hermit or Paul the Anchorite. He is generally considered to be one of the earliest Christian Desert Fathers and thus a pioneer of Christian monasticism. Born to wealthy parents at a place called Thebaid, he lost his parents at a young age. His sister's husband made plans to have him handed over to persecutors during the era of Decius and Valerianus in 250. It was at this time, when he was approximately 23, that he fled to the deserts in eastern Egypt to avoid martyrdom. Settling down in a cave a short distance from the Red Sea, he found that he loved the life of prayer and the isolation that simplified everything. He lived in isolation as a monk for approximately 90 years until his death in 341/342 at the age of 113. He stayed in the deserts even after Christianity was made legal in the Roman Empire in 313. For many years he was sustained by a raven that brought him half a loaf of bread daily.

Even though St Anthony the Great is often recognized as the father of monasticism, it is Paul who started the movement. Paul went to the desert around the time Anthony was born and stayed there for longer than him. The main difference between their approaches – which may be why Anthony is usually acknowledged as the father of the movement – is that Anthony had disciples around him who built their monastery close to his. Paul was in isolation until the end of his life. Of course, Paul and Anthony were friends, especially as Paul approached his death. The two of them shared a deep spiritual connection. Anthony treated Paul as an older and more experienced friend. Paul is recognized as a saint in both the Eastern Orthodox and Roman Catholic Churches. What he started was then picked up by a younger generation of monastic leaders. Anthony was one of those younger disciples. He died only 15 years after Paul in 356, by which time there were thousands of men and women praying, fasting, fighting the devils, making disciples and farming in the deserts. When Anthony went to the desert, he sought to battle with the demons on their own turf – he was not escaping the sin-sick city to the quiet safety of the wilderness. His life, for many decades, would be characterized by a series of encounters with devils that wanted to distract and discourage him. Athanasius tells of one occasion when the devil visited Anthony with a host of demons including 'the ease of pleasure', 'the friend of whoredom' and 'the spirit of lust'. They beat him so mercilessly that he lay helpless on the ground from the extreme torment, nearly dead. He was rescued by a friend who habitually brought him food, taking him to a nearby village. As soon as he awoke he requested to be returned to the tomb he called home, where the battle continued. Eventually the roof of the tomb gave way to a beam of light, and the demons disappeared. The relieved Anthony then asked God why he had delayed in helping him. God answered that he needed to see Anthony's battle, and then he promised Anthony, 'I will ever be a succour to thee, and will make thy name known everywhere.'[2]

The monastic movement was in full gear. Hundreds of monasteries appeared in the sands of the Egyptian and Libyan deserts, with disciples flocking to them to be close to the living saints who had dedicated their lives to God in such a practical manner. Before long monasticism became a key method for propagating the Christian faith in Europe, with many monasteries mushrooming up and down Western Europe, from Ireland to Switzerland, as far as Scotland and Latvia and beyond. When the Jesuits emerged in the 1540s, with 'We are not monks' as part of their motto, they were the first in a long time to set up a non-monastic mission strategy. They did not want to build monasteries, and this was the start of a new era in mission. This happened at a time when many monasteries were suppressed, dissolved or confiscated by governments or rulers. For example, during the Protestant Reformation many monasteries were closed or suppressed by Protestant rulers, such as in Denmark (1528), Sweden (1527) and Switzerland (1520s–1530s). This was often accompanied by confiscation of their properties and assets. During the English Reformation under Henry VIII (1509–47), nearly 900 monasteries were closed, confiscated and sold off to fund his military campaigns. In England this process, known as the Dissolution of the Monasteries, took place between 1536 and 1541.[3] In wider Europe the dissolving of monasteries went on for much longer. During the French Revolution of 1789, their National Assembly declared that church property was at the disposal of the nation and used it to back a new currency. Many monasteries were subsequently sold or confiscated and their properties redistributed.[4]

Another 'mission' is possible

I introduce Paul of Thebes and Anthony of Egypt immediately after talking about the Apostle Paul's focus on Rome not necessarily to compare them or to suggest that we all ought to follow the way of Paul of Thebes. I believe there is a space for some form of monasticism in the hyper-connected world of ours – the new monastic movement is on to something helpful. However, the point I seek to make is that while the Apostle went to Rome, Thebes went into the desert. While one was focused on reaching the heart of the empire, the other went in the opposite direction to the extreme margins. God used them both, but to some extent the movement that Paul of Thebes started served the wider Christian communities beyond the empire better. The foundations of Ethiopian Christianity, for example, were built on the work of the nine monks who built their monasteries on the tops of mountains.[5]

Notes

1 St Jerome of Stridon, 'Life of St. Paul the First Hermit', *The Australian Province of the Order of Saint Paul the First Hermit*, https://paulinefathers.org.au/about/st-paul/life-paulus-first-hermit/, accessed 24.03.2025.

2 Saint Athanasius, 'The Life of St. Anthony the Great', in Philip Schaff and Henry Wace (eds), *Nicene and Post-Nicene Fathers*, Vol. 4, *Athanasius, Select Works and Letters* (Grand Rapids, MI: Eerdmans, 1987), p. 221.

3 Geoffrey Baskerville, *English Monks and the Suppression of the Monasteries* (New Haven, CT: Yale University Press, 1937). Also see George W. Bernard, 'The Dissolution of the Monasteries', *History* 96, no. 324 (2011). Another interesting resource for this is Hugh Willmott, *The Dissolution of the Monasteries in England and Wales* (Sheffield: Equinox, 2020).

4 Liise Lehtsalu, 'Rethinking Monastic Suppressions in Revolutionary and Napoleonic Italy: How Women Religious Negotiated for Their Communities', *Women's History Review* 25, no. 6 (2016).

5 See Rugare Rukuni and Erna Oliver, 'Ethiopian Christianity: A Continuum of African Early Christian Polities', *Theological Studies* 75, no. 1 (2019).

4

To Dominate and Christianize

Starting in the era of the Greeks, Europeans had been aware of the Eastern empires, especially that of the Persians. Alexander spent most of his 13 years as ruler of the Greeks seeking to expand the Macedonian Empire to Asia. He overthrew the Achaemenid Dynasty (having killed Darius III in 330 BCE), and then went on to attempt to fulfil his dream of reaching the 'ends of the world and the Great Outer Sea'. He invaded India and defeated Porus at the Battle of the Hydaspes in 326 BCE.[1] Alexander turned back from his Asian campaign at Beas River in the modern-day area of Punjab because his soldiers had become homesick after being away for more than a decade. After Alexander's death in 323 BCE, the Macedonian Empire was divided among the four Diadochi and with this move started its decline just as the Roman Republic was on the rise (evidenced by the series of Roman–Greek wars from 280 (against Pyrrhus) to 30 BCE (Battle of Alexandria).

For the many centuries of the Roman and Byzantine Empires, Europeans had a very limited knowledge of the world beyond the boundaries of their continent. North Africa and the Middle East had been known to Europeans from the days of the Greek civilization, but not much beyond that. The Greek historian Herodotus (484–425 BCE) visited Egypt in the 440s BCE and published an account of his travel that is a valuable historical resource of Egyptian geography as well as ethnography of the fifth century BCE. His theories about the Nile and its significance for Egyptian life, largely verified over the centuries, have made Herodotus a somewhat reliable historian of ancient Egypt. In 332 BCE, Alexander the Great invaded Egypt, taking it from the Persians who had ruled it during the brief period of the Second Egyptian Satrapy (or the Thirty-first Dynasty, 343–332 BCE). After Alexander's death, the Ptolemaic Dynasty – which had started with Ptolemy himself in 305 BCE – ruled Egypt until 30 BCE, when the last Ptolemaic queen, Cleopatra, died.

After the fall of the Macedonian Empire the Romans expanded their rule to cover vast areas beyond the Mediterranean basin, from Babylon to York and as far down as the borders of the kingdom of Kush in the Sudan region of north-east Africa. Within the geographical limits of this area the Romans were, for the most part, occupied enough and saw no need to expand further. Between the fourth and the eleventh centuries CE, Europeans spread Christianity northwards to evangelize the peoples of the Germanic tribes and Nordic tribes, as well as those of Britannia, Ireland, Scotland and the Slavs. Rome fell to the Vandals in 476 CE. Constantinople rose in its place to become the new Rome, the capital of the Eastern Roman Empire (which would later be known as the Byzantine Empire). For most of the Roman and Byzantine eras, Europeans were busy among themselves and were largely unaware of the broader world beyond their part of the Eurasian landmass. The Ottoman Empire ended the Byzantine Empire in 1453, a development that forced Europeans to find other means to get to Asia for spices and led to an awareness of the Americas, Africa beyond what had been Roman Africa or Byzantine Africa, and the landmasses of Asia. Before we talk about the Ottomans, it will be helpful to discuss the wider impact of Islam on Byzantine North Africa and its Christianity.

Apart from Egypt the wider North African region had played an increasingly significant role in the affairs of the Mediterranean world. While the Greeks ruled in Egypt, Carthage asserted itself around the Mediterranean Sea, from Libya to Spain and beyond. By 300 BCE, through its vast patchwork of colonies, vassal states and satellite states, held together by its naval dominance of the western and central Mediterranean Sea, the Carthaginian Empire controlled the largest territory in the region – much larger than the Roman Republic (long before the Roman Empire came into existence) and the Greek Empire (which was fracturing after the death of Alexander). At its peak the Carthaginian Empire included the coast of north-west Africa, southern and eastern Iberia and the islands of Sicily, Sardinia, Corsica, Malta and the Balearic archipelago.[2] It was in the Punic Wars (264–146 BCE) that the Romans defeated the Carthaginians and created the colony of Roman Africa.[3] Later, in 30 BCE, after the death of Mark Antony and Cleopatra, Augustus would take over Egypt and give the Roman Empire the right to claim all North Africa as a colony. The Romans ruled North Africa until the Vandals took it over beginning in 429 CE. The Byzantine Emperor, Justinian I, took North Africa again in 534 CE and Constantinople would rule it until the rise of Islam. Throughout this period, European contact with Africa was limited to North Africa even though there was an awareness of the large human populations south of Roman Africa. A thriving trading collaboration had been established between the Berbers of North Africa and those Africans who lived to their south, beyond the desert.

Europeans pushed back from North Africa

The rise of Islam in the Middle East in 610 CE reshaped the map of European influence around the Mediterranean. By the 630s CE, Muslim Arabs embarked on a campaign to conquer Syria and take the Levant from Byzantine rule. The conflicts started while Muhammad was alive, with the first one taking place at a village called Mu'tah, east of the Jordan River. After Muhammad's death in 632 CE, and under the leadership of the Rashidun Dynasty, they went on to hold a siege against Jerusalem (which they conquered in 638 and ruled unchallenged until the First Crusade in 1099). Under the leadership of Caliph Umar, Islamic forces of the Arabs quickly took control of Mesopotamia in 638, Syria in 641, Egypt in 641–42 and Armenia in 642. Alexandria was, until this time, the second most important city of the Byzantine Empire, hosting one of its main naval bases. After ransacking Alexandria in 641, the Arabs collected enormous spoils, including '4,000 palaces, 4,000 baths, 400 theatres, 12,000 sellers of green vegetables, and 40,000 tributary Jews'.[4] The fall of Alexandria marked the end of Byzantine maritime control and economic dominance of the eastern Mediterranean, shifting geopolitical power in favour of the Rashidun Caliphate. The fall of Alexandria had far-reaching implications for Byzantium, affecting not only its economy, geopolitics, culture and military but also its religious influence. The loss of this strategic city and its trade networks disrupted Byzantium's access to its breadbasket of Egypt and, later, the Maghreb.

Continuing westwards along the coast of North Africa, they captured Cyrenaica in 642 and Tripoli in 643. In the few years between 644 and 650, Caliph Uthman led the Arab Muslims to conquer Cyprus and Tripoli in North Africa, giving them control of the eastern Mediterranean, including Armenia and parts of the Caucasus. Having captured these lands, the Arab armies wanted more. These victories were understood to be a sign of God's favour. Under the Ummayad Caliphs (661–750), Uqba ibn Nafi led thousands of Muslim warriors into North Africa. In 670 he established a new garrison town at Kairouan, south of the great Byzantine city of Carthage. From Kairouan the Arabs organized and controlled all their operations. In 698 they took Carthage. In 707 they carried out a siege against Tangier, which they took in 711. Thus, within a few short decades – about 100 years since its inception – Islam had become the dominant religion in North Africa and the Arabs had taken control of the Mediterranean Sea, whose many islands they had captured. The three key Byzantine strongholds of Tripoli, Carthage and Tangier had all fallen to the Arabs and their inhabitants been forcibly converted to Islam. They governed North Africa from three bases:

al-Fustat in Egypt, Kairouan in Ifriqiya and Tangier in the Maghreb. In 711 they marched into Europe across the straits of Gibraltar.[5]

All in all the rise of Islam and the resultant Byzantine loss of the Levant and North Africa to the Arabs left Europe pretty limited. The rise of the Ottoman Empire in the thirteenth century would effectively close off the Levant and North Africa to the Europeans. Before this though, the southern European countries that had embraced Christianity during the Roman era started to shift their focus to the north. It is for this reason that a great deal of the Christianization of the Nordic and Slavic countries happened after Islam made North Africa and the Middle East somewhat inaccessible to the Europeans. Indeed, the Slavs received the gospel in waves from the seventh to the twelfth centuries.[6] The Christianization of the Nordic countries started in the ninth century and was completed in the twelfth century.[7] Some of these conversions were forced – people were told to convert to Christianity or else they would be killed.[8]

In the centuries between 500 and 1500, Europeans were busy spreading Christianity among themselves, spending most of their efforts Christianizing their neighbours. During this period, in the ninth and tenth centuries, some Vikings sailed west via the Shetland and Faroe Islands to establish colonies in Iceland and Greenland – away from Africa and the Middle East. Around 1000, a group of Vikings led by Leif Erikson reached a place they called 'Markland' and 'Vinland'.[9] He is believed to be the first European to reach the Americas, having done so 500 years before Christopher Columbus. The exact location of the places he visited is unclear, though they could probably be around Nova Scotia and Newfoundland.[10] Later on, in 1271, a Venetian merchant by the name Marco Polo (1254–1324) set out on a journey along the Silk Road, from Italy to Asia (with his father and uncle who had just returned from Asia in 1269).[11] Upon reaching Cathay (China), the Mongolian emperor Kublai Khan (1215–94) entrusted Marco with a position of imperial authority as a foreign emissary. In this capacity, Polo travelled quite extensively, throughout the empire and beyond, as far as present-day Myanmar, India, Indonesia, Sri Lanka and Vietnam. He left China in 1291 and got back to Venice in 1294 when the Venetians were engaged in a war with Genoa. Marco Polo was unfortunate enough to be captured. While in a Genoese prison he narrated his story to a friend, who published it as *The Travels of Marco Polo* (also known as *Book of the Marvels of the World* and *Il Milione*).[12] Marco Polo was not the first European to visit China; he only stands out because of the detailed account that he left behind, both of the travels themselves and the geography and ethnic customs that he saw in Asia, including the first Western record of porcelain, gunpowder, paper money and some Asian plants and exotic animals.[13] He gave the Europeans their first comprehensive look into Asia. He opened up, for the European mind, the idea of Asia as a rich continent that had great resources and had had expansive civilizations for centuries.

Finding new ways around the world

The era of European expansionism took off in the fifteenth century. For many centuries before this, Europe had been relatively self-contained and self-absorbed. Europeans were somewhat content and busy with the fair dose of their own political and religious drama that had characterized their landscape since the heydays of the Roman Empire. Two hundred years after Marco Polo, in 1492, Christoper Columbus, a fellow Italian of Genoese origin, docked in the Caribbean islands on his way to India.[14] His goal was to get to India without having to face the unfriendly Muslims who controlled most of the Mediterranean Sea and North Africa, and had just taken Constantinople and thus strengthened their hold on the Middle East. Columbus died in 1506 still believing that he had reached India. Columbus' reaching of the West Indies is almost as consequential as the fall of Constantinople, of which it is an outcome. It inaugurated a new chapter in Europe's self-awareness and its relations with the rest of the world. In many ways, that voyage changed the world.[15] Yet it must be acknowledged that Columbus' voyage was decades in the making.

Starting in the early decades of the fifteenth century, the Portuguese had slowly expanded their maritime efforts. They established themselves, under the leadership of Prince Henry the Navigator (1394–1460), as the leading empire of Europe. As a young teenager, Henry influenced his father to capture the Muslim port city of Ceuta across the Straits of Gibraltar to reconquer the Muslim lands of North Africa and thereby extend Iberian Christian influence on the Mediterranean. He also sought to suppress the Barbary pirates, whose raids on Portuguese coastal settlements resulted in the capture and enslavement of their inhabitants within the Moorish slave markets of North Africa. In 1415 Ceuta fell to the Portuguese and Henry became even more intrigued about Africa.[16] Henry was keen to know the extent of the Muslim territories in Africa, to find out if it was possible to reach the source of the lucrative trans-Saharan caravan gold trade, trans-Middle Eastern caravans, and possibly wheat, as well as to find and join forces with the legendary Christian kingdom of Prester John rumoured to exist somewhere to the east.[17]

In 1420 Henry was appointed to be the governor of the Military Order of Christ (the Portuguese rebranding of the Knights Templar, also known as the Poor Fellow-Soldiers of Christ and of the Temple of Solomon).[18] With this appointment he was encouraged to continue exploring trading opportunities with Africa and possibly with Asia. Driven by the desire to find Prester John's Christian kingdom, Henry fortified Portugal's maritime fleet. His Christian faith would be critical to his military identity (which would, in return, drive his exploration work). In the end all these became an expression of his faith. Exploration and military conquest were part of his service to the Lord. By the 1430s, Portuguese sailors were making efforts to reach West Africa, first making a landing on the islands of Madeira and Azores, off the coast of Morocco, in 1434.[19] In the same year, Gil Eannes passed Cape Bojador, which until then was considered the point of no return. It was, in the maritime mind of the time, an unbreachable barrier beyond which death awaited any human who dared to cross. Some believed that beyond Cape Bojador was the edge of the earth and that ships would fall off into a ditch and never come back. Many believed that the sun was boiling hot at the equator and could potentially burn to ashes any ships that came close. Eannes' courageous passing of the cape in 1434 opened a new era of exploration. Before long, Portuguese vessels pushed southwards, with Alvise Cadamosto reaching the Gambia River in 1456. Later, Diogo Cao reached the mouth of the Congo River in 1482. He would reach Cape Cross in Namibia in 1486. Bartolomeu Dias rounded the Cape of Good Hope at the southern tip of Africa in 1488. Ten years later, Vasco da Gama sailed around the cape to reach India in 1498.[20]

While the Portuguese were going around Africa to India, the other maritime empire of the era, the Spanish, were seeking the way to Asia by going West. In October 1492 Christopher Columbus reached the island now called the Bahamas and believed he had reached India (and from this error we get the term West Indies, which originally applied to all the Americas).[21] He reports of this landing in a letter to Queen Isabella:

> Thirty-three days after my departure from Cadiz I reached the Indian Sea, where I discovered many islands, thickly peopled, of which I took possession without resistance in the name of our most illustrious monarch by public proclamation and with unfurled banners. To the first of these islands, which is called by the Indians Guanahani, I gave the name of the blessed Saviour (San Salvador) relying upon whose protection I had reached this as well as the other islands; to each of these I also gave a name.[22]

To dominate and Christianize

Christopher Columbus understood his task to be of service both to Queen Isabella and to God. He was a devout Catholic man, a Third Order Franciscan who, according to Bartolomé de las Casas, 'observed the fasts of the church most faithfully, confessed and made communion often, read the Divine Office like a churchman, hated blasphemy and profane swearing, and was most devoted to Our Lady and the seraphic father St. Francis'.[23] To justify his voyage to the Crown of Spain, he offered the wealth that would be gained from the voyage to fund a new crusade to liberate the Holy Land from Muslim rule to recover the Holy Sepulchre to bring glory to Ferdinand and Isabella.[24] He believed – or hoped – as many did that the year 1500 would bring a new and final crusade that would liberate the Holy Land before the End Times.[25] In the introduction to the English publication of Columbus' *Libro de las Profécias*, Delno West says:

> The vision of Columbus was one of a missionary and a crusader ... [This] is present in writings that survive from the early period of his life, in notes written on the margins of books he owned that are dated as early as 1481, and in letters to a wide range of people throughout his lifetime ... His contemporary biographers agree in recognizing this vision and the spiritual discipline of his life.[26]

Michael Bradley argues that Columbus' goal was a crusade not to liberate the Jerusalem in the Holy Land but to establish a new one in the New World:

> The legal agreement that Columbus signed with Ferdinand and Isabella on April 17, 1492, reveals something of his innermost motivations and single-minded obsession. His voyage was a crusade and, if it was successful, it would establish a New Jerusalem in a New World, not provide gold to re-take the old Jerusalem in the Holy Land.[27]

If Bradley is right, Columbus was wildly successful in setting European eyes to the New World. Upon his death, much of his fortune was bequeathed to the cause of a new crusade in the Holy Land and the spreading of the gospel in the New World. Essentially then, a key part of Columbus' work was dedicated to religious purposes. This was not unique to Columbus. Many of the sailors of the century, whether Portuguese or Spanish, understood their role to be that of expanding both Christendom and European civilization. Paul Vickery observes:

[Columbus'] quest for gold and conversions was one and the same, with neither aspect of the endeavour meant to justify the other. Columbus, on behalf of Isabella and Ferdinand, sought nations to convert and lands and gold to seize, to expand Christendom and to fund missions to nations to convert and lands and gold to seize, to expand Christendom, and so on.[28]

Columbus himself said in his journal of the 'Indians': 'They would be good servants, and of good disposition, for I see that they repeat very quickly everything which is said to them. And I believe that they could easily be made Christians, for it seems to me that they have no belief.'[29] Later, after reaching Cuba, he added:

> having devout religious persons, knowing their language, they would all at once become Christians, and so I hope in Our Lord that Your Highnesses will take action in this matter with great diligence, in order to turn to the Church such great peoples and to convert them, as you have destroyed those who would not confess the Father and the Son and the Holy Ghost, and after your days, for we all are mortal, you will leave your realms in a most tranquil state and free from heresy and wickedness, and you will be well received before the eternal Creator, whom may it please to give you long life and great increase of many kingdoms and lordships, and the will and inclination to spread the holy Christian religion, as you have done up to this time.[30]

The popes and bulls

The story of the voyages of discovery started with the Portuguese first capturing Ceuta in Morocco and then slowly, in several attempts, sailing southwards around West Africa. By this time the Ottoman Empire had been expanding across Anatolia (Turkey) and the Balkan region as far as the Adriatic Sea. Constantinople, which was only a shadow of the great city that it once was, having lost almost all its colonies, was a small Christian town surrounded by massive Muslim lands. The land route to Asia was effectively closed down as the Ottomans controlled much of southern Europe and the Mediterranean Sea. Ottoman leaders had unsuccessfully tried to capture it 12 times. To a great extent the writing was on the wall. It was only a matter of time before the Muslims took Constantinople. The European rulers of the time were not strong enough to prevent the fall of the once-beloved capital of the Byzantine Empire. This made the need for a new route to India quite urgent for the Europeans.

As a result the Roman Catholic Church was keenly interested in the Portuguese voyages of discovery. In 1452, one year before the fall of Constantinople, Pope Nicholas V issued a papal bull entitled *Dum Diversas*. He was very aware of the potential significance of the voyages. They would capture new lands for Christendom, having lost most of the original heartland to the Muslims. Those lands and their resources could fund the crusade that would stop Sultan Mehmet II, the 20-year-old ruler of the Ottomans who had just inherited the throne in 1451 and made it his most important goal to take Constantinople. (In a provocative move, Mehmet II had just built the Rumelihisari fortress on the European side of the Bosporus to cut out Constantinople to prevent it from receiving military support.) It was also critical for Nicholas V to ensure that those people and lands found on the way to India were sufficiently brought into Christendom to prevent them from falling into the hands of the Muslims. As such, he gave the power and rights to the King Afonso of the Portuguese to not only claim those lands for Portugal but also to capture and enslave them. He wrote:

> Justly desiring that whatsoever concerns the integrity and spread of the faith, for which Christ our God shed his blood, shall flourish in the virtuous souls of the faithful ... we grant to you by these present documents, with our Apostolic Authority, full and free permission to invade, search out, capture and subjugate the Saracens and pagans and any other unbelievers and enemies of Christ wherever they may be, as well as their kingdoms, duchies, counties, principalities, and other property ... and to reduce their persons into perpetual slavery, and to apply and appropriate and convert to the use and profit of yourself and your successors, the Kings of Portugal, in perpetuity, the above-mentioned kingdoms, duchies, counties, principalities, and other property and possessions and suchlike goods.[31]

Essentially, the world was theirs for the taking and they had the blessings of the Pope in all their endeavours. They – the Portuguese kingdom – had the rights to all territories they would claim along the West African coast and, as later bulls declared, going east, as far as Asia. They could also reduce any non-Christians they found in those lands to slaves indefinitely and make their lands perpetual colonies of Portugal.

Two years later, in 1454 (one year after the fall of Constantinople), Pope Nicholas V issued another bull, *Romanus Pontifex*, that repeated a great deal of what had been said in *Dum Diversas*, giving the King of Portugal full rights to all present and future Portuguese territorial possessions overseas.[32] The bull's primary purpose was to forbid other

Christian nations from infringing the King of Portugal's rights of trade and colonization in what were considered Portuguese territories overseas. This was done to prevent conflict between the Portuguese and the Castilians (Spanish), who were also beginning to explore new lands. With *Romanus Pontifex*, the Portuguese had a monopoly on trade in the new areas in Africa and Asia. Repeating parts of *Dum Diversas*, it confirmed the Pope's permission for the Crown of Portugal to dominate *all lands south of Cape Bojador in Africa. It also* encouraged the seizure of the lands of Saracen Turks and non-Christians and the enslavement of all whom the Portuguese would conquer. In the end *Romanus Pontifex* made the King of Portugal and his representatives direct agents of the Pope's (and the Catholic Church's) ecclesiastical administration and expansion. The Portuguese authorities sent to colonize lands were not only commanded to convert people and build churches, monasteries and holy places for them. They were also authorized to:

> send over to them any ecclesiastical persons whatsoever, as volunteers, both seculars, and regulars of any of the mendicant orders (with license, however, from their superiors), and that those persons may abide there as long as they shall live, and hear confessions of all who live in the said parts or who come thither, and after the confessions have been heard they may give due absolution in all cases, except those reserved to the aforesaid see, and enjoin salutary penance, and also administer the ecclesiastical sacraments freely and lawfully.[33]

Romanus Pontifex was followed by the first *Inter Caetera*, which Pope Calixtus III wrote on 13 March 1456. This *Inter Caetera* (not to be confused with Pope Alexander VI's *Inter Caetera* of 1493) reiterated *Dum Diversas* and *Romanus Pontifex*. It continued to recognize Portugal's rights to the territories it had discovered along the West African coast as far as the Indies (*usque ad Indos*) – that is, Asia – and encouraged the reduction of the 'infidels and non-Christian' territories to perpetual vassals of the Christian monarch. It also gave the Order of Christ (of which Prince Henry was governor) 'all power, dominion and spiritual jurisdiction' over all regions claimed by Portugal 'from Capes Bojador and Nam through the whole of Guinea and beyond its southern shore as far as to the Indians'. Thus, again, the Portuguese had every right to convert and civilize the people they would find in other parts of the world. It was in their best interest to extend Christendom. Anyone who challenged this decree was threatened with excommunication. In addition, *Inter Caetera* prohibited all Christians from trading with the Saracens, or from navigating, trading or fishing without the permission of the King of Portugal.[34]

Several other bulls and treaties followed between the first *Inter Caetera* and Christopher Columbus' arrival in the Bahamas, geared towards maintaining peace between Portugal and Spain as they competed to claim new lands. For instance, in 1479 they signed the Treaty of Alcáçovas, which led to the cessation of hostilities between the Portuguese and the Castilians. In 1481 Pope Sixtus IV issued a new bull, *Aeterni Regis*, 'sanctioning Portugal's claims to exclusive rights in Guinea (West Africa) while also confirming ... the Treaty of Alcáçovas whereby the sovereigns of Castile promised not to disturb Portugal in Guinea or in certain of the Atlantic islands or in Morocco'. Some of the bulls were intended to gather an army of European Christians for a new crusade to take back Constantinople and defend Belgrade from the Ottoman armies. In the end it was Spain that benefited from the crusading impulse. Its long campaign against the last remaining Muslim sultanate of Granada led to a decisive victory in 1492. Only a few weeks later, Queen Isabella gave a royal warrant to Christopher Columbus for his voyage across the Atlantic. On the day following Columbus' departure from Spain, all Jews were expelled from Spain, and their property and lands confiscated.

Columbus came back from the West Indies bearing good news. In response, Pope Alexander VI issued a new bull, *Inter Caetera* (1493), establishing: (1) the Church had the political and secular authority to grant Christian kings a form of title and ownership in the lands of infidels; (2) European exploration and colonization was designed to exercise the Church's guardianship duties over all the earthly flock, including infidels; (3) Spain and Portugal held exclusive rights over other European Christian countries to explore and colonize the entire world; and (4) the mere sighting and discovery of new lands by Spain or Portugal in their respective spheres of influence and the symbolic possession of these lands by undertaking the rituals and formalities of possession, such as planting flags or leaving objects to prove their presence, were sufficient to create rights in these lands.[35] *Inter Caetera* states:

> Among other works well pleasing to the Divine Majesty and cherished of our heart, this assuredly ranks highest, that in our times especially the Catholic faith and the Christian religion be exalted and be everywhere increased and spread, that the health of souls be cared for and that barbarous nations be overthrown and brought to the faith itself. ... [W]e ... assign to you and your heirs and successors, kings of Castile and Leon ... all islands and mainlands found and to be found, discovered and to be discovered towards the west and south, by drawing and establishing a line from ... the north ...to ... the south ... the said line

to be distant one hundred leagues towards the west and south from any of the islands commonly known as the Azores and Cape Verde.[36]

With that line, first drawn at 100 leagues west of Cape Verde and later shifted to 370 leagues by the Treaty of Tordesillas in 1494 (to accommodate Portugal's claim for Brazil, which had not been discovered yet), the world was divided between the two main European maritime nations of that era, to conquer and Christianize. Essentially, *Dum Diversas*, *Romanus Pontifex* and 1493 *Inter Caetera* have together been interpreted as the foundational justification for both the doctrine of discovery and the age of imperialism. Not only did they serve to justify the beginnings of European imperial domination of the world, they also provided the basis for the enslavement of the nations by Portugal and Spain.

A violent mission to civilize the world for God

It is quite evident in the papal bulls of the fifteenth century that the motivations behind the European efforts to evangelize the world were mixed. If anything, the original drive behind their maritime voyages was not to evangelize: they mostly needed to find a sea route to India where they could continue to trade in the spices they needed for their livelihood in Europe. They were not strong enough to fight the Ottoman Empire, which had blocked off land access to Asia, but they hoped to find in the explorations resources that could fund new crusades at first to liberate the Holy Land from Muslim rule and, after 1453, to take Constantinople back from the Ottomans. A third understated motive was to find the legendary Christian kingdom somewhere towards the east – maybe in Ethiopia or in India – led by Prester John.

Having captured Cape Verde in 1403 and Ceuta in 1415, the Portuguese were determined to pioneer the way to the east by going around Africa – it would take them several attempts to reach the bottom end of Africa in the many decades it took them to dock at the Cape of Good Hope. All this happened when European Christendom constantly needed soldiers (who, being European, were also Christian) to defend it from the threat of the Muslims. However, the need for an army of Christian soldiers had shaped a great deal of the Roman Empire's history since the conversion of Constantine.

Beginning with Constantine's decision to align with Christianity in 312 CE, a new relationship emerged between the Christian faith and Roman imperial power. His choice set in motion events that led to his becoming sole ruler of the Roman Empire in 325 CE, bringing imperial violence into Christianity's story. He embraced Christianity amid a bloody conflict with Maxentius, one of his three co-emperors, at the Battle of Milvian Bridge. With the deaths of Maxentius in 312 and Licinius – the other co-emperor – in 324, Milvian Bridge proved consequential for Christianity. On the crucial day before the epic battle, Christ appeared to Constantine in a vision with a cross in heaven with the words, 'In this sign, conquer.' In his biography of Constantine, Eusebius says:

> About the time of the midday sun, when the day was just turning, he said he saw with his own eyes up in the sky and resting over the sun, a cross-shaped trophy formed from light, and a text attached to it which said, 'By this conquer' (τούτῳ νίκα). Amazement at the spectacle seized both him and the whole company of soldiers which was then accompanying him on a campaign he was conducting somewhere, and witnessed the miracle.[37]

Later that night Constantine had a dream in which Christ spoke to him:

> The Christ of God appeared to him with the sign which had appeared in the sky, and urged him to make himself a copy of the sign which had appeared in the sky, and to use this as a protection against the attacks of the enemy.[38]

Constantine followed the instructions and conquered Maxentius. Jesus, who had died at the hands of Roman soldiers on the hill of Golgotha, had helped Constantine claim the throne for himself. At that moment Jesus was incorporated into Rome's imperial violence, first of one Roman against another, but would soon be on the side of the Roman military machine against outsiders – the Visigoths, the Vandals and indeed the Muslims. From then on Constantine was one of the three rulers of the empire, with Maxentius and Licinius.[39] Constantine and Licinius issued the Edict of Milan in 313 CE, which gave to the Christians as well as to all (others) free permission to follow the religion that each one chose, in order that whatever deity there is on the heavenly throne may be propitiated and show itself favourable to themselves and to all who are under their power.[40] With that edict, Christianity was made legal throughout the Roman Empire. As a result, many Christians – who made up at least 10 per cent of the empire's population – had to take part in the empire's violence. Christian thought and identity had to adapt to accommodate the use of violence against enemies of the empire.

Empires survive by violence. It is through conquest that they achieve their peace. Empires rise and fall on the power of their armies. The Roman Empire itself came into existence after Augustus defeated Mark Antony and Cleopatra in Egypt (and quickly killed Caesarion, Julius Caesar's son with Cleopatra). A few smaller battles followed before the era of the Pax Romana finally became a reality. Pax Romana was only possible because of the many legions the empire had (some say as many as 34 legions existed), each camped at a strategic location throughout the empire yet each being mobile enough (travelling on the wide-reaching network of Roman roads), ready to face any enemy within and without the empire. The violent nature of the Roman Empire was on full display every time persecution broke out in any part of the empire. This was the case in 64 CE when Nero blamed Christians for the fires that ransacked Rome in 64 CE and martyred many Christians (including Peter and Paul). Such persecutions were a normal part of Christian life in the Roman Empire until Constantine and Licinius, through the Edict of Milan.

In the decades that followed, the idea of Christian soldiers became a normal part of life in the empire. Later, in 1095, under the leadership of Pope Urban II, Christian soldiers from Europe launched the Crusades intended to liberate Jerusalem from the Muslims after the Byzantine emperor, Alexios I Komnenos, called for help. As is normal for imperial violence, fellow Christians were not spared. In 1204, during the Fourth Crusade (1202–04), Latin Christian soldiers ransacked Constantinople on their way to Jerusalem, dealing the city a decisive blow from which it never recovered. As a result, when the fifteenth century came – and with it a much stronger enemy in the form of the Ottoman Empire – the need for strong Christian men in Europe was stark.

European racial and religious supremacy

The Christian imagination of the Europeans at this point reflected that of the empires that had shaped it and which it had shaped for centuries – Greek, Roman, Byzantine. It was one in which the Supreme Pontiff himself could call for the domination and enslavement of those he called the enemies of Christ, as Nicholas V did in *Dum Diversas*. This should not be a surprise. Even the Apostle Paul, himself a native of the empire, took some aspects of the imperial life to be normal and acceptable even for followers of Christ. He could not condemn slavery – he sent Onesimus back to Philemon with nothing more than an exhortation to treat him as a beloved brother in the Lord. Slavery was part of the violence that kept the machinations of the empire running. In parts of the

Greek Empire, citizenship was tied to owning slaves. Those who were lucky enough to survive when their armies were conquered were, as a general rule, taken into slavery. The Egyptians, the Babylonians and the Persians enslaved those they conquered. The Greeks did the same, and so did the many other conquering empires. The Roman Republic practised slavery. The Roman Empire perfected the art of enslaving numerous peoples and spreading them throughout the empire for their labour. Many centuries later the Ottoman Empire enslaved many people, European Christians included, especially during the transatlantic slave trade era, which extended from the 1440s until the late 1800s (with Brazil outlawing slavery in 1888, although the last slave ships left West Africa in the 1890s). The Ottoman Muslims, who occupied the Barbary Coast of North Africa, raided European towns and villages and enslaved many of their people. Mention has to be made also of the Arab slave trade that ravaged eastern Africa for many centuries and only came to an end in the early years of the twentieth century.[41]

At the heart of the papal bulls of the fifteenth century were several key issues. First, the Europeans were afraid of the Muslims, who proved to be militarily superior to them for many centuries. Alongside this was the fear of losing some more Christian land to the Ottomans (and, possibly, the Moors, who were still present in Spain until 1492). Second, the Portuguese and the Spanish worked with the popes to extend Christendom to non-Christian parts of the world to replace the lands lost to the Muslims by the Roman and Byzantine Empires. The Muslims had taken the Holy Land, North Africa, Anatolia and Constantinople, and were knocking on the doors of Italy. In return, European Christians could convert many other peoples in Africa, Asia and Latin America, and while at it claim ownership of the land and subject its peoples to colonial subjugation to prevent them from falling into the hands of the Muslims. To do this effectively the papal bulls provided authority. The Pope had said it – conquer, capture, enslave – and they had the superiority to do it. Many Christian soldiers, unable to engage the Muslims in Asia Minor, the Levant and North Africa, turned to the many non-Christians overseas. The imperial violence that had shaped much of Europe's Christian imagination since Constantine was unleashed on the wider world. Years before the fall of Constantinople, Prince Henry the Navigator was selling African men and women as slaves in Lisbon.[42]

The doctrine of discovery, enshrined in the papal bulls *Dum Diversas*, *Romanus Pontifex* and the 1493 *Inter Caetera*, was grounded on the belief that God had given the world to Europeans to dominate, Christianize and civilize. Pope Nicholas V, King Afonso of Portugal, Isabella and Ferdinand of Castille, Columbus, Pope Alexander VI, and many others in Europe believed that the kingdom of God ought to be extended into non-Christian lands, which could easily be done using colonial violence: claim the land and Christianize the people through civilization or civilize the people through Christianization. Non-Christian lands were deemed to be *terra nullius* – vacant land – that could be claimed just by sight. Doing something more, such as planting a flag or naming a river, gave them an added advantage. Whenever a piece of land was claimed by either Portugal or Spain, it was theirs to dominate, civilize and Christianize. This was well established in the European mind by the 1490s, as Robert Miller argues: 'The idea that the Doctrine [of discovery] granted European monarchs ownership rights in newly discovered lands and sovereign and commercial rights over Indigenous peoples due to first discovery by European Christians was now established international law, at least to Europeans.'[43] In the decades that followed *Inter Caetera* of 1493, Portugal and Spain used the papal bulls to claim that the popes had given them exclusive rights to whatever lands and peoples they found on their voyages.

By the sixteenth century the English, the French and other European nations were joining the frenzy, with the French king disputing the Portuguese and Spanish claims, declaring in 1541: 'The Popes hold spiritual jurisdiction, and it does not lie with them to distribute land amongst kings' and that 'passing by and discovering with the eye was not taking possession'.[44] Later, in 1580, Elizabeth I of England would argue that 'The Pope had no prerogative to grant the New World to Spain or to oblige princes who did not owe the Pope obedience' and that 'The Spaniards have touched here and there, have erected shelters, have given names to a river or promontory: acts which cannot confer property.'[45] In the end Spain and Portugal continued to rely on the papal bulls to claim any non-Christian lands they saw, while the British and the French preferred symbolic acts, colonial charters and occupation.[46]

Civilizing mission in Africa

Because of its origin in the fifteenth and sixteenth centuries, the European understanding of mission has always been tied to the idea of civilization (and this depends to a very large extent on domination and Christianization). It was by and large a *civilizing* mission.[47] The term 'civilizing mission' did not emerge until later, during the French Revolution. From the time of the voyages of discovery and the early Jesuit missions, the philosophical foundations of Christian missionary work were rooted in the European belief in their right to dominate and 'civilize' or 'lift up' other societies. Edward Said once wrote that the rhetoric of the civilizing mission is 'what has been called "a duty" to natives, the requirement in Africa and elsewhere to establish colonies for the "benefit" of the natives, or for the "prestige" of the mother country'.[48] This sense of duty to lift societies up would be used to justify anything and everything – from the enslavement of Africans to the colonization of the continent and everything in between – that the Europeans did overseas as something that would eventually make life better for the local people (as, more importantly, it benefited the Europeans). The civilizing mission would come to be called 'The White Man's Burden', as argued by Rudyard Kipling:

> Take up the White Man's Burden
> Send forth the best ye breed
> Go bind your sons to exile
> To serve your captives' need;
> To wait in heavy harness
> On fluttered folk and wild
> Your new-caught, sullen people, half devil and half child.[49]

In this poem Kipling sought to justify Western imperialism and to encourage the United States to join forces with the British to share the 'white man's burden' of 'extending civilisation to peoples considered incapable of governing themselves'. In the end, by the conclusion of the nineteenth century the idea of a 'civilizing mission' was inextricably linked to imperialism through the work of Western Christian missionaries (especially the British and the French). For example, Jean-Paul Wiest states:

> The French government and French missionaries collaborated in combining the two notions of *Gesta Dei per Francos* (The Deeds of God through the French) and *Mission Civilisatrice* (Civilizing Mission). From a nineteenth-century French perspective, Christian missionaries saw themselves as undertaking a civilizing mission that aimed not only to evangelize and export European culture but also to facilitate French colonial and economic expansion.[50]

Most nineteenth-century missionaries saw the idea of 'civilizing mission' as legitimate, believing they brought education and the gospel even as they advanced colonial expansion. As Eric Hobsbawm says, 'the idea of superiority to, and domination over, a world of dark skins in remote places was genuinely popular' in the nineteenth century.[51] He adds:

Whether trade followed the flag may still be debated, but there is no doubt at all that colonial conquest opened the way for effective missionary action – as in Uganda, Rhodesia (Zambia and Zimbabwe) and Nyasaland (Malawi). And if Christianity insisted on the equality of souls, it underlined the inequality of bodies – even of clerical bodies. It was something done by whites for natives, and paid for by whites. And though it multiplied native believers, at least half the clergy remained white.[52]

However, Christian missionaries were a special breed of heroic persons bringing Christ to foreign lands.[53] Right from the 1400s, the lands claimed by the Europeans were to be civilized. That civilization was, and still is, defined in European and Western terms means that to be civilized was then, in the European mind, to be Europeanized. To paraphrase Brian Stanley, missionary beliefs were derived primarily from the Bible: non-Christians required conversion for salvation, their religious systems constituted little more than 'pagan idolatry'; Western civilization was both superior to and had a capacity for improving others; and the commitment to the monogenist interpretation of human origins.[54] Andrew Walls stated that missionaries were:

> representative Christians trying ... to do Christian things, things that were specifically, characteristically Christian. They were trying to share the knowledge of Christ; and more than any other group of Westerners in the period of Western expansion, they were trying to make Christian choices and live in a Christian way.[55]

However, as Alison Twells has put it:

> Their missionary strategy was further consolidated by the dynamic secular theory of cultural change which ... saw all societies moving through distinct stages of development. In particular, the polarity of the 'civilised' and the 'savage' within Enlightenment thought mapped onto the biblical dichotomy of the 'Christian' and the 'heathen', emphasising the capacity for progress and salvation of all peoples and providing a framework for missionary intervention.[56]

In the end Jean and John Comaroff are right to declare that:

> The very nature of the 'mission', with its endeavor to change a culture and to replace it not only with Christian belief and practice but with 'civilized' cultural practices, was shaped by a meta-narrative of social

progress, which made it a vehicle of the West's 'post-Enlightenment imagination.[57]

Today, in the era of international development and non-governmental organization, that civilizing mission continues. Among Christians, the United States' influence on global Christianity makes that civilization look Western. In their defence, Stephen Neill states that:

> Even the most blameless of missionaries was liable, in the epoch of Cecil Rhodes and Bismarck, to be caught up in the stream of the time, and half consciously to identify his own country's interests with the interests of the kingdom of God ... The concern of the missionaries was primarily for the African.[58]

To justify this civilizing agenda, Europeans created a hierarchy of civilizations with the European civilization at the top – they defined and modelled civilization – and everyone else beneath them according to their cultures (at least as these were understood and defined by the Europeans). At the bottom of that hierarchy were the Africans. If Samuel Huntington's *The Clash of Civilizations* theory is correct, there is no – and has never been – African civilization.[59] Tied to this idea of the hierarchy of civilizations is the concept of the hierarchy of the races, with white people (and whiteness) defining what it means to be human and black people being not fully human, a primitive race of children at the very beginning of human evolution. Needless to say, race (and its offspring of racism) is, and has always been, the fulcrum of the 'civilizing mission'. Racism, being a belief that denotes the superiority of some races over others and that the inferior races need to be treated with different standards, was the major incentive of imperialism. As Robert Johnson says:

> [The] black skin [of the African] was 'evidence' of being a 'human fossil' or 'infantile'. The absence of literature or technology was seen as evidence of ignorance. Rebellion or resistance to white rule, and therefore to civilisation, was used as proof of underdevelopment, impulsiveness and immaturity.[60]

In essence, the African needed to be civilized and, at least as they understood at the time, God had granted the Europeans the duty to do that civilizing, and the missionaries were doing part of that work. This civilizational rationale, supported and nurtured by old and resilient racialized outlooks, was particularly instrumental in the creation and institutionalization of a system of colonial labour, which became the cornerstone of the organization of the new imperial and colonial political economies in the aftermath of the legal abolition of the transatlantic slave trade.[61] For those Africans who wanted to be civilized, progress happened in stages and had several facets. First, societies had to transition their modes of production from hunting and gathering to a commercial economy. But this required a middle stage of domesticating animals and settled agriculture. Furthermore, such societies had to change their social institutions to reflect the cultures of European commercial economies.

The journey towards civilization also reflected a shift in the peoples' religious inclinations from idolatrous polytheism to monotheism. Unfortunately for Africans, their religious heritage was at first denied – 'an untutored African can never understand God'[62] – and later demonized: it was called devilish and animism.[63] This created a beneficial way of understanding Africans (and many other people around the world). Without a religion, they were not human at all. If they were, they existed at the earliest primitive evolutionary stages of being human. Indeed, once their humanity was negated – once they had been dehumanized – the Africans could easily be enslaved, colonized and demonized. They were, since the beginning of the European slave trade, believed to be neither human nor to have been created in the image of God (whom Europeans understood to have made the white race superior to all other races) and, therefore, needed no religion, or whatever they had was not religion at all. When they came to settle in Africa, many Europeans were convinced that Africans were neither human nor had any religion.

For instance, the first Dutch settlers at the Cape of Good Hope in the seventeenth century did not evangelize the Africans among whom they settled because they believed them to have no souls (which meant they could not be converted). They ignored the Christian kingdom that existed in the Congo-Angola area at the time. The Dutch people's denial of African humanity (and religiosity) set the trends for the next two centuries. As Europeans settled in southern Africa with their eyes set on trade, they had no interest in evangelizing Africans. In the nineteenth century, 200 years after the Dutch had arrived in South Africa, Europeans were largely still dismissive of African humanity:

> At the pinnacle of civilisation was urban, western Europe, placed there by its commercial, civic and domestic successes and values, happily unhindered by its neighbouring peasant, Catholic and orthodox populations. India was characterised as an ancient civilisation reduced by idolatrous religion to a nation of human sacrifice and widow-burning.

The idol worship, promiscuous sexuality and homosexual practices of the South Pacific were mitigated by the absence of corruption by slavery and apparent openness to Western ideas and influence. *Fewer peoples were lower than Africans in this scale of civilisation, their 'barbarism' tragically reinforced by slavery and by their blackness which was long associated with disadvantage and degradation.*[64]

This denial of African humanity was not properly articulated until much later, in the seventeenth and eighteenth centuries. Racist quotes of Europeans saying ridiculous things about Africans abound. For example, Georg F. W. Hegel (1770–1831), one of Europe's foremost philosophers, called Africans a race of children. He wrote in his *Philosophy of Mind*:

> [Black Africans] are to be regarded as a *nation of children* who remain immersed in their state of uninterested naïveté. They are sold, and let themselves be sold, without any reflection on the rights or wrongs of the matter. The Higher which they feel they do not hold fast to, it is only a fugitive thought. This Higher they transfer to the first stone they come across, thus making it their fetish and they throw this fetish away if it fails to help them. Good-natured and harmless when at peace, they can become suddenly enraged and then commit the most frightful cruelties. They cannot be denied a capacity for education; not only have they, here and there, adopted Christianity with the greatest gratitude after a long spiritual servitude, but in Haiti they have even formed a State on Christian principles. But they do not show an inherent striving for culture. In their native country the most shocking despotism prevails. There they do not attain to the feeling of human personality, their mentality is quite dormant, remaining sunk within itself and making no progress, and thus corresponding to the compact, differenceless mass of the African continent ... It is in the Caucasian race that mind first attains to absolute unity with itself. Here, for the first time mind enters into complete opposition to the life of Nature, apprehends itself in its absolute self-dependence, wrests itself free from the fluctuation between one extreme and the other, achieves self-determination, self-development, and in doing so creates world history.[65]

Of course, for him North Africa did not have any of these problems. He believed that even though Africa appears to be a 'landmass belonging to a compact unity', North Africa, up to the boundary of the sandy desert, is not proper Africa.[66] The inhabitants of North Africa were to him not Africans, 'that is, negroes, [*die Neger*]', but were rather 'akin to Europeans' in character.⁶⁷ Later, he says, 'the fiery heat [of Africa] is a force of a too powerful nature for man to resist, or for [the human] spirit to achieve free movement and to reach a degree of richness which the precondition and source of a fully developed mastery of reality.'⁶⁸ He adds:

> Africa proper, as far as History goes back, has remained – for all purposes of connection with the rest of the World – shut up; it is the Gold-land compressed within itself – *the land of childhood*, which lying beyond the day of self-conscious history, is enveloped in the dark mantle of Night.⁶⁹

This 'Africa proper' is not part of history. He says:

> Africa, is no historical part of the World; it has no movement or development to exhibit. Historical movements in it – that is in its northern part – belong to the Asiatic or European World. Carthage displayed there an important transitionary phase of civilization; but, as a Phoenician colony, it belongs to Asia. Egypt will be considered in reference to the passage of the human mind from its Eastern to its Western phase, but it does not belong to the African Spirit. What we properly understand by Africa, is the Unhistorical, Undeveloped Spirit, still involved in the conditions of mere nature, and which had to be presented here only as on the threshold of the World's History.⁷⁰

Another racist European philosopher is Emmanuel Kant (1724–1804). His list of racist comments about black Africans is long. Let us hear from Kant himself in this quotation:

> The Negroes of Africa have by nature no feeling that rises above the ridiculous. Mr. Hume challenges anyone to adduce a single example where a Negro has demonstrated talents, and asserts that among the hundreds of thousands of blacks who have been transported elsewhere from their countries, although very many of them have been set free, nevertheless not a single one has ever been found who has accomplished something great in art or science or shown any other praiseworthy quality, while among the whites there are always those who rise up from the lowest rabble and through extraordinary gifts earn respect in the world. So essential is the difference between these two human kinds, and it seems to be just as great with regard to the capacities of mind as it is with respect to color. The religion of fetishes which is widespread among them is perhaps a sort of idolatry, which sinks so deeply into the ridiculous as ever seems to be possible for human

nature. A bird's feather, a cow's horn, a shell, or any other common thing, as soon as it is consecrated with some words, is an object of veneration and of invocation in swearing oaths. The blacks are very vain, but in the Negro's way, and so talkative that they must be driven apart from each other by blows.[71]

Elsewhere, Kant adds that black Africans are stupid (because of being 'black from head to foot'[72]), vain and careless:[73]

> The Negro race, one could say, is exactly the opposite of the American; they are full of affect and passion, very lively, talkative and vain. They acquire culture, but only a culture of slaves; that is, they allow themselves to be trained. They have many incentives, are also sensitive, afraid of beatings, and also do many things out of honor.[74]

In 1785 he wrote:

> The purpose [of race] is nowhere more noticeable in the characteristics of race than in the Negro; merely the example that can be taken from it alone justifies us also in the supposition of seeing an analogy in this race to the others. Namely, it is now known that human blood becomes black, merely [because] it is loaded with phlogiston ... the strong stench of the Negro which cannot be removed through any amount of washing, gives us reason to suppose that their skin removes a great deal of phlogiston from the blood and that nature must have organized this skin in such a way that the blood can be dephlogistonized to a much greater degree than is the case with us.[75]

David Hume (1711–76), another racist European thinker, wrote:

> I am apt to suspect the Negroes to be naturally inferior to the Whites. There scarcely ever was a civilized nation of that complexion, nor even any individual, eminent either in action or speculation. No ingenious manufactures amongst them, no arts, no sciences. On the other hand, the most rude and barbarous of the Whites, such as the ancient Germans, the present Tartars, have still something eminent about them, in their valour, form of government, or some other particular. Such a uniform and constant difference could not happen, in so many countries and ages, if nature had not made an original distinction between these breeds of men. Not to mention our colonies, there are Negro slaves dispersed all over Europe, of whom none ever discovered any symptoms of ingenuity; though low people, without education,

will start up amongst us, and distinguish themselves in every profession. In Jamaica, indeed, they talk of one Negro as a man of parts and learning; but it is likely he is admired for slender accomplishments, like a parrot who speaks a few words plainly.[76]

Europeans called Africa the 'Dark Continent', a term popularized by Henry Morton Stanley when he made it the title of his best-selling books, *Through the Dark Continent* and *In the Darkest Africa, Volumes 1 and 2*.[77] Of course, this was still pretty much how most Europeans understood Africa at the turn of the twentieth century. It was part of the philosophical justification for colonialism – another sad part of Africa's history of which Henry Morton Stanley is a co-architect. It was Stanley who carved out the entire Congo for King Leopold of Belgium as his personal property, and in the process started the domino of events that culminated in the dividing up of the African continent among European countries at the Berlin Conference in 1884. This 'Dark Continent' propaganda quickly gained traction and, in 1902, some two decades after Stanley's *Through the Dark Continent*, another European, József Teodor Konrad Korzeniowski, using an anglicized version of his name, Joseph Conrad, published a novel, *The Heart of Darkness*,[78] in England to a very warm reception. In it, Africans are described as primitive savages and cannibals who deserve to be violently colonized by the Europeans. The continent itself is portrayed as the antithesis of Europe and, therefore, of civilization – Africa is the 'other world' where humanity's intelligence and refinement are mocked by triumphant bestiality. *The Heart of Darkness* remains one of the popular English titles today.

All this was to justify the need first to kidnap and enslave Africans during the transatlantic slave trade and later to colonize, civilize and Christianize them, starting in the first half of the nineteenth century and going on until the 1960s and 70s. For a long time, in the Congo-Angola region where Portuguese slave traders ran rampant, many Africans were kidnapped and shipped off as slaves to the Americas even after they converted to Christianity. This was the scourge of the Christian kingdom that existed in the Congo area from the 1490s to the early 1700s. While that Christianity thrived for a good 200 years, with many people converting through the ministry of Portuguese priests and a strong Jesuit presence, Portuguese slave traders continued to empty the entire country of its population. By the 1800s, Portuguese slave traders had depopulated a great deal of the Congo-Angola region of Africa and had to go to the eastern coast of Africa, to the Mozambique area, to find people they could enslave.

Immediately, Europeans sought to dominate and colonize the Americans (using enslaved Africans for free plantation labour) and parts of Asia (at first, using trading companies). Right from the start, European Christians were involved in this expansion project, providing the philosophical (and theological) justification for the domination of the world. Columbus had the papal mandate to expand Christendom. A few decades later, the Society of Jesus came into existence (and with it, 'mission' got to be defined in the way we understand it today). The Portuguese established the Christian Kingdom of the Kongo and built Fort Jesus at Mombasa before establishing trading colonies in India. Later, in the 1800s, European expansionism reached its peak with a quarter of Europe's population migrating to the Americas, Africa and parts of Asia. The main drive was colonialism, but they were Christians. In the end colonialism and mission became one thing, and this would be the case right to the end of the twentieth century.

Following the beginnings of 'mission' among the Jesuits in the 1540s, to engage in mission was to extend God's kingdom among the nations, and in most cases the earthly expression of that kingdom of God was the European civilization. Just as European Christendom was Christianity on the map, European civilization was the kingdom of God geographically defined. To be a European was to be a Christian as well as to be civilized. European, Christian and civilized were essentially interchangeable. As a result, for many, Europe was the standard of civilization, a standard that was achieved because of Christianity. Therefore, to Christianize others was to cause them to aspire to the European civilized life. To civilize people was also to Christianize them. The two worked together. They were two sides of the same coin.

These European origins of mission mean that mission talk among Westerners has been shaped by a paternalistic attitude towards the rest of the world. The language of mission has always been that of the civilizer. It speaks down to the unconverted, often treating them as less human than Christians or, indeed, enemies of Christ himself. In 1452 Pope Nicholas V said, 'Invade, search out, capture and subjugate *the Saracens and pagans and any other unbelievers and enemies of Christ* wherever they may be, as well as their kingdoms, duchies, counties, principalities, and other property ... and ... reduce their persons into perpetual slavery.'[79] Later, in 1540, Ignatius of Loyola added:

> This entire Society and each one individually are campaigning for God under [the pope] and the other Roman Pontiffs who will succeed him ... whether he sends us among the Turks or to other infidels, even to

the land they call India, or to any heretics or schismatics, or to any of the faithful ... as the *militia* of Jesus Christ.[80]

Today this patronizing language can be heard when a group of North American Evangelical Christians talk about mission among what they call 'unreached people groups' around the world, or the unevangelized peoples living in the 10–40 Window (mainly North Africa, the Middle East and Asia) or the least evangelized and half-evangelized parts of the world (such as sub-Saharan Africa).[81] It can also be heard when British missionaries boast about their time teaching English in Colombia or serving at a hospital in Uganda, or indeed helping Nigerian women set up microfinance projects. Locally, in the West, we also hear it when Westerners take pride in renting their church facilities to an immigrant church with which they cannot find the courage to develop a more relational multicultural worship community, while complaining about their smelly foods and refusing them access to the kitchen.

In the mission communities in the West, there is an obsession with evangelizing people in other parts of the world while ignoring those very people when they find their way to the West. This is a testament to their commitment to mission as civilization. Many British agencies, for example, do not really know what to do with the reality of the global diaspora that has emerged to be a critical part of the country's religious landscape. One mission agency has formed an African Diaspora *task force* whose only purpose is to evangelize Africans in the United Kingdom, but to the surprise of many, there are no Africans on their team even though there are numerous mission-minded African leaders around the country. Many of these African, Afro-Caribbean, Latin American and Asian Christians can trace their faith journey to the work of British mission agencies. Numerous Anglicans from Jamaica, St Kitts, Nigeria, Kenya, India and Sri Lanka, just to name a few, live in the UK now – they have been here for two, three or four generations already – and are still struggling for recognition in the Church of England as well as its mission agencies. We could say the same about Presbyterians, Methodists, Baptists and many other denominations. It appears once these diaspora peoples arrive in Europe, the civilizing aspect of mission becomes irrelevant. So we ignore them and continue to focus on civilizing those living overseas. As a matter of fact, this is the same reason Westerners are generally not so good at evangelizing fellow Westerners. Most of their strategies are designed for a different audience. They cannot civilize fellow Westerners, especially working-class Westerners. In parts of Africa and maybe elsewhere in the world, the civilizing aspects of mission continue to be the main mission strategy.

Mission schools often required parents to convert before their children were allowed access to education. Mission hospitals did the same. Often only Christian converts would be seen at the hospital.

Notes

1 The Macedonian and Persian Empires together formed much of the known world at the time.

2 Adrian Goldsworthy, *The Fall of Carthage: The Punic Wars 265–146 BC* (London: Weidenfeld & Nicolson, 2012).

3 The Punic Wars were a series of three wars fought between the Roman Republic and the Punic (Carthaginian) Empire between 264 and 146 BCE. The first Punic War took place between 264 and 241 BCE. The second one ran from 218 to 201 BCE. The third one was much shorter, running from 149 to 146 BCE. It resulted in a resounding victory for the Romans, the destruction of the city of Carthage, the enslavement of its people and the establishing of the Roman hegemony around the western Mediterranean.

4 After conquering Alexandria, Amr Ibn Al-Aas sent a letter to the Caliph in which he stated, 'I have taken a city of which I can but say that it contains 4,000 palaces, 4,000 baths, 400 theatres, 12,000 sellers of green vegetables, and 40,000 tributary Jews.' Alfred Butler explains, 'While these round numbers contain an obvious overstatement, which was probably not in the original letter but has arisen from copyists' errors, they show clearly enough what an impression the city made upon its conquerors. But amazed as they were at the size and splendour of Alexandria, they were even more struck by its extraordinary brilliancy ... If we read 400 palaces and baths, 40 theatres, 1,200 sellers of vegetables, and 40,000 Jews, there is nothing improbable in the estimate.' Alfred Joshua Butler, *The Arab Conquest of Egypt and the Last Thirty Years of the Roman Dominion* (Oxford: Oxford University Press, 1978), p. 368.

5 This fascinating history has been covered extensively in many books. I found particularly helpful Hugh Kennedy, *The Great Arab Conquests: How the Spread of Islam Changed the World We Live In* (Philadelphia, PA: Da Capo Press, 2007). You can also read a general history of the Arab people: Albert Hourani, *A History of the Arab Peoples* (London: Faber & Faber, 2013).

6 See Thomas John Drobena and Wilma Samuella Kucharek, *Heritage of the Slavs: The Christianization of the Slavs and the Great Moravian Empire: A History of Political and Religious Events AD 800–899* (Columbus, OH: Kosovo Publishing Company, 1979).

7 See Anders Winroth, *The Conversion of Scandinavia: Vikings, Merchants and Missionaries in the Remaking of Northern Europe* (London: Yale University Press, 2012).

8 Henry Kamen, *The Spanish Inquisition: A Historical Revision* (New Haven, CT: Yale University Press, 2014).

9 Gwyn Jones, *A History of the Vikings* (Oxford: Oxford University Press, 2001), p. 303.

10 For more on this, see the classic narrative, Eben Norton Horsford, *The Landfall of Leif Erikson, AD 1000: And the Site of His Houses in Vineland* (Boston, MA: Damrell & Upham, 1892).

11 See Noah Brooks, *The Story of Marco Polo* (New York: Cosimo, 2008). There are numerous other books written about Marco Polo and the controversies that have followed his story for centuries. One that I found helpful is Robin Brown, *Marco Polo: Journey to the End of the Earth* (Stroud: The History Press, 2011).

12 Marco Polo, *The Travels of Marco Polo* (DigiCat, 2022).

13 John Larner, *Marco Polo and the Discovery of the World* (London: Yale University Press, 1999).

14 In the year that Columbus reached the West Indies, Spain managed to liberate Granada from Muslim rule by pushing the Moors back into Morocco.

15 See David Arnold, *The Age of Discovery, 1400–1600* (London: Routledge, 2013).

16 Ceuta was a trading port with links to the interior of Africa. It was ruled by the Portuguese from 1415 to 1688 when it was ceded to Spain. It continues to be an autonomous enclave of Spain in Morocco until today.

17 Anthony R. Disney, *A History of Portugal and the Portuguese Empire: From Beginnings to 1807*, vol. 2 (Cambridge: Cambridge University Press, 2009), pp. 1–2. Also see Robert Silverberg, *The Realm of Prester John* (Athens, OH: Ohio University Press, 2020).

18 This idea of an army made of real soldiers who would fight for the cause of Christ has a long history. The Knights Templar were founded in 1119 to protect Christian pilgrims going to the Holy Land. But they were also good at organizing money and banking. As such, they were a military outfit known for their economic acumen. They were disbanded in 1309 due to the turning of fortunes both in the Holy Land, where Muslims were in control of Jerusalem (1244–1917), and in France, where the politics between the pope and King Philip had become unfavourable to the Templars. See Jochen Burgtorf, Shlomo Lotan and Enric Mallorquí-Ruscalleda, *The Templars: The Rise, Fall, and Legacy of a Military Religious Order* (London: Routledge, 2021).

19 The Portuguese had reached the Canary Islands in 1336, which had a missionary bishop from Majorca from the 1350s to about 1400. The Canary Islands were colonized by the Castilians in about 1402. Pope Nicholas V awarded the islands to Portugal but after a strong revolt, the Portuguese and the Castilians signed the Treaty of Alcáçovas in 1479, letting Castile keep the Canary Islands while giving the Azores, Madeira and Cape Verde to Portugal.

20 For a fascinating read of this journey, see Vasco da Gama, *Em Nome de Deus: The Journal of the First Voyage of Vasco da Gama to India, 1497–1499*, ed. and trans. Glenn J. Ames (Leuven: Brill, 2009). The title of the book, which translates 'in the name of God', gives away the Christian foundations of Vasco da Gama's motivation for the adventure. Yes, it was partly to find a new trade route to India, but all this was done to serve God by propagating the gospel among the unevangelized.

21 C. Graham Clarke and Bridget M. Brereton, 'West Indies', *Encyclopedia Britannica*, 23 August 2024, https://www.britannica.com/place/West-Indies-island-group-Atlantic-Ocean, accessed 24.03.2025.

22 Christopher Columbus, *Letters*, trans. Richard H. Major (London: Hakluyt Society, 1847), pp. 1–17.

23 George Grant, *The Last Crusader* (Wheaton, IL: Crossway Books, 1992), p. 85.

24 Edward Everett Hale, *The Life of Christopher Columbus: From His Own Letters and Journals and Other Documents of His Time* (La Vergne, TN: True Sign Publishing House, 2023), p. 128.

25 Pope Alexander unsuccessfully called for a crusade in 1500. The Ottomans were well established in Constantinople. European armies were still not strong enough to face the Muslims.

26 Christopher Columbus, *Libro de las Profecias*, trans. Delno C. West and August Kling (Gainesville, FL: University of Florida Press, 1991), pp. 2–3.

27 Michael Bradley, *The Columbus Conspiracy: An Investigation into the Secret History of Christopher Columbus* (Willowdale, Ontario: Hounslow Press, 1991).

28 Paul S. Vickery, *Bartolomé de las Casas: Great Prophet of the Americas* (Mahwah, NJ: Paulist Press, 2006), p. 10.

29 Hale, *The Life of Christopher Columbus*.

30 Christopher Columbus, *The Journal of Christopher Columbus*, trans. Cecil Jane (New York: Bonanza Books, 1989), p. 57.

31 John Francis Maxwell, *Slavery and the Catholic Church: The History of Catholic Teaching Concerning the Moral Legitimacy of the Institution of Slavery* (London: Barry Rose, 1975), p. 53. There are several translations of *Dum Diversas* available on the internet. While it is mentioned in many of the resources used in this book, I could not find any full translation of the bull. As such, for this discussion I used an internet translation, Unam Sanctam Catholicam, 'Dum Diversas (English Translation)', *Defending the Goodness, Truth and Beauty of Catholicism*, 2011, https://unamsanctamcatholicam.blogspot.com/2011/02/dum-diversas-english-translation.html, accessed 14.04.2025. Instead of 'servitude', many other translations have 'slavery'.

32 The best version that I could find of the *Romanus Pontifex* is in Frances Gardiner Davenport, *European Treaties Bearing on the History of the United States and Its Dependencies to 1684* (Washington DC: Carnegie Institution of Washington, 1917). A newer translation can be found at https://www.nativeweb.org/pages/legal/indig-romanus-pontifex.html, accessed 14.04.2025.

33 Davenport, *European Treaties*, p. 24.

34 Davenport, *European Treaties*, pp. 30–2.

35 Davenport, *European Treaties*, Doc. 7.

36 Davenport, *European Treaties*, Doc. 7.

37 Eusebius, *Life of Constantine*, trans. Averil Cameron and Stuart Hall (Oxford: Clarendon Press, 1999), Book 1, p. 81.

38 Eusebius, *Life of Constantine*, Book 1, p. 81.

39 Constantine would later defeat his co-ruler, Licinius, in 324 CE. Licinius was married to Constantine's younger sister, Flavia Julia Constantia.

40 Francis S. Betten, 'The Milan Decree of A. D. 313: Translation and Comment', *The Catholic Historical Review* 8, no. 2 (1922), p. 192.

41 In most cases African chiefs were incentivized to sell off their captives and, indeed, some of their own people (those unwanted by their societies), to the European slave traders and their slave raiders. A great deal of David Livingstone's missionary work in East and Central Africa in the 1850s and 60s was driven by a passion to bring the slave trade to an end. He called the slave trade in Africa the open sore of the world and prayed for blessings on anyone – American, English, Turk – who would help to heal this open sore (Tim Jeal, *Livingstone* (New Haven,

CT: Yale University Press, 2013), p. 367). While I do not support the hagiographic aspects of Jay Milbrandt's book, I appreciate that it tells Livingstone's story in ways that make sense to many Westerners. See Milbrandt, *The Daring Heart of David Livingstone: Exile, African Slavery, and the Publicity Stunt that Saved Millions* (Nashville, TN: Nelson Books, 2014).

42 Willie James Jennings, *The Christian Imagination: Theology and the Origins of Race* (New Haven, CT: Yale University Press, 2010), ch. 1.

43 Robert J. Miller et al., *Discovering Indigenous Lands: The Doctrine of Discovery in the English Colonies* (Oxford: Oxford University Press, 2010), p. 12.

44 Brian Slattery, 'Paper Empires: The Legal Dimensions of French and English Ventures in North America', in John McLaren, A. R. Buck and Nancy E. Wright (eds), *Despotic Dominion: Property Rights in British Settler Societies* (Vancouver, British Columbia: University of British Columbia Press, 2005), pp. 58–9.

45 Slattery, 'Paper Empires', p. 67.

46 Kent McNeil, 'The Doctrine of Discovery Reconsidered: Reflecting on Discovering Indigenous Lands: The Doctrine of Discovery in the English Colonies', *Osgoode Hall Law Journal* 53, no. 2 (2016), p. 707.

47 'Civilizing mission' emerges from the French Revolution as a secular term – *mission civilisatrice*. However, what it embodies had been going on in the world since the fifteenth century. See Alice Conklin, *A Mission to Civilize: The Republican Idea of Empire in France and West Africa, 1895–1930* (Stanford, CA: Stanford University Press, 2000).

48 Edward W. Said, *Culture and Imperialism* (New York: Vintage Books, 1994), p. 108.

49 Rudyard Kipling, 'The White Man's Burden', 1899. Kipling, an Indian-born British man, wrote the poem in 1899, intending to persuade the United States to annex and colonize the Philippines Islands. See Christopher Hitchens, *Blood, Class and Empire: The Enduring Anglo-American Relationship* (New York: Bold Type Books, 2004).

50 Jean-Paul Wiest, 'Catholic Activities in Kwangtung Province and Chinese Responses, 1848–1885' (PhD dissertation, University of Washington, 1977), pp. 34–5, 252–4.

51 Eric J. Hobsbawm, *The Age of Empire: 1875–1914* (New York: Vintage Books, 1989), p. 70.

52 Hobsbawm, *The Age of Empire*, p. 71.

53 Wiest, 'Catholic Activities', p. 656.

54 Brian Stanley, *Christian Missions and the Enlightenment*, Studies in the History of Christian Missions (Grand Rapids, MI: Eerdmans, 2001), p. 8.

55 Andrew F. Walls, *The Missionary Movement in Christian History: Studies in the Transmission of Faith* (Maryknoll, NY: Orbis Books, 1996), p. xviii.

56 Alison Twells, *The Civilising Mission and the English Middle Class, 1792–1850: The 'Heathen' at Home and Overseas* (London: Palgrave Macmillan, 2009), p. 25.

57 Jean Comaroff and John Comaroff, *Of Revelation and Revolution: Christianity, Colonialism, and Consciousness in South Africa*, vol. 1 (Chicago, IL: University of Chicago Press, 1991), p. 310.

58 Stephen Neill, *Colonialism and Christian Missions* (New York: McGraw Hill, 1966), p. 280.

59 Samuel P. Huntington, *The Clash of Civilizations and the Remaking of World Order* (New York: Touchstone, 1997).
60 Robert Johnson, *British Imperialism* (London: Springer, 2003), p. 109.
61 Miguel Bandeira Jerónimo, *The 'Civilising Mission' of Portuguese Colonialism, 1870–1930*, trans. Stewart Lloyd-Jones (London: Springer, 2015), p. 2.
62 Edwin W. Smith (ed.), *African Ideas of God, A Symposium* (Edinburgh: Edinburgh University Press, 1950), p. 1.
63 Edward B. Tylor, *Primitive Culture: Researches into the Development of Mythology, Philosophy, Religion, Language, Art, and Custom*, 2 vols, 4th edn (London: J. Murray, 1993). A summary version of his argument appears as an excerpt in Michael Lambek, *A Reader in the Anthropology of Religion*, and that shorter essay, written by Tylor himself, informs this paragraph. See Michael Lambek, *A Reader in the Anthropology of Religion*, 2nd edn, Blackwell Anthologies in Social and Cultural Anthropology (Malden, MA: Blackwell Publishers, 2008).
64 Twells, *The Civilising Mission*, p. 15 (my emphasis).
65 Georg Wilhelm Friedrich Hegel, *Philosophy of Mind*, trans. W. Wallace and A. V. Miller, revised with Introduction and Commentary by Michael Inwood (Oxford: Clarendon Press, 2007), pp. 41–2 (my emphasis).
66 Hegel, *Philosophy of Mind*, p. 40.
67 Hegel, *Philosophy of Mind*, p. 40.
68 Georg Wilhelm Friedrich Hegel, *Lectures on the Philosophy of World History*, trans. H. B. Nisbett with an introduction by Duncan Forbes (Cambridge: Cambridge University Press, 1984), p. 155.
69 Georg Wilhelm Friedrich Hegel, *The Philosophy of History*, trans. J. Sibree (Kitchener, Ontario: Batoche Books, 2001), p. 109 (my emphasis).
70 Hegel, *The Philosophy of History*, p. 117.
71 Immanuel Kant, *Immanuel Kant: Observations on the Feeling of the Beautiful and Sublime and Other Writings*, ed. Patrick R. Frierson and Paul Guyer (Cambridge: Cambridge University Press, 2011).
72 Kant, *Observations*, p. 61.
73 Kant, *Observations*, p. 181.
74 Immanuel Kant, *Lectures on Anthropology*, trans. Robert R. Clewis and G. Felicitas Munzel, ed. Allen W. Wood and Robert B. Louden (Cambridge: Cambridge University Press, 2012), p. 320.
75 Immanuel Kant, *Von den Verschiedene Racen der Menschen: Zur Ankündigung der Vorlesungen der physischen Geographie im Sommerhalbjahr 1775*, reprinted in Fritz Schultze, *Kant und Darwin*, pp. 58–79, quoted in Emmanuel C. Eze, *Achieving Our Humanity: The Idea of the Postracial Future* (Abingdon: Routledge, 2013), pp. 101–2.
76 David Hume, *Essays: Moral, Political and Literary* (Oxford: Oxford University Press, 1963), pp. 213–14.
77 Henry Morton Stanley, *Through the Dark Continent: Or, The Sources of the Nile Around the Great Lakes of Equatorial Africa, and Down the Livingstone River to the Atlantic Ocean*, 2 vols. (New York: Harper, 1878); Henry Morton Stanley, *In Darkest Africa: Or the Quest, Rescue, and Retreat of Emin Governor of Equatoria*, vol. 1 (London: Sampson Low, Marston, Searle & Rivington, 1890). In addition, Henry Morton Stanley, *In Darkest Africa: Or the Quest, Rescue, and Retreat of Emin Governor of Equatoria*, vol. 2 (London: Sampson Low, Marston, Searle & Rivington, 1890).

78 Joseph Conrad, *Heart of Darkness* (London: Legend Press, 2020).

79 *Dum Diversas*, English translation – see note 31 (my emphasis).

80 The Formula: https://jesuitportal.bc.edu/research/documents/1540_Formula/, accessed 14.04.2025 (my emphasis).

81 Current missiological discourse has shifted somewhat; both terms are often critiqued for their colonial connotations. For instance, my critique of the term 'unreached people groups' has been popularized by Holly Fletcher. When she asked me about how I understand the term 'unreached people groups', I asked her, 'Unreached by whom?' In asking her that question, I wanted to make a point that we ought to be clear that we mean unreached by Westerners, especially North Americans, because, of course, God has always been present among God's people in the whole wide world. The Spirit of God has already reached all of us. Acts 14.17 says, 'Yet [God] has not left himself without a witness in doing good – giving you rains from heaven and fruitful seasons, and filling you with food and your hearts with joy.'

5

Whoever Wishes to Serve as a Soldier

> Whoever wishes to serve as a soldier of God beneath the banner of the cross in our Society, which we desire to be designated by the name of Jesus, and to serve the Lord alone and his vicar on earth, should keep in mind that once he has made a solemn vow of perpetual chastity he is a member of a community founded chiefly for this purpose: to strive especially for the progress of souls in Christian life and doctrine and for the propagation of the faith by the ministry of the word, by spiritual exercises and works of charity, and specifically by the education of children and unlettered persons in Christianity.[1]

In this chapter, I seek to establish the Jesuit origins of the two words at the centre of the argument of this book: *mission* and *missionary*. To do this I will explore some aspects of the early history of the Society of Jesus, paying particular attention to their sense of purpose, their commitment to obedience and service to the popes, and the military language that reflects a great deal of their self-understanding and identity and coloured the way they developed their engagement in mission. I will argue that what we call 'mission' today is to a large extent a product of the European military situation of the fifteenth and sixteenth centuries, which was primarily dominated by the fall of Constantinople to Sultan Mehmed II in 1453. Mission was thus conceived within the long history of the Roman Catholic Church's response to what happened when the Byzantine capital was breached and destroyed on 29 May 1453. In addition, the Jesuit development of mission was to some extent a response to the start of Martin Luther's Reformation on 31 October 1517, when he nailed his 95 theses on the cathedral door at Wittenberg in Germany.

The Jesuit origins of mission

The idea of mission as the sending of Christians to propagate the Christian faith in unevangelized lands emerged in the 1540s with the start of the Society of Jesus (also known as the Jesuits). With the support of six of his companions, Ignatius of Loyola (1491–1556) founded a society in 1534 in Paris where they were studying. Later, in 1539, after moving to the outskirts of Rome with his companions, Ignatius wrote an initial document called the *Formula of the Institute* (Lat. *Formula Instituti*, also known in English as the *Formula*) to propose the establishment of the Society of Jesus to Pope Paul III.

On 27 September 1540, the Society of Jesus was recognized by Paul III. In the papal bull that established it, *Regimini Militantis Ecclesiae*, the Society's purpose is stated in the exact words of the *Formula*: 'To strive especially for the progress of souls in Christian life and doctrine and for the propagation of the faith by the ministry of the word, by spiritual exercises and works of charity, and specifically by the education of children and unlettered persons in Christianity.'[2] A second papal bull, entitled *Exposcit Debitum*,[3] issued in 1550 by Pope Julius III, incorporates the words of *Regimini Militantis Ecclesiae* (meaning 'To the Government of the Church Militant') but adds the words *et defensionem* (meaning 'the defence') to the purpose of the Society. The Society was not only to propagate the Christian faith, it was to defend the faith as well.[4] Thus, in *Exposcit Debitum*, the Society is:

> To strive especially for *the defense* and propagation of the faith and for the progress of souls in Christian life and doctrine, by means of public preaching, lectures, and any other ministration whatsoever of the word of God, and further by means of the Spiritual Exercises, the education of children and unlettered persons and the spiritual consolation of Christ's faithful through hearing confessions and administering the other sacraments.[5]

This was a radical and significant shift from the original purpose stated in 1539 and 1540. In the years between 1539 and 1550 the need for the Jesuits to engage in the work of defending the gospel had become quite visible. Consequently they had to add 'the defence' of the faith to their original purposes (placing 'defence' before 'propagation'). To a great extent the need to defend the faith was targeted at the Reformers and their impact on the Roman Catholic Church. But the general climate in Europe at the time was one of fear of the Ottomans, who had captured and destroyed Constantinople only a few decades before the formation of the Society of Jesus. The Jesuits would have to defend the faith from the Muslims in Western Asia and the Reformers (called heretics and schismatics) back home in Europe. Many Jesuit scholars downplay the role the Reformation played in shaping the agenda of the early Jesuits, including that of Ignatius.[6] John O'Malley is persuaded that:

> Aware as [the original Jesuits] were of the Reformation, it played no palpable role in the future they then designed for themselves ... they make few references to it when they describe their years in Paris ... When, in 1534, they took a vow to spend some time in ministry in a distant place, they set their eyes on Jerusalem, not Wittenberg.[7]

He concludes that 'the direct impact of the Reformation on the Jesuits ranged from minimal to non-existent.'[8] Of course, there is overwhelming evidence to the contrary. Looking at the development of their missiological thought, from the *Formula* to *Exposcit Debitum* (and later to the *Constitutions*), it appears that the growing influence of the Protestant movement in Europe was of great concern to both the popes (Paul III and Julius II) and by extension to the Society. Jean Lacouture sounds right when he says:

> The shock to the papacy was all the harder because Luther was at that very moment wresting a third of Europe from Roman sway; the Turk, scimitar in hand, was laying siege to Balkan and Danubian Christendom; and the giddy rise of Charles V's empire was outshining the Vatican's.[9]

It was not only Martin Luther taking a third of Europe away from the Roman Catholic faith. While Lutheranism was catching on in Germany, Calvinism was expanding in Switzerland and all the Protestant Reformers – the entire Reformation movement – was chipping away at Roman power, and the Catholic Church had to do something about it. The Reformers were still alive and *still* reforming the Church. One understated effect of the Reformation was the loss of Catholic land. Whenever people converted to Protestantism, the Catholic Church lost control of not only the people but also the land and everything that came out of that land. Starting in 1526, nine years after Martin Luther burned the Pope's bull and nailed the 95 theses in Wittenberg, Saxony and Hessen adopted Protestantism. In the 1530s, Lüneburg, Brandenburg-Ansbach and Anhalt followed suit.[10] In England, King Henry VIII broke away from Roman Church authority in 1534, starting what would be called the English Reformation. Without a doubt there was a great deal of heartache, anxiety and anger about this. The Counter-Reformation came into existence to minimize it. Armed conflict followed and many people died.

The emergence of the Jesuits made possible the Roman Counter-Reformation, a movement that embodied so much of the Jesuit identity that it was often used synonymously with it. The Jesuits became known as the 'the shock-troops of the Counter-Reformation'.[11] Back in 1556, a younger member of the Society, Jerónimo Nadal, began to make an explicit connection between the rise of the Jesuits and the Reformation. In 1562 he wrote, 'God called our Father Ignatius in about the same year that Luther left his convent and contracted his scandalous marriage ... From this fact we understand in a special way how the Society was raised up to help the Church in Germany, in India or wherever.'[12] In 1564 Ignatius' long-term secretary, Juan Alfonso de Polanco, wrote:

> When God, because of our sins, permitted Martin Luther in Germany to declare war on the apostolic Holy See and the Catholic religion ... at the very same time, his divine Providence began to prepare an antidote, so to speak, to counter this poison, in the striking conversion of Fr Ignatius Loyola.[13]

It is extremely likely, indeed, that the Society was turned into a defence movement very early in its existence at a time that called for a justifiable paranoia against the Muslims as well as the Protestants. The seeds of this Jesuit theological innovation helped the expansionist agenda that shaped a great deal of the European mind throughout the fifteenth century. It is impossible fully to understand how the Jesuits conceived of mission without an in-depth conversation about their military ethos.

A soldier becomes a missionary

Ignatius served as a soldier before he converted to become a missionary. His conversion happened in 1521 while he was recovering from a cannon fracture that he suffered in battle in the defence of Pamplona against a French army. He started his missionary journey with a passion to evangelize the Muslims, saying, as Joseph McCabe argues, 'After all the Crusades, the sites in the Holy Land were still trodden by the feet of blaspheming Turks.'[14] After a failed trip to Jerusalem in 1537, where he had hoped, together with his companions, he could help the service of the knights at a hospital, they decided to ask the Pope for guidance. The Pope would have them stay in Rome but send them on 'missions' – as emissaries with special assignments to get certain tasks done – around the world. Those tasks would be centred on the defence and propagation of the Christian faith, and this is what came to be called 'missions' and those sent on these 'missions' became called 'missionaries'.

In the *Formula* (1539) Ignatius made explicit the Society's dedication to 'missions anywhere in the world' by a special vow that obliged them to be ready to travel 'among the Turks or to other infidels, even to the land they call India, or to any heretics or schismatics, or to any of the faithful'.[15] Before long though, he shifted his eyes and became concerned about the spread of Protestantism in Europe where, as he realized, '[People] talked much of Luther and Calvin, little of Mohammed.'[16] Joseph McCabe observes:

> In its hour of greatest need, at the very outbreak of the Reformation, the Society of Jesus was formed as one of these auxiliary regiments, and in the war which the Church of Rome has waged since that date, the Jesuits have rendered the most spirited and conspicuous service.[17]

Richard W. Thompson opens his book *Footprints of the Jesuits* with a quote from one Nicolini of Italy saying, 'The Jesuits, by their very calling, by the very essence of their institution, are bound to seek, by every means, right or wrong, the destruction of Protestantism. This is the condition of their existence, the duty they must fulfil, or cease to be Jesuits.'[18] As McCabe argues, it is rather needless to say that the Society was 'in essence and details, a regiment enlisted to fight Protestantism'.[19] He adds, 'At its institution, on 27 September 1540, *Regimini Militantis Ecclesiae* placed the Society of Jesus at the service of the Counter-Reformation.'[20]

Ignatius was often invoked as the antidote to Martin Luther. One Jesuit historian, Pedro de Ribadeneira, wrote to this effect in his biography (in 1572 and elaborated further in 1583). He emphasized the military aspects of Ignatius and of the Church he served, portraying Catholicism as a kingdom at war that God provides with reinforcements. Ignatius, he affirmed, was the great reinforcement sent by God to do battle with Luther.[21] Later on he described the Jesuits as 'the squadron and company of soldiers' always ready 'like light infantry ... to meet the enemy in battle'.[22] It seems fair to conclude, as the great German historian Leopold von Ranke does, that 'Loyola formed his society into a sort of religious standing army; selected carefully man by man, enrolled under the influence of the religious fantasy, each one trained for the especial service he was intended to perform, and commanded by himself.'[23] Forty years after the birth of the Society, at the death of its fourth general, Everard Mercurian celebrated that:

> The ten Jesuits had become a formidable army of 5000 *socii* (including novices and lay-brothers) ... all over Europe, in a fanatical zeal for the papacy, extending its influence through the laity by means of sodalities and confraternities ... [They] *were the backbone of the*

counter-Reformation, formidable alike by the simple and austere devotion of some, the brilliance and learning of others, and the unscrupulousness of yet others in the service of the Church. And every man, and every movement of every man, was registered in that central bureau at Rome, where four sagacious heads directed the strategy and tactics of this planet-scattered regiment.[24]

The Jesuit vows to obey

The Ignatian Society started with three vows – chastity, poverty and obedience – enshrined in the *Formula*. The first two vows were quite easy to decide. There was, however, a long discussion before the vow of obedience was agreed upon by the members, but in the end it seemed wise to them all to require members to vow obedience to the Superior General. By the time *Regimini Militantis Ecclesiae* was issued, the conversation had shifted to a point where a fourth vow was needed (and was added to the *Formula*). It was the vow of obedience to the Pope (at least that is how many scholars read it).[25] Thus, right from its start the Society was shaped by an extreme commitment to obedience. They were to 'obey the superior of the Society ... [who] should issue the [mission] commands'. It further asks members to 'promise never to carry on negotiations with the Roman Pontiff about missions directly or indirectly'. Today, a Jesuit making the vow will include something like this:

> I vow to your divine Majesty, before the most holy Virgin Mary and the entire heavenly court, perpetual chastity, poverty, and obedience in the Society of Jesus. I further promise a special obedience to the Sovereign Pontiff in regard to the missions according to the same apostolic letters and Constitutions.

Jesuits make the promise to submit 'to the will and judgment of the Supreme Pontiff, for we knew that he possessed greater knowledge of what was most meet for all Christendom'.[26] Jean Lacouture adds:

> In addition to that ordinary bond of the three vows, we [i.e. the fully professed Jesuits] are to be obliged by a special vow to carry out whatever the present and future Roman pontiffs may order which pertains to the progress of souls and the propagation of the faith; and to go without subterfuge or excuse, as far as in us lies, to whatsoever provinces they may choose to send [*mittere*] us – whether they are pleased to send us among the Turks or any other infidels, even those who live

in the region called the Indies, or among any heretics whatever, or schismatics, or any of the faithful.[27]

It is in this context of the emergence of the Society of Jesus that the word 'missionary' (and therefore 'mission') began to take root. Of course, 'missionary' does not appear in either the *Formula* (1539) or *Regimini Militantis Ecclesiae* (1540). What we call mission today was before *Regimini* referred to simply as 'propagating the faith' or 'journeying to the infidel'.[28] Generally, where both these terms are used in both the *Formula* and *Regimini*, they can be translated to mean 'travel for the sake of the ministry'. John O'Malley suggests that, 'By the time of the *Constitutions* [written by Ignatius with the help of his secretary Juan Alfonso de Polanco about ten years after *Regimini Militantis Ecclesiae*], "mission" has displaced the older terms, and it dominates the Seventh Part, the section devoted to "the distribution of members in the vineyard of the Lord," which some commentators consider the heart of the document.' He observes:

> In the first official document of the order, submitted to Pope Paul III and incorporated by him in the bull of approval *Regimini Militantis Ecclesiae* of 1540, the first Jesuits spoke of this aspect of their goals as 'propagation of the faith', but later in the document used 'missions' in that same regard. In subsequent years in their correspondence among themselves, they employed 'mission,' 'journey,' and 'pilgrimage' almost as synonyms to designate travel for the sake of ministry.[29]

By the time we get to the *Constitutions*, the word 'missioned' is used to mean 'sent'. Much of this concerns the fourth vow – the vow of obedience to the Sovereign Pontiff regarding the missions. The Pope sent them on missions. Thus, in the context of this vow the word 'missions' meant 'itinerant ministry' or 'ministry throughout the world' for the greater help of souls.[30] For O'Malley:

> The Jesuits' Fourth Vow was, in essence, a vow of mobility, that is, a commitment to travel anywhere in the world for the 'help of souls.' The *Constitutions*, in fact, assume that these 'missions' would generally last no longer than three months. The Fourth Vow was thus one of the best indications of how the new order wanted to break with the monastic tradition.[31]

O'Malley later concludes that the *Constitutions* also make it clear that such 'missions' might also become permanent so that Jesuits 'may carry on their labour, not by travelling but by residing steadily and continually in certain places where much fruit of glory and service to God is expected'.[32] All in all, for O'Malley, 'The Jesuits were among the first, if not the first, to develop [the concept of mission] and were extremely influential in its evolution.'[33] Later on he adds that 'the modern definition of missions as "the propagation of the faith"' is mostly due to the Jesuits who 'were among the first to inaugurate the new usage and were the group initially perhaps most responsible for its widespread propagation'.[34] Part of this shift in the way the work of propagating the faith was understood had to do with the Jesuit belief that they were *not* monks – they were not called or sent to set up monasteries. They were called to be mobile (and thus agile), so that the Pope could send them to where he felt their ministry was needed. One of the first rhetoricians of the Jesuits, Jerónimo Nadal, used to repeat to young Jesuits across Europe that they were not monks and their home was the world (not a monastery).[35] Indeed, for Nadal the essence of the monk was 'to flee the company of other human beings', but the essence of the Jesuit was to seek their company 'in order to help them':[36]

> In other orders, the members lived in monasteries or convents. Jesuits lived in 'houses' or 'colleges,' but they differed from the others most pointedly in that their 'best house' was their 'pilgrimages' and their 'missions,' that is, their journeying for ministry. In these various ways, Jesuits followed more closely the lifestyle of the early preachers of the Gospel. The Apostles did not wear a monastic habit ... They did not spend their time [in choir] chanting psalms and hymns.[37]

Whoever wishes to be a soldier and *et defensionem*

The very first words of the *Formula* call for 'whoever wishes to serve as a *soldier of God beneath the banner of the cross* in our Society' (my emphasis). It goes on to outline, in a rather military manner, the vows that the new soldier for Christ would need to make. It needs all members of the Society to remember that the 'entire Society and each [member] individually are campaigning for God under [the Pope]'.[38] In keeping with popular Catholic and Protestant theology, and the general context of Europe at the time, the Church needed to be militant. Catholic theology has something known as the 'three states of the church': church militant, church suffering and church triumphant.[39] The church militant consists of those Christians (and these had to be Catholic in the context of the sixteenth century) who are 'pilgrims' on earth. It is thus also called the pilgrim church. These Christians are soldiers of Christ against sin, the devil and 'the rulers of the world of this darkness, against the spirits of wickedness in the high places'. The word 'militant' here comes from the Latin word *milito*, which is translated as 'to be a soldier, perform military service, serve as a soldier'.[40] Central to this theology of a militant church is the idea of Christians being pilgrims on earth, engaging in constant spiritual warfare against the wiles of the evil one. More often, the church militant refers to spiritual warfare. Yet this spiritual warfare usually turned physical and led to armed conflicts (like the Thirty Years War, which took place among European Christians between 1618 and 1648). Before their suppression in 1773, the Jesuits were recorded to have been involved in armed conflict, either directly or indirectly, in some parts of Europe.

Ignatian missiology makes frequent use of military language. Ignatius seems at home speaking in military terms – he was a soldier for a long time before he became a missionary. His writing, starting with the *Spiritual Exercises* (largely composed between 1522 and 1524 but not fully completed until 1535), all the way to the *Constitutions*, contains a significant number of words that can be attributed to military exercise, warfare and conquest. The tenor of his autobiography portrays a man who was proudly, above all else, a soldier for Christ.[41] Indeed, his identity is peppered with such words as 'soldier' and 'knight'. Michael Mullet suggests that Ignatius was informed, 'on the one hand, by values such as endurance, a rigid, intolerant, *militant* Catholicism, self-sacrifice, loyalty and dour hardihood that shaped his childhood in Spain [which only managed to free Granada from Muslim rule in 1492 when Ignatius was only a baby] ... and, on the other hand, by the fictitious knights in a novel called *Amadis de Gaula*'.[42] Mullet writes:

> The knightly values of the culture that shaped him were set out in a best-seller published in Zaragoza in 1508. This book was a late flowering of chivalric romanticism and heroic knightliness, *Amadis de Gaula*, a work of fiction of whose attitudes Loyola's 'whole mind was full', as he later recalled, for, as 'a man given over to the vanities of the world', with a 'great vain desire to win fame ... especially in the exercise of arms', his mind was a prisoner of his reading and his goals were those of honour won through valour ... Loyola's response to this work was to alter the focus of his emulation from knightly champions, as in Amadis, to great saints, especially Francis and Dominic.[43]

The military nature of the Jesuit identity has been discussed quite extensively over the centuries since the inception of the Society. For instance,

Jonathan Wright's popular history of the Jesuits is entitled *God's Soldiers*.[44] He goes on to tell of the adventures of the Society and the power that it has exuded across the world over the past 500 years. Like many others, Wright identifies the Jesuits as God's soldiers because of their willingness to follow the orders of the Superior General or the Pope to do any kind of work anywhere in the world. For this reason others have called the Jesuits 'The Company of Jesus', 'God's Marines' and the Church's 'Storm Troopers'.[45] A great deal of Jesuit history is entangled in this military identity.

The crusading spirit behind mission

The language of a militant church did not necessarily emerge with the Jesuits. It was there before Ignatius or Luther. When Paul III called his 1540 bull *Regimini Militantis Ecclesiae*, he invoked a term in wide circulation in the sixteenth century. It had been in use for centuries before the Jesuits arrived on the scene. It shaped a great deal of the Christian expansion that happened not only in the fifteenth and sixteenth centuries but also throughout the existence of the Church. Long before the Jesuits, during the Crusades, the theology of a militant church undergirded European attempts to liberate the Holy Land – and the Middle East – from the Muslims. It had been central to the expansion of Christianity in Europe and the Christianization of the Slavs and the Nordic countries. The militant church was the church of the Roman Empire when it forcibly converted people, making them submit to Christ, his servants, the Pope and the emperor. When the church militant speaks of Christians being constantly engaged in a spiritual battle against the principalities, powers and rulers of this world, it becomes the story of the entire Church from the New Testament to the twenty-first century. It was Paul who admonished the disciples in Ephesus to stay strong in the Spirit, 'For our struggle is not against enemies of blood and flesh, but against the rulers, against the authorities, against the cosmic powers of this present darkness, against the spiritual forces of evil in the heavenly places' (Eph. 6.12). These words of Paul still stand today. Unfortunately, as noted earlier this struggle against spiritual powers often spills over into physical conflict. Although there is no likelihood that Paul would have in mind any ideas to start a revolution against the emperor – his words were really about spiritual warfare – many use this language to justify physical conflict against unbelievers.[46]

Military language among Christians shaped the expansionist adventures of the fifteenth and sixteenth centuries when Europeans were waking up to the possibilities of dominating and civilizing the world, believing this to be their God-given mandate. As such the Church had to be militant against the people they called pagans and 'Mohammedans'. One famous author of the era, Desiderius Erasmus (1466–1536), published *Handbook of the Militant Christian* in 1503.[47] Erasmus' *Handbook* was quite influential both for Martin Luther and the other Reformers, and for Ignatius and the Jesuits. Written for an actual soldier, the *Handbook* speaks about the general Christian life, urging Christian readers to 'inject into the vitals' the teachings of Christ by studying and meditating on the Scriptures and using the spiritual interpretation favoured by the 'ancients' to make the text pertinent to moral concerns.[48] Erasmus believed that the life of a good follower of Christ ought to reflect that of a knight who, in Europe, was a popular figure in the people's self-understanding; the idea of knights had been central to European Christian identity since the Crusades.

Just a few decades before Ignatius was born, pope after pope had unsuccessfully called for crusades to take back Constantinople and, possibly, the Holy Land from the Ottomans. Both Nicholas V (who was pope in 1453 when Constantine fell) and Calixtus III (who held the papacy between 1455 and 1458) called for crusades to liberate Constantinople. In 1452, with the siege of Constantinople impending, Emperor Constantine XI asked Pope Nicholas for help to stop Mehmed II. Pope Nicholas V's bull, *Dum Diversas*, gave authority to King Afonso V of Portugal to 'attack, conquer, and subjugate Saracens, pagans and other enemies of Christ wherever they may be found'.[49] In the weeks preceding 29 May 1453 (when Constantinople fell to the Turks), Nicholas ordered ten papal ships to sail with ships from Genoa, Venice and Naples to defend the city.[50] Unfortunately, the city fell before the ships could offer any aid. Nicholas, who was a humanist bibliophile, was doubly affected – the fall of Constantinople was a blow to Christendom as well as to Greek literature. His friend Aeneas Silvius wrote to him, 'It [the fall of Constantinople] is a second death to Homer and Plato.'[51]

> The news of the loss of Constantinople caused a great terror among Christians, and the pope immediately sent word to the Signoria that the Venetians should arm five galleys against the Turks at his expense, and he launched the crusade. Those who went in an armada or by land against the Turks should receive the full benefits of the jubilee. If any soldier refused recruitment and declined to go, he was excommunicated.[52]

From then on Nicholas V preached the need for a crusade. On 30 September 1453 he followed through with another papal bull, *Etsi Ecclesia Christi*,[53] in which he explicitly summoned all the Christian princes for a crusade against the Turks and their ruler, Mehmed, 'son of satan, perdition, and death', to reverse the fall of Constantinople.[54] He confirmed it with another bull, *Ad Summi Apostolatus Apicem*, in 1455.[55] Callixtus III, who became pope after the death of Nicholas, was said to 'speak and think of nothing but the crusade ... Other affairs he despatches with a word, but he treats and speaks of the crusade continually.'[56] On 29 June 1456 he issued a bull entitled *Cum His Superioribus Annis* (also called *Bulla Turcorum*), in which he announced the fall of Constantinople and exhorted the faithful to make processions in every diocese on each first Sunday of the month in order to pray that the threatened Turkish invasion might be averted.[57] He sent ambassadors to preach the crusade and collect tithes to several provinces of Spain and Germany, for Portugal, Poland, Dalmatia, Norway, Denmark and Sweden, even to Ireland and to the distant shores of Scotland.[58] He also ordered bells to be rung at midday to remind the faithful that they should pray for the welfare of the crusaders.[59]

After Callixtus III came Pius II. In 1459 Pius II issued a papal bull, *Vocavit nos Pius*, calling European rulers to the Council of Mantua to galvanize an army to take back Constantinople from the Turks.[60] The Council happened, but the effort for a fresh crusade was unsuccessful as European kingdoms were busy fighting their own internecine wars. In 1460 he declared a three-year crusade that would end up a failure. In 1463 Pius II renewed his efforts to organize a crusade against the Ottomans. Again, in 1464 he issued another bull, *Ezechielis Prophetae*, in which he called Christians to pick up arms and fight against the Ottoman Empire, offering Plenary Indulgence to those who 'personally join the expedition, and remain in the field for at least six months, as well as those who should give money according to their power'.[61] He chided them:

> O stony-hearted and thankless Christians! Who can hear of all these things, and yet not wish to die for Him Who died for you. Think of your hapless brethren groaning in captivity amongst the Turks, or living in daily dread of it. As you are men, let humanity prompt you to help those who have to endure every sort of humiliation. As you are Christians, obey the Gospel precept which bids you love your neighbour as yourself. Think of the miseries inflicted on the faithful by the Turks. Sons are torn from their fathers, children from their mother's arms, wives are dishonoured before the eyes of their husbands, youths

are yoked to the plough like cattle. Take pity on your brothers: bring help to those who are suffering. But if nothing in their situation moves you, at least consider your own safety. Don't think that you are safe because you have obtained, perhaps, an abode that is distant from the Turks. No one is so remote that he cannot be found. If you dismiss your neighbour when he is in danger, the one who in front of you is closest to the fire, you too will be dismissed likewise by the neighbour who dwells behind you. We should behave towards others as we wish them to behave towards us. Don't expect the French to help you, Germans, unless you yourselves help the Hungarians, nor the Spaniards to help you, men of France, unless you help the Germans. For the same measure that you have meted out will be meted out again for you. And let no one flatter himself because he is powerful in principality or kingdom. The emperors of Constantinople and Trebizond, the king of Bosnia and the lords of Rascia, and many other rulers who were captured and cruelly put to death teach you what to expect. Nothing is so repugnant to Mehmed as the name of king: having won the empire of the East, he hastens toward the empire of the West.[62]

As before, there was no real response to the call. Even after these powerful words – *in the form of a papal bull* – the rulers of Europe did not get their armies together to fight Mehmed II. In the end Pius II died in Ancona in 1464, as he tried to make one last effort to launch the crusade by his own example.

In 1481 Pope Sixtus IV issued a fresh bull, *Cogimur Jubente Altissimo*, again calling for a crusade against the Ottomans.[63] Five years later, in 1486, Pope Innocent VIII sent another bull, *Catholice Fidei Defensionem*, granting plenary indulgences to whoever took part in the war against the Ottoman Empire.[64] In 1487 Innocent issued another bull, *Universo Pene Orbi*, in which he 'dilated upon the seriousness of the Turkish threat to Germany and Italy, affirming his determination to leave no stone unturned to arouse Christendom to offensive action. He announced the emperor's readiness to go on the crusade with imperial churches and churchmen.'[65] As late as 1500, Pope Alexander VI promulgated a fresh bull, *Quamvis ad Amplianda*, calling for a crusade against the Ottomans in response to their invasions of Venetian territories in Greece.[66]

The mission of the church militant

The trauma of the loss of Constantinople to the Ottomans in 1453 weighed too heavily on the hearts of virtually all popes who followed Nicholas V until the end of the fifteenth century. There was the continued threat that the Turks would continue pushing westwards to conquer Rome – Mehmed II had attempted to assume the title of the Emperor of the Eastern Roman Empire (calling himself *Kayser-i Rum* – Caesar of Rome). Having captured Constantinople, Mehmed continued his campaigns, engaged in a long war with Venice (1463–79), later receiving Shkodra from the Venetians in the Treaty of Constantinople (1479), and besieged Otranto, occupying it from July 1480 to September 1481. His long series of wars included those with Serbia (1454–59), Morea (1458–60), Trebizond (1460–61), Wallachia (1459–62), Bosnia (1463), Moldavia (1475–76), Albania (1466–78) and Italy (1480). Rome was always a potential target. If Mehmed had not died after taking Otranto, the Ottomans would have had the chance to keep advancing towards Rome, hoping to expand the Ottoman Empire to include Italy and the western Roman Empire, with the possibility of expanding Islamic rule into Western Europe as they had done in North Africa.[67] As a result, almost all the popes of the second half of the fifteenth century, from Nicholas V to Alexander VI, issued bulls seeking to galvanize European Christians to raise an army for new crusades to liberate Constantinople.[68] They felt the need to do everything in their power to take Constantinople from the Turks, hoping this might stop their possible further advance towards the West.[69]

Consequently there was always an urgent need for Christian knights to rise up and defend the West. In this situation a theology calling for the Church to be militant was needed, justifiable and often widespread. Nevertheless the princes of Europe were neither strong nor courageous enough to go against the Turks, whose empire was at its strongest in the fifteenth and sixteenth centuries. In addition to the Ottoman threat, Martin Luther's Reformation in Germany in 1517 sparked a new threat to the control and power of the Roman Catholic Church in Europe itself. The Christian soldiers would have to fight on two fronts – against the Ottomans on the one hand and the Protestants on the other. This is why the Jesuits vowed to go anywhere in the world, be it among the 'Turks and the other infidels, even to ... India' or 'any heretics or schismatics'.[70] A younger student of Loyola, St Robert (1542–1621), would publish an ecclesiological book entitled *On the Militant Church* as a part of the *De Controversiis Tomus III* trilogy.[71]

The Jesuits are recognized to be among the most successful missionary arms of the Roman Catholic Church. Their impact around the world is beyond a doubt.[72] The fact that we are discussing their history and its implications for how we understand, talk about and engage in the work of propagating the good news of Christ around the world almost 500 years after Ignatius started the Society is quite significant. With Pope Francis having been the first Jesuit to occupy the highest seat of the Roman Catholic Church, and with more than 15,000 missionaries active in the world today, the Society is, without a doubt, a force to reckon with. Reading their long history serving the Catholic Church (and the popes) over the centuries, it is pretty evident that a great deal of that success comes from Ignatius Loyola's genius in placing the Society directly under the Supreme Pontiff. This happened at a time right in the aftermath of the Reformation when Paul III needed to find ways to decrease its influence in Europe. It worked well for him and for Julius III, who followed him, and for many other later popes. With the popes on their side and the papal authority entailed thereby, and the freedom to serve in the entire world without geographical restrictions – 'we are not monks, the world is our house'[73] – the Jesuits managed to get a lot done. Serving the popes in a direct manner like this gave them access to power that the other orders did not enjoy. In addition it allowed them access to the popes' coffers. Of course, they also used their connection to Rome to raise even more funds for the Society (even though every Jesuit took the vow of poverty).[74] It is for this reason that McCabe suggests:

> [The Jesuits] stand out from the other religious congregations of the Roman world only in the attainment of greater power and wealth, and the means by which they attain them. Here alone is there a distinctive strand in the story of the Jesuits, perceptible from the foundation of the Society. Unquestionably, they did far more for their Church in the first century after the Reformation than any other religious body; and they did this specifically by seeking wealth and power. They strained every nerve to secure the ears of popes, princes, and wealthy people.[75]

Their mission strategy is quite telling. They were basically a group of brothers (with few distractions from family, wives and children), vowed to poverty and obedience (and therefore with no concern for economic survival), agile and ready to spring into action at the Pope's request (no questions asked). In a world that needed Christian soldiers to defend the West from the threat of the Ottomans, the Jesuits were the men to work for the popes to make this happen. They had access to all the resources they would need. They could get around the world, wherever they were sent to go. Their understanding of 'mission', even as they fashioned that word and gave it its meaning, was shaped for a people whose circumstances were drastically different from those of many who call themselves 'missionaries' today.

That, I believe, is easy to understand. Not many of us Protestants can enjoy similar circumstances in our efforts to propagate the good news to the world. Yes, many Western missionaries will never be very rich, but most of them live relatively comfortably and retire with enough resources saved up to keep them going until death. Many of them will also have family commitments – parents, spouses and children. Many do go on the mission field unmarried or without their partners, but in most cases this is different from the chastity vows that the Jesuits make. Even though many will have some mighty supporters behind their work – including the American dollar, the British pound or the German euro – their power cannot be compared to that enjoyed by the early Jesuits through their connection with the Vatican. Later, in the eighteenth century, when nation-states began taking shape, the Society's international (or global) nature and the fact that it was only answerable to Rome made it highly suspicious to European princes and rulers. Because of its power and riches the Society was perceived to be full of conniving tricksters bent on nothing less than world domination. As a result the Jesuits were banned in Portugal, France and Spain. Later, in 1773, Pope Clement XIV suppressed the Society and made its 22,000 members illegal in many countries until the early nineteenth century.[76]

Conclusion

It is my argument here that the early Jesuit missiology worked largely because it was conceived and executed in the context of power. It was 'mission' because it was done from a position of power. Yes, God sends people, but Jesuits, in addition to being sent by God, were sent by the popes on the popes' missions. Their missiology served the popes as a means of serving God. It was a powerful missiology. Individually some missionaries may have been weak and powerless but as a Society, with the backing of the Vatican and sent out by the Pope to take care of the Pope's business, they were extremely powerful. It is in this context that the work of propagating the gospel to others became mission. This language, embedded in military thought, was picked up by William Carey in 1792 and has continued to inform our thinking about what God is doing in the world. Mission continues to be something that Westerners do to people around the world with the backing of their economies in the West.

Notes

1 'The Formula of the Society of Jesus'. An English translation of *Regimini Militantis Ecclesiae*, the papal bull of 27 September 1540 establishing the Society of Jesus, is found in John Olin, *The Catholic Reformation: Savonarola to Ignatius Loyola: Reform in the Church, 1495–1540* (New York: Harper & Row, 1969), pp. 203–8. Also see Saint Ignatius of Loyola, *The Constitutions of the Society of Jesus and Their Complementary Norms: A Complete English Translation of the Official Latin Texts*, trans. George E. Ganss SJ (St Louis, MO: Institute of Jesuit Sources, 1996).

2 https://jesuitportal.bc.edu/research/documents/1540_Formula/, accessed 15.04.2025.

3 https://jesuitportal.bc.edu/research/documents/1550_formula/.

4 See John W. O'Malley, *The First Jesuits* (London: Harvard University Press, 1993), p. 5.

5 https://jesuitportal.bc.edu/research/documents/1550_formula/ (my emphasis).

6 This is quite common among Jesuit scholars. For instance, see Jean Lacouture, *Jesuits: A Multibiography*, trans. Jeremy Leggatt (Washington DC: Counterpoint, 1995). Also see Robert Aleksander Maryks, *A Companion to Ignatius of Loyola: Life, Writings, Spirituality, Influence*, Brill's Companions to the Christian Tradition (Leuven: Brill, 2014). Chapter 9 of Maryks' book is devoted to the discussion of Ignatius and Luther and how the Society emerged in the context of the Reformation (and Counter-Reformation).

7 O'Malley, *The First Jesuits*, p. 16.

8 O'Malley, *The First Jesuits*, p. 17.

9 Lacouture, *Jesuits: A Multibiography*, p. 61.

10 Joachim Whaley, *Germany and the Holy Roman Empire: Volume I: Maximilian I to the Peace of Westphalia, 1493–1648* (Oxford: Oxford University Press, 2012), p. 255.

11 John W. O'Malley, *The Jesuits: A History from Ignatius to the Present* (London: Rowman & Littlefield, 2014), p. 21.

12 Jerónimo Nadal, 1562, quoted in Philip Endean, 'Ignatius in Lutheran Light', *The Month* 24 (1991), p. 271.

13 Juan Alfonso de Polanco, 1543, translated and quoted in Terence O'Reilly, 'Ignatius Loyola and the Counter-Reformation: The Hagiographic Tradition', *Heythrop Journal* 31, no. 4 (1990), p. 465.

14 Joseph McCabe, *A Candid History of the Jesuits* (Louisville, KY: Bank of Wisdom, 1913).

15 In *Exposcit Debitum*, the special vow obliged them to travel 'among the Turks or any other infidels, even those who live in the regions called the Indies, or among any heretics whatever, or schismatics, or any of the faithful'. See Saint Ignatius of Loyola, *The Constitutions*, p. 7. Of course, the 'heretics' and the 'schismatics' refer to the Protestants (and the Reformers).

16 McCabe, *A Candid History of the Jesuits*, p. 16.

17 McCabe, *A Candid History of the Jesuits*, p. v.
18 Richard W. Thompson, *The Footprints of the Jesuits* (Cincinnati, OH: Cranston & Curts, 1894), p. i.
19 McCabe, *A Candid History of the Jesuits*, p. 8.
20 McCabe, *A Candid History of the Jesuits*, p. 25.
21 O'Reilly, 'Ignatius Loyola: The Hagiographic Tradition', p. 441.
22 O'Reilly, 'Ignatius Loyola: The Hagiographic Tradition', p. 442.
23 Leopold von Ranke, *History of the Popes: Their Church and State*, vol. 1 (New York: Colonial Press, 1901), pp. 158–9.
24 McCabe, *A Candid History of the Jesuits*, pp. 104–5 (my emphasis).
25 Jesuit scholars interpret it as a vow to mission.
26 Lacouture, *Jesuits: A Multibiography*, p. 64.
27 For a short and focused conversation on this, see Kevin Flannery's essay, 'Circa Missiones: On the Founding of the Society of Jesus', https://www.scribd.com/document/96719873/Circa-Missiones, accessed 15.04.2025. For more on the subject, see John W. O'Malley, *Saints or Devils Incarnate? Studies in Jesuit History*, vol. 1 (Leuven: Brill, 2013), ch. 13.
28 The word 'infidel' appears in most English translations of both the *Formula* and the *Regimini Militantis Ecclesiae*.
29 O'Malley, *Saints or Devils Incarnate?*, 1, pp. 217–18. Also see Mario Scaduto, 'La strada e i primi gesuiti' in AHSI 40 (1971), pp. 323–90, now available in an abridged translation, 'The Early Jesuits and the Road', *The Way* 42, no. 1 (2003), pp. 71–84, and John Olin, 'The Idea of Pilgrimage in the Experience of Ignatius Loyola', *Church History* 48, no. 4 (1979), pp. 387–97.
30 O'Malley, *The First Jesuits*, pp. 298–9.
31 O'Malley, *The First Jesuits*, p. 299.
32 O'Malley, *The First Jesuits*, p. 299.
33 O'Malley, *The First Jesuits*, p. 126.
34 O'Malley, *Saints or Devils Incarnate?*, 1, p. 217.
35 Maryks, *A Companion to Ignatius of Loyola*, p. 6.
36 O'Malley, *The First Jesuits*, p. 68.
37 O'Malley, *The First Jesuits*, p. 67.
38 https://jesuitportal.bc.edu/research/documents/1540_Formula/.
39 *Catechism of the Catholic Church* (2nd edn), Vatican Publishing House, 2019, paragraph 954.
40 Latin Dictionary, 'milito', https://www.online-latin-dictionary.com/latin-english-dictionary.php?parola=milito, accessed 24.03.2025.
41 Saint Ignatius of Loyola, *The Autobiography of St. Ignatius of Loyola*, trans. Joseph F. O'Callaghan (New York: Fordham University Press, 1992).
42 Michael A. Mullett, *The Catholic Reformation* (London: Routledge, 1999), p. 75 (my emphasis).
43 Mullett, *The Catholic Reformation*, p. 75.
44 Jonathan Wright, *God's Soldiers: Adventure, Politics, Intrigue, and Power – A History of the Jesuits* (London: Image Books, 2005).
45 The Week Staff, 'The Jesuits: "God's Marines"', *The Week* (8 January 2015), https://theweek.com/articles/466362/jesuits-gods-marines, accessed 24.03.2025.
46 Paul had no intention to rebel against Rome. In his letter to the Romans he advised them to obey their government, for 'there is no authority except from God, and those authorities that exist have been instituted by God' (Rom. 13.1).

47 In Dutch, the original language of the book *Enchiridion Militis Christiani*, the word 'enchiridion' is translated as either 'handbook' or 'manual'. It can, however, also mean a 'handy sword' or a 'dagger'. Desiderius Erasmus, *Handbook of the Militant Christian*, trans. John P. Dolan (Notre Dame, IN: Fides Publishers, 1962). Other translations of the book have been entitled *Handbook of a Christian Knight* and *The Manual of a Christian Knight*.

48 Erasmus, *Handbook of the Militant Christian*, p. 41.

49 *Catholicam Dum Diversas* (English Translation), *Defending the Goodness, Truth and Beauty of Catholicism*, 2011, https://unamsanctamcatholicam.blogspot.com/2011/02/dum-diversas-english-translation.html, accessed 14.04.2025.

50 Ludwig Pastor, *The History of the Popes from the Close of the Middle Ages*, vol. II (London: Kegan Paul, Trench, Trübner & Co., 1899), p. 261.

51 Kenneth M. Setton, *The Papacy and the Levant, 1204–1571: The Fifteenth Century*, vol. II (Philadelphia, PA: American Philosophical Society, 1978), p. 150.

52 Setton, *The Papacy and the Levant*, II, p. 140.

53 Norman Housley, *Crusading and the Ottoman Threat, 1453–1505* (Oxford: Oxford University Press, 2013).

54 Setton, *The Papacy and the Levant*, II.

55 Pastor, *The History of the Popes*, II, p. 349.

56 Pastor, *The History of the Popes*, II, pp. 348–9.

57 Pastor, *The History of the Popes*, II, p. 400.

58 Pastor, *The History of the Popes*, II, p. 353.

59 Pastor, *The History of the Popes*, II, pp. 400–1.

60 Nancy Bisaha, *From Christians to Europeans: Pope Pius II and the Concept of the Modern Western Identity* (London: Routledge, 2023), p. 184.

61 Ludwig Pastor, *The History of the Popes: From the Close of the Middle Ages*, vol. III (London: Kegan Paul, Trench, Trübner & Co., 1923).

62 Pastor, *The History of the Popes*, III, p. 332.

63 Ludwig Pastor, *The History of the Popes from the Close of the Middle Ages*, trans. Frederick Ignatius Antrobus, vol. IV (London: Kegan Paul, Trench, Trübner & Co., 1900), pp. 340–1.

64 Norman Housley (ed.), *The Crusade in the Fifteenth Century: Converging and Competing Cultures* (London: Routledge, 2016), p. 201.

65 Setton, *The Papacy and the Levant*, II, p. 403.

66 Setton, *The Papacy and the Levant*, II, p. 527.

67 By the time Mehmed attacked Constantinople, the Ottoman Empire controlled much of the Balkan Peninsula, including modern-day Bulgaria, Greece, Albania, Macedonia and parts of Romania, Serbia and Hungary. They had captured Bursa in 1326 and effectively established a foothold in Europe. They expanded into the Balkans by conquering Serbia in 1389 and Bulgaria in 1396.

68 Only Paul II, who was pope between 1464 and 1471, did not issue a bull for the crusades. He was too busy fighting internal issues.

69 The Turks did indeed engage in a war with the Venetians from 1463 to 1479 and another one between 1499 and 1503. See Caroline Finkel, *Osman's Dream: The History of the Ottoman Empire* (London: Hachette UK, 2007).

70 The *Formula*, the *Regimini Militantis Ecclesiae* and the *Exposcit Debitum* mention this. Essentially the Reformation changed the battlefield, so to speak. The 'heretics' and the 'schismatics' are Martin Luther and his fellow Reformers and their followers.

71 Robert Bellarmine, *On the Church Militant*, trans. Ryan Grant (Post Falls, ID: Mediatrix Press, 2016).

72 See Thompson, *The Footprints of the Jesuits*.

73 O'Malley, *The First Jesuits*, p. 67.

74 This vow does not mean that the Society was poor. On the contrary, the Society has always been well resourced, with much money coming from donors from Europe and beyond.

75 McCabe, *A Candid History of the Jesuits*, p. 197.

76 McCabe, *A Candid History of the Jesuits*, pp. 334–63.

6

Mission and Colonialism in the Nineteenth and Twentieth Centuries

... in the nineteenth century, Europeans explored and subjugated Africa, they completed the conquest of India and Ceylon, they blasted open the doors of China and threatened to partition the empire among themselves, they induced the Japanese to admit their merchants, diplomats, and missionaries, they made themselves masters of the islands of the Pacific and in Australia New Zealand built new nations of European stock, they further developed Siberia, and they completed their occupation of the Americas. By A.D. 1914, all the land surface of the world was politically subject to the European peoples except a few spots in Africa, some of the Asiatic states, Japan, a little corner of South-eastern Europe, and the jungles of the some of the largest islands of the Pacific. Even the lands which had not submitted politically had been touched by the commerce of Europeans and most of them had been modified by European culture.[1]

I started this book in Chapter 1 talking about Magomero, the UMCA mission station that became the Livingstones' colonial farm. It is, of course, a story of my village. I know that some of my ancestors worked on Bruce Estates. Many in the surrounding area have stories about their parents' and grandparents' work at the estates. All the stories are generally negative. They tell of the brutality that shaped their existence close to a colonial farm that was owned by the most powerful colonial landowners in the country. Although Bruce was not involved in the government, he had the colonial office's special attention. After the death of William Livingstone in 1915, the British government in Malawi took special care of Bruce. His status as the grandson of one of Britain's most popular missionaries made him untouchable. Indeed, in its reaction to the Chilembwe Uprising in 1915, the British government sought to make a statement. The leaders, many of whom, like Chilembwe, were Christians, were summarily killed to show all locals the fate that awaited anyone who dared raise a finger against the British government. They sought to instil fear among all they had colonized, not only in Malawi but also throughout their colonies in Africa and beyond.

The Magomero story was multiplied thousands of times across Africa and the other colonies overseas. All colonial powers did something similar. The Germans had killed off thousands of people in Namibia – something of genocidal proportions.[2] There was an ongoing genocide in the Congo.[3] The French were even more ruthless in their pacification of the colonies (and, indeed, their economic colonization of their former colonies continues well into the twenty-first century).[4] The British government's colonial policies would lead to the starvation of millions in India in the 1940s.[5] Soon after this, in the 1950s, the British established concentration camps in Kenya to stop the Mau Mau revolt.[6] All these countries were part of European Christendom – they were Christians, and these atrocities are a part of the story of the spread of Christianity. Colonial theology has confined these atrocities to the past, buried them in inaccessible historical archives and convinced us that we are wrong to think that mission and colonialism were closely interconnected.

Magomero was in so many ways a very good demonstration of the template that had shaped a great deal of the colonized peoples' perception of mission. In Africa colonial violence was especially brutal because, as I have argued in Chapter 1, Africans were at the bottom of the social hierarchy. The inhumane brutality of plantation slavery was imported back to Africa from the Americas and the West Indies. The science of breaking the colonized and keeping them in oppression had been perfected in Latin America in the centuries following the 1400s and in India since the 1700s. It was, in the nineteenth and twentieth centuries, unleashed on to the African continent. Knowingly or unknowingly, many missionaries participated in imperial mission. Like the enslavers in North America who used the Slave Bible to teach the people they enslaved to be subservient and to work hard for them, colonizers in Africa used those parts of the Bible that could justify white supremacy. Until today, in the twenty-first century, more than 50 years after gaining political independence, the doctrine of the Curse of Ham continues to play a large role in shaping some Africans' Christian identity.[7] I have heard some people around Magomero say, 'As black people, we are cursed to serve white people and there is nothing we can do about it.' The doctrine of white supremacy was well executed in many parts of Africa and the Bible was the most effective tool for this. Mzee Jomo Kenyatta did not exclude the colonialists when he said, 'When the missionaries came to Africa, they had the Bible and we had the land. They said, "Let us pray." We closed our eyes. When we said Amen and opened our eyes, we had the Bible and they had the land.'[8]

Mission in the heyday of colonialism

Stephen Neill begins his chapter entitled 'The Heyday of Colonialism' in the book *A History of Christian Missions* with a list of many influential figures of the nineteenth century, and for each of them Neill places an emphasis on their age with reference to the all-important year of 1858.[9] In August 1858 the British Empire established the Raj in India, making it its first official colony. India would remain a British colony until 1947. In the course of the century, Britain would acquire many other colonies around the world. Colonialism extended the British Empire so much that at one time it had a credible quarter of the world's population under its government.[10] It has been said that at the peak of its power, because of its span across the globe, the sun was always up on at least one of its numerous territories. At the height of British colonial rule the Queen of England had more Muslim subjects than any Muslim ruler.[11]

The advent of colonialism would for ever change the relationship between the missionaries and the locals. Neill says that the great expansion of Christianity coincided in time with the worldwide expansion of Europe; that the colonizing powers were Christian powers; that a whole variety of compromising relationships existed between governments and missionaries; and that in the main, Christianity was carried forward on the wave of Western prestige and power.[12] Whatever their theological views it was virtually impossible for the missionaries to avoid promoting European values and influence, whether actively or passively.

Other Western historians, such as Arthur Schlesinger Jr[13] and William Hutchinson,[14] have identified missionaries and their ideas as agents of cultural imperialism. Hutchinson says that missions provided the 'moral equivalent for imperialism'.[15] Schlesinger observes that imperialism in missionary work encouraged some missionaries to embody Conrad's brutal statement from *Heart of Darkness*, 'Exterminate all the brutes!' and then quickly adds Winwood Reade's, 'Leave the native nothing of the African except his skin.'[16] Dana Robert adds, 'Missionary goals of religious conversion and social change, when functioning in a colonialist context, became a prime means of social control by expansionist powers over their non-Western victims.'[17] Hilary Carey observes that missionaries continued to be defined as agents for the colonization of the mind, who institutionalized Western hegemony through their control of missions, schools, Bible translation and publishing houses.[18] However, in spite of all this suspicion, the seeds of the faith were planted and they would blossom worldwide, especially after the process of political decolonization. The preaching of God's word itself, even in the context of colonialism, would end up having some probably unintended positive consequences for the spread of Christianity. The global events taking place in the 50 years between 1914 and 1964 would have massive unforeseeable effects on missions worldwide.

The problems start at the beginning

I have argued earlier that the problem of colonialism in our missiology goes back many centuries. If we are to pinpoint where it started we could say it was with Pope Nicholas V and his bull *Dum Diversas*, because I am convinced that Ignatius and the Jesuits were just following the trend set forth in the bulls of the fifteenth century. However, we could also go as far back as the fourth century when Christianity was legalized in the Roman Empire. It was this *imperialization* of the Christian faith which followed the Edict of Milan that changed the ways Christians (and their sense of mission) related to the world. This connection between mission and colonialism becomes clearly visible during the era of the British Raj in India (beginning in 1858) and that of European colonialism in Africa (beginning in the 1880s). It is generally well accepted that the missionaries and colonial agents worked hand in hand in sub-Saharan Africa. However, it has also become quite evident that while the missionaries started the work of evangelizing Africa during the colonial era, the conversion of Africans to Christianity has really happened after the collapse of European colonization of Africa. Thus, I often wonder about the effect of European colonialism on their mission in Africa. If colonialism had not happened, how would the continent respond to the missionaries? If European colonialism in Africa had not come to an end, what would become of African Christianity in the twenty-first century?

Unfortunately for us, Western mission in the nineteenth and twentieth centuries was shaped by so many unchristian motives that its very theological basis is questionable. Essentially, it was a continuation of the Crusades, just done differently. Otherwise how could they justify the need to evangelize and colonize a people at the same time? A century earlier we could ask how they justified evangelizing Africans while keeping them enslaved, or how they erected a chapel above a slave dungeon at the Cape Coast Castle in Ghana. A theology that struggled to critique this unholy union between mission and the European destruction of humankind – for example, Africans, Native Americans, Indians – ought not to be trusted in the twenty-first century. This is the same theology that claims military power is a God-ordained tool for compelling the world to embrace Christianity, framing violence and conquest as acceptable means of advancing the gospel even when this contradicts Jesus' message. It is as bankrupt today as it was 200 years ago.

Unfortunately again, a great deal of our understanding of mission today is still shaped by nineteenth-century talk. Mission is still about civilizing and Christianizing the heathens – and many of us still believe that the heathens are somewhere in the world, but not in Western Europe, North America, Australia and New Zealand. We believe this despite the many reports that suggest that Europe and some parts of the West are mission fields, currently in desperate need of evangelism. Many Christians in the world still believe that only certain people can be missionaries, and those people are generally white Westerners. I have heard African Christians wonder if a black person can actually be a missionary. Everything else is never in question. They know that Africans can be pastors, evangelists and even apostles. However, it seems hard to imagine an African doing the work of a missionary in their part of the world. To some extent this is because they associate the missionary with white skin, Western origin and high status in their community – and these cannot be rightly attributed to a black African.

I have also on quite a few occasions been informed that many European Christians still cannot fathom an African being a missionary – let alone serving as a missionary in Europe. These Europeans have two hurdles to negotiate. The first is that they do not believe that Europe is a mission field. To them, mission work has to be done elsewhere. The fact that Europe is indeed a post-Christian and largely secularized continent is still a far-fetched idea to them. Then, even if Europe is indeed a mission field, they believe that God will not send Africans as missionaries for, of course, mission is still a white person's mandate.

Most European Christians will need a paradigm shift to begin to understand that to invite a person to Christianity is also to invite them to engage in God's mission, regardless of their race or geographical location. And with this invitation comes the requirement that they will serve in mission wherever God wants them, be it in their own community or in a country halfway around the world. This means that many of my European friends need to understand that God can use people of other races for mission, and can send missionaries to Europe from other parts of the world just as God sent missionaries from Europe. I know that for Europeans it is a bit easier to understand if the missionaries working among them are fellow white men and women from the United States or Canada. For various reasons they find it difficult to receive when God sends them some non-white missionaries. This is more so if the missionary has come from Africa because very many of Europe's colonial racist attitudes about Africa and Africans still persist today. To many Europeans, Africa (as a continent) and Africans (as a people) are still at the bottom of the social hierarchy and thus have nothing of import to say. If they are Christians, their Christianity is half-baked and the gospel they preach is suspicious.

Mission and migration: a European story

William Carey was born in Northamptonshire in 1861 to an Anglican family of weavers. As a young man he joined the Dissenters. He became a shoemaker and while working as a cobbler he taught himself Hebrew, Greek and several other languages.[19] In addition he spent a great deal of his time collecting whatever data he could find that helped him understand the world better, especially its religious landscape. In 1792 he published an essay entitled *An Enquiry into the Obligations of Christians to Use Means for the Conversion of the Heathens*.[20] He had been informed by the travel journals of Captain James Cook (1728–79), a British explorer, cartographer and naval officer who made three voyages between 1768 and 1779 across the Pacific Ocean to Australia and New Zealand. He was also informed by the work of the Moravian missionaries who had been sent around the world from Bavaria.

Once he asked the leaders of the Northampton Baptist Association to consider 'whether the command given to the apostles to teach all nations was not binding on all succeeding ministers to the end of the world, seeing that the accompanying promise was of equal extent'. A sharp rebuke followed: 'Young man, sit down ... When God pleases to convert the heathen, He will do it without consulting you or me. Besides, there must first be another Pentecostal gift of tongues!'[21] Despite this, Carey and his like-minded friends founded the Baptist Missionary Society (BMS) in 1792. He became its first missionary and spent the rest of his life in India. In the wake of his essay and departure from the UK, many other new agencies emerged: the London Missionary Society (1795), the Church Missionary Society (1799) and the Netherlands Missionary Society (1797). His impact was immediate: within ten years of the formation of the BMS there were more than a dozen mission societies formed on both sides of the Atlantic. His ideas were so influential that many call him the 'father of modern Protestant missions'. Several Protestant missions and mission societies had been founded long before his work was published, but it was Carey's thinking on the Great Commission, made concrete by his visionary work, that launched what eventually became today's missionary societies and agencies. His lasting influence is still seen today – the Baptist Mission Society is still in operation. Other mission agencies that came into existence soon after the BMS are also very active today. Both the London Missionary Society (LMS) and the Church Missionary

Society (CMS) are still engaged in world mission today, with sister CMSs in Ireland, Africa, Asia and Australia. The LMS went into a partnership with the Commonwealth Missionary Society (established in 1836 as the Colonial Missionary Society) to become the Congregational Council for World Mission in 1966, and evolved to become the Council for World Mission in 1977.

Carey's essay touched a people who were ready to move. It does not appear to me that he was intentionally trying to spark some form of migration trend, neither was he aware of a wave of migration happening. It was sheer happenstance that he wrote right at the end of the eighteenth century when, in just a few decades, hundreds of thousands of Europeans would be migrating to the Americas, Africa, Asia, Australia and New Zealand. Only a small number of them would be missionaries. The rest of them would be what we would consider today as economic migrants going for gold in South Africa, land in Montana, diamonds in Zimbabwe and various other things. Mission agencies helped but in the end it was just European Christians migrating for whatever reasons that expanded the Christian faith worldwide. In the case of Zimbabwe it is helpful to remember that at some point in the twentieth century, 6,000 British farmers owned the fertile 60 per cent of Zimbabwe's land.[22]

Consequently we can safely say that the spread of Christianity that occurred during the nineteenth century is different from that of the first century. The Galileans did not form a mission agency. There is no such thing as the Capernaum City Mission, neither is there such a thing as the Nazareth Mission Society in the Bible. They spread for economic reasons across the empire and beyond. William Carey's mission strategy of sending missionaries made sense in a world where Europeans were migrating to other parts of the world. Nineteenth-century mission history underscores the connection between migration and mission. The great missionary endeavours of the nineteenth century took place in the context of the great migration of Europeans to all parts of the world. It is impossible to overlook the great era of Christian missions that occurred as people of European origin extended their political and economic control until it encompassed 84 per cent of the land surface of the globe.[23]

The scattering of European peoples to all the corners of the world for the purposes of trade, civilization and to take care of the imperial interests of the West provided a backdrop for the missionary activities of the nineteenth century. Indeed, as Edmund Dunn put it, 'The missionary surge took place during an era when Europe was the faith and the faith was Europe.'[24]

Andrew Walls is rather kind in his assessment: 'The missionary movement from the West was a semi-detached part of the European migration – semi-detached because its essential motor derived not from the economic, political, and strategic interests that produced the migration, but from the nature of the Christian message.'[25] However, in the eyes of most of the colonized, the missionaries made way for the colonizers. Many people in Africa, Asia and Latin America believe that the Christian message was used to pave the way for the colonizer and reduce resistance from the indigenous people. For example, Mongo Beti says the missionaries were sent before the colonial agents to make way for colonization in Cameroon.[26] The semi-detachment that Walls is talking about brings into question the whole structure of 'commerce, civilization and Christianity', which provided the moral justification for colonization. Even then colonization really took shape when both the great migration and the missionary movement were at their peak.

When Kenneth Latourette explored the 'Great Century of Mission of 1815–1914', he outlined 13 'sets of factors' that in his opinion characterize the spread of Christianity that occurred then.[27] In a nutshell, they have to do with development in the fields of science and knowledge, the industrial revolution, the improvement in transport systems and the consequent expansion of the Western empires worldwide. Central to these sets of factors are scientific discoveries and industrialization. These two factors together precipitated permanent changes in the social interactions of the world population. As industrial towns began to emerge and the need for raw materials and markets became more evident in the West, Europe had to explore further than its limited geographical space. The great European migration followed.

Mungo Park's publication, *Travels in the Interior Districts of Africa* (1799), alerted Europeans to the vast continent of Africa with a great deal of resources that might as well be a vast mission field waiting to be harvested. It thus brought to the attention of Europe the many opportunities that lay on the other side of the seas. Just like William Carey, who was informed by the travel journals of James Cook, the later works of missionary explorers like David Livingstone and Ludwig Krapf (a German missionary who worked for the British Church Missionary Society in Kenya) further attracted more explorers and missionaries from Europe. The invention of the steamboat meant that the rivers of Africa, which had previously been impassable, became exciting routes for exploration inland, raising awareness of the many civilizations, lakes and mountains beneath the coastal regions that were already known to Europeans.

Knowledge about the economic potential of trading with the rest of the world, coupled with the hardening economic circumstances in Europe, famine and commercialization of agriculture, among many factors, led to the massive European emigration of the nineteenth century.[28] Essentially, the need to leave an overcrowded Europe (which was not really overpopulated at all) and the promise of a better life overseas trading in precious minerals or with access to fertile farmlands (in the Americas, Africa, Australia and New Zealand) made emigration from Europe rather attractive. The extent of the emigration was such that Dudley Baines says that while only 4 per cent of ethnic Europeans were living outside Europe and Siberia around 1800, the number shot up to 21 per cent by the First World War.[29] In the second half of the nineteenth century alone, one in five Europeans left Europe to settle down elsewhere. Baines suggests that up to 60 million emigrated in the period between 1815 and 1930.[30] In fact it is likely that an even larger number than this migrated from Europe. Baines is largely working with data from the Americas and Australia. He makes very little mention of migration to the non-Western world in his book, even though it is known that a great number of these European immigrants settled in the colonies of the European powers in Africa and the Middle East.

This great migration brought to a climax the migration of Europeans out of Europe that had already been in progress for three centuries. It had started with the discovery of the Americas and went on until the mid-twentieth century, when it slowed down dramatically and the reversal started. The missionary aspect of this migration was immense. By the time it came to an end, Western Christianity had been exported to the rest of the world. In the belief of the day, Christianity was the only way to true civilization – it had to be part of the colonial civilizing mission process. Andrew Walls further observes that the great European migration produced great effects on religion, creating Hinduism in India as the entity we know today, setting afoot a Buddhist renaissance in Sri Lanka, facilitating a rapid spread and intensification of Islam and establishing Christianity as a world religion.[31] Indeed, by the time this great European migration came to an end in the middle of the twentieth century, it had 'made the modern world as we know it, establishing a world political and economic order and a new cultural entity called the West'.[32]

Since 1950 the Majority World has arisen and, with it, the reversal of the old migration pattern. Millions of people from Latin America, Africa and Asia began to migrate to the West, and this may continue for decades to come. However, it is important to note that this migration too has missionary impulses. In this age of migration, where world travel is easier than ever before and cheap instantaneous communication shapes the shrinking global village, even those religions that were historically limited to narrow geographical territories are being practised in countries very distant in space and culture from their original heartlands. Islam, Hinduism and Buddhism, among many other non-Western religions, are flourishing in New York, Atlanta, Minneapolis, London, Munich, Zurich and many other Western cities. Today it is possible to find massive gurdwaras, mosques, temples and synagogues in almost all major cities in the West. Migration clearly plays a very significant role in the spread of religions. Historically, migrations spread and preserve religions. For instance, in the case of Africa, Jehu Hanciles suggests a possibility that the phenomenal growth of Christianity has been impacted by such tremendous transfers of human populations.[33] Indeed, Africa has had the greatest number of migrants and displaced peoples in the world in the past century; however, at the same time it has also seen the greatest growth in Christianity and Islam.

Is mission after colonialism possible?

The sharing of the good news of Jesus does not require imperial powers to make it impactful. The first Galileans sent to make disciples of all nations were not backed up by any power. As Galileans, citizens of a colonized country, they had no power to colonize anybody. They could only share the news about the Messiah without bringing their own cultural baggage with it. This is what Jesus started – a movement of the colonized to change the world. The imperial structures came centuries later and, unfortunately, they have stayed until today. However, in a nutshell, it is possible to imagine mission without conquest; indeed, mission without domination is possible. To get there we must accept that mission, as it is today, stands too closely connected to the spread of Western civilization with its empires. Perhaps Ludwig Rütti was right when he wrote that the entire modern missionary enterprise is so polluted by its origin and close association with Western colonialism that it is irredeemable; we have to find an entirely new image today.[34]

Essentially, we need to rethink mission for a world in which the images of a blue-eyed blond-haired Jesus are not only questionable but rejected. It is not being 'politically correct' or 'woke' to say Jesus was not a white man; it is not a narrow 'Black Lives Matter' stance to imagine a Jesus who is 'God With Us' for all humanity. The challenge we face is to reimagine mission in a world where the missionary movement of the Western civilization has reached its limits. We need to learn to engage in mission when all that the missionary brings is the liberating gospel of Jesus Christ, without a superior culture that seeks to civilize in the name of empire. Of course, empires must colonize others in order to be. Colonization is empire doing empire things. Religious empires use religion to colonize. Effective colonization of a people must involve changing the people's life philosophy, self-identification and culture.

Christianity has been synonymous with Europe for centuries. It was part of the Roman Empire, became part of the Byzantine and, since the 1400s, has been an integral part of the expansion of European empires. The world Christianity that we celebrate today has emerged because of the past 600 years of Western domination of other parts of the world: the Spanish/Iberian Empire that colonized Latin America; the Portuguese Empire that colonized Brazil and parts of Africa and India; at its peak the British empire stretched across all time zones. The era of European political colonization of Africa was short, largely running from the 1880s to the 1960s, but it has had drastic effects of the continent, many of which are yet to be resolved. Of course, economic and ideological colonization continue until today.

We are now living through the age of the American empire, but the tides are changing. The era of the American empire is being challenged from within and without. From within it, its democratic foundations are being tested by the polarization of its people. From outside, the rise of BRICS (an economic block that was started by Brazil, Russia, India, China and South Africa) poses a challenge. Samuel Huntington suggested in his 1996 book, *The Clash of Civilizations*, that the Western civilization now faces competition from other civilizations.[35] This is more evident today than it probably was when Huntington wrote *The Clash*. Both Russia and China have become even more influential players on the global political scene. As I write this, there is a conversation about BRICS seeking to establish their own currency and de-dollarize their economies, a move that some in the West consider economic aggression.

The greatest challenge those of us thinking about mission in the new religious and geopolitical landscape of the world need to negotiate is that it has historically (at least in the past 200 years) been too closely attached to Western expansionism. Originally started by Westerners as a way to study mission around the world, the discipline of missiology continues to be a white-dominated subject even though white Christians form less than a third of world Christians. It is again for this reason that our very definitions in missiology, for instance, that of a missionary, are still shaped by Eurocentric ideas – British Christian teachers teaching English in Uganda are missionaries while Ugandan Christian nurses working in Britain are migrants. The thousands of Nigerian pastors leading churches in the UK will never be recognized as serving in mission while a UK gap-year student working at an orphanage in Nigeria is a missionary. It is also for this reason that when we talk about mission, we always generally speak in terms of sending European missionaries to other parts of the world like Africa, even though the heathen – to use the European language of the last century – is now also in Europe. European mission organizations are still focused on converting Africans, Asians and Latin Americans.

There will most definitely be an eclipsing of Western missionary work in the world. This is already apparent in many European countries. Many European mission agencies find it difficult to recruit new missionaries – their catchment area has shrunk quite significantly. If they find new missionaries, they often struggle to sustain the lists of their donors. Again, their donor bases are shrinking – many of them are ageing – as younger Europeans are not as interested in giving money to missions. If, in the end, mission will be open to non-Western Christians – Brazil and South Korea are among the top three mission-sending countries, the other one being the United States – it must be doable by people who are not white, not rich and definitely not in the West, like the old Galileans. Today – non-Western Christianity (which forms almost 70 per cent of world Christianity – is a religion with little to no imperial powers. Of course, it helps to remember that Jesus Christ was executed in his home country by a colonial power. He started the movement that became Christianity among people who will easily identify with the rest of the world today.

Notes

1 Kenneth Scott Latourette, *A History of the Expansion of Christianity*, vol. 4, *The Great Century: Europe and the United States* (Grand Rapids, MI: Zondervan, 1970), p. 13.

2 Casper Erichsen and David Olusoga, *The Kaiser's Holocaust: Germany's Forgotten Genocide and the Colonial Roots of Nazism* (London: Faber & Faber, 2010).

3 Adam Hochschild, *King Leopold's Ghost: A Story of Greed, Terror, and Heroism in Colonial Africa*, 1st Mariner Books edn (Boston, MA: Houghton Mifflin, 1999).

4 See Herbert Ingram Priestley, *France Overseas: A Study of Modern Imperialism* (London: Routledge, 2018).

5 Janam Mukherjee, *Hungry Bengal: War, Famine and the End of Empire* (Oxford: Oxford University Press, 2015). Also see Aziz Rahman, Mohsin Ali and Saad Kahn, 'The British Art of Colonialism in India: Subjugation and Division', *Peace and Conflict Studies* 25, no. 1 (2018).

6 Aoife Duffy, 'Legacies of British Colonial Violence: Viewing Kenyan Detention Camps through the Hanslope Disclosure', *Law and History Review* 33, no. 3 (2015). See also Peter Karari, 'Modus Operandi of Oppressing the "Savages": The Kenyan British Colonial Experience', *Peace and Conflict Studies* 25, no. 1 (2018).

7 The Curse of Ham doctrine teaches that dark-skinned people (taken to be black Africans) were cursed to serve white people all their lives. It was used to justify both slavery and colonialism. Garrett Kell observes that the Baptist pastor and Southern Seminary trustee Iveson L. Brookes (1785–1868) taught that 'Negro Slavery is an institution of heaven and intended for the mutual benefit of master and slave, as proved by the Bible … God himself … authorized Noah to doom the posterity of Ham.' He adds that Patrick Mell (1814–88), the fourth president of the Southern Baptist Convention, proposed: 'From Ham were descended the nations that occupied the land of Canaan and those that now constitute the African or Negro race. Their inheritance, according to prophecy, has been and will continue to be slavery … [and] so long as we have the Bible … we expect to maintain it.' Garrett Kell, 'Damn the Curse of Ham: How Genesis 9 Got Twisted into Racist Propaganda', *The Gospel Coalition*, 9 January 2021, https://www.thegospelcoalition.org/article/damn-curse-ham/, accessed 25.03.2025.

8 This citation is often attributed to several African leaders like Desmond Tutu and Jomo Kenyatta. However, Nicholas Otieno suggests that it is the Mau Mau Fighters who made it popular in their anti-colonial struggles in Kenya. See Nicholas Otieno and Hugh McCullum, *Journey of Hope: Towards a New Ecumenical Africa* (Geneva: WCC Publications, 2005), p. 7. Tutu and other South African Black theologians have insisted that the task of Black Christians is to get back the land without losing the Bible.

9 Stephen Neill and Owen Chadwick, *A History of Christian Missions*, The Pelican History of the Church (New York: Penguin Books, 1986), p. 273.

10 See Kehinde Andrews, *The New Age of Empire: How Racism and Colonialism Still Rule the World* (London: Allen Lane Publishing, 2021).

11 Jehu J. Hanciles, *Beyond Christendom: Globalization, African Migration, and the Transformation of the West* (Maryknoll, NY: Orbis Books, 2008), p. 255.

12 Neill and Chadwick, *A History of Christian Missions*, p. 414.

13 See Arthur Schlesinger Jr, 'The Missionary Enterprise and Theories of Imperialism', in John King Fairbank (ed.), *The Missionary Enterprise in China and America*, Harvard Studies in American–East Asian Relations (Cambridge: Harvard University Press, 1974), pp. 336–73.

14 William R. Hutchison and Torben Christensen, *Missionary Ideologies in the Imperialist Era, 1880–1920* (Aarhus, Denmark: Aros, 1982). Also see William R. Hutchison, *Errand to the World: American Protestant Thought and Foreign Missions* (Chicago, IL: University of Chicago Press, 1987), ch. 4.

15 Hutchison and Christensen, *Missionary Ideologies in the Imperialist Era, 1880–1920*.

16 Fairbank, *The Missionary Enterprise in China and America*, p. 362. Winwood Reade, *The Martyrdom of Man* (New York: E. P. Dutton & Co., 1926), p. 330. William Reade (1838–75) deserves his own mention. He ranks high among the key thinkers of Victorian Britain. While he was an explorer in Africa he wrote *Savage Africa* (London: Smith, Elder & Co., 1864) and *The African Sketch-Book* (London: Smith, Elder & Co., 1873). As the titles indicate, he is known for his racist ideologies that sought to justify slavery and colonialism.

17 Dana Lee Robert, *Converting Colonialism: Visions and Realities in Mission History, 1706–1914*, Studies in the History of Christian Missions (Grand Rapids, MI: Eerdmans, 2008), p. 2.

18 Hilary M. Carey, *God's Empire: Religion and Colonialism in the British World, c.1801–1908* (New York: Cambridge University Press, 2011), p. 23.

19 See Thomas Schirrmacher, *William Carey: Theologian, Linguist, Social Reformer* (Eugene, OR: Wipf & Stock Publishers, 2018). There are also numerous biographies of William Carey; for example, Timothy George, *Faithful Witness: The Life and Mission of William Carey* (Birmingham, AL: New Hope, 1991).

20 William Carey, *An Enquiry into the Obligations of Christians to Use Means for the Conversion of the Heathens in which the Religious State of the Different Nations of the World, the Success of Former Undertakings, and the Practicability of Further Undertakings are Considered* (London: Carey Kingsgate, 1961).

21 A. Christopher Smith, 'Carey, William', in Gerald H. Anderson (ed.), *Biographical Dictionary of Christian Missions* (New York: Macmillan Reference, 1998), p. 115.

22 Simbarashe Moyo, 'A Failed Land Reform Strategy in Zimbabwe. The Willing Buyer Willing Seller', *Public Policy and Administration Review* 2, no. 1 (2014), p. 71.

23 David Smith, *Mission After Christendom* (London: Darton, Longman & Todd, 2003), p. 90.

24 Edmond J. Dunn, *Missionary Theology: Foundations in Development* (Washington DC: University Press of America, 1980), p. 151.

25 Frieder Ludwig and J. Kwabena Asamoah-Gyadu (eds), *African Christian Presence in the West: New Immigrant Congregations and Transnational Networks in North America and Europe* (Trenton, NJ: Africa World Press, 2011), p. 409.

26 See Mongo Beti, *The Poor Christ of Bomba* (Long Grove, IL: Waveland, 1971).

27 Avoiding the male-dominated language of his day, here is Latourette's list in a gender-sensitive language: (1) humankind's knowledge of the universe, (2) people's mastery of their physical environment, (3) the development of scientific methods, (4) alteration in the structure of human life, (5) attempts to reorganize society based on ideologies, (6) intellectual currents, (7) nationalism, (8) peace, (9) optimism, (10) the expansion of the Northern and Western European people, (11) the disintegration of non-European cultures under the culture of the Occident, (12) the beginning of a world culture, and (13) the 'outstanding-ness' of the English-speaking peoples. See Kenneth Scott Latourette, *A History of Expansion of Christianity, Volume 4: The Great Century, A.D. 1800–A.D. 1914, Europe and the United States of America* (London: Harper & Brothers, 1941), pp. 9–15.

28 Dudley Baines, *Emigration from Europe, 1815–1930*, New Studies in Economic and Social History (New York: Cambridge University Press, 1995), pp. 21–30.

29 For a more detailed discussion of how ideas of Western superiority played a role in the self-understanding of missionaries in colonial Africa, see Andrew N. Porter, *The Imperial Horizons of British Protestant Missions, 1880–1914*, Studies in the History of Christian Missions (Grand Rapids, MI: Eerdmans, 2003).

30 Baines, *Emigration from Europe*, p. 7. But he worked only with data from the Americas. The numbers would increase significantly if his data included Africa and Asia.

31 Andrew F. Walls, 'Towards a Theology of Mission', in Frieder Ludwig and J. Kwabena Asamoah-Gyadu (eds), *African Christian Presence in the West: New Immigrant Congregations and Transnational Networks in North America and Europe* (Trenton, NJ: Africa World Press, 2011).

32 Ludwig and Asamoah-Gyadu, *African Christian Presence*, pp. 407–8.

33 Hanciles, *Beyond Christendom*, p. 5.
34 Cited in David Jacobus Bosch, *Transforming Mission: Paradigm Shifts in Theology of Mission*, American Society of Missiology Series (Maryknoll, NY: Orbis Books, 1991), p. 518.
35 Samuel P. Huntington, *The Clash of Civilizations and the Remaking of World Order* (New York: Touchstone, 1997).

7

Decolonizing Mission Language

Missiological discourse in the West has for a long time been shaped by a focus on two critical issues. First, much energy and ink have been poured into discussing the history of missions. While this is a long history that goes back 2,000 years, when limited to the centuries following the fall of Constantinople it has really been about the works that Western missionaries have done in other parts of the world. Mission historians such as Kenneth Latourette, Dale T. Irvin, Scott Sunquist, Brian Stanley, Jehu Hanciles and numerous missionary biographers have written quite extensive records of how Christianity has spread around the world. Of course, this function of missiology is not complete. It will continue to include the stories of what Western missionaries are currently doing and what they will do in the future. If it is faithful to its task, the telling of the story of the expansion of Christianity must always include names and voices of numerous non-Western followers of Christ who have, over the centuries, preached the gospel in new contexts. Many of them will agree that the work of evangelization has been most effective when it is carried out by local Christians. As such the emergence of world Christianity is a testament to the missionary work of millions upon millions of African, Asian and Latin American evangelists.

The second key theme in missiology is the study of other peoples around the world, their cultures, languages and religious systems. This aspect of missiology has intended to inform and equip Westerners for cross-cultural mission so that they have some understanding of the peoples they work with. It is in this regard that missiology is understood to be the mother of such disciplines as anthropology and sociology of religion. It is out of these efforts that disciplines such as cultural anthropology – the study of humanity, human cultures, societies and linguistics – emerge.[1] Often the cultures of people groups around the world are dissected and put under a microscope (like a virus in the laboratory), with their languages and religious systems scrutinized and their very personhood and sense of humanity put on the scales. All this happens in the context of a theological discourse that is almost entirely informed by Western thought. As a result, for most of the past decades (and centuries), the study of mission has been almost entirely geared towards helping Western missionaries to be effective in their work of converting non-Westerners and making them disciples of Christ in the unevangelized parts of the world. Most students of mission have spent their time seeking to understand the cultures of other peoples around the world to discern how best to relevantly communicate the gospel to them.

Andrew Walls and the rule of palefaces in missiology

The discipline of mission studies today, generally speaking, continues to place a great emphasis on what is currently known as *cross-cultural* mission (which basically means mission that happens overseas, in foreign countries and cultures). More often than not, when Westerners talk about cross-cultural mission they mean the work of Westerners in other parts of the world. To a Western mind this is a normative way of describing mission because in most of our language, and indeed our understanding of what it is that we do, cross-cultural mission is the work of white people, often among black and brown peoples of the world – even though there are today numerous non-Westerners sharing the good news of Christ among the nations of the world. Most of our mission language is still shaped not only by Western thinking but also whiteness. This is a result of the historical fact that, as we have seen above, the concept of mission emerged in Europe in the context of great military tensions. The world of mission today is still dominated by Westerners. Their language has been exported to all parts of the world.

Andrew Walls once spoke about what he called 'the untroubled rule of palefaces over the academic world'.[2] He was speaking of the academic world of theology, missiology and world Christianity. The point he sought to make was that in a world where there are more black and brown Christians, the fields of theology, missiology and world Christianity must include the voices of more than just white scholars. He was right. However, there are too many barriers for scholars in the Global South to participate effectively. It is not just the numbers. Many Westerners have been involved in the study of missions but there have emerged some eloquent scholars in Africa, Asia and Latin America who can contribute. Of great concern, at least to me, are the gatekeepers who have vested interests in keeping the field white and Western either because they do not want to be challenged by what they consider inferior, non-Western knowledge or are fearful of losing their relevance and influence.

In a later article, Andrew Walls continued: 'Western theological leadership of a predominantly non-Western church is an incongruity.'[3]

Writing this paragraph today, these words by Walls seem even more relevant to us. In their 2006 book *Globalizing Theology: Belief and Practice in an Era of World Christianity*, Craig Ott and Harold Netland identified this problem of Western domination of the theological disciplines as located in four areas: (1) the West's 'hegemony postulate'; (2) the West's self-perception that it is 'the centre'; (3) the perception of Third World scholars as 'purveyors of exotic, raw intellectual material to people in the North'; and (4) the 'dialogue of the deaf' between the West and the rest of the world.[4] Each of these four areas is critical and all shape the theological dialogue between the West and the rest of the world. Of immediate interest to me in missiology is the fourth area. How can we remove the communication barriers between the West and the rest in missiology? On the one hand, how can we convince our Western colleagues to listen and engage non-Western missiological contributions with the respect and seriousness they deserve? On the other, how shall we convince non-Western scholars to bring their authentic missiology to the discourse and avoid sharing only those resources that they believe their Western counterparts want to hear (or to fund)? The greatest challenge in this work will be to get Western scholars to realize that there is some good missiology out there that can enhance their own understanding of what God is doing in the world *if only* they can hear it.

Bursting the bubble of Western missiological discourse

Western missiological scholarship, in this twenty-first-century context of world Christianity, generally speaking fails to sufficiently engage voices outside its own white and Western echo chambers. This becomes evident when we take a serious look at the key voices shaping missiological discourse in the world today. Annual compilations of key textbooks in missions and missiology published in the past 20 years reveal a list dominated by Western scholars with only a handful of non-Westerners, many of whom focus on issues that are of marginal interest to Westerners. In addition the lists of scholars contributing to five key journals in mission and missiology: *Missiology*; *International Missions Board Review*; *Mission Studies*; *Evangelical Mission Quarterly*; *Practical Theology* (this is a British journal that publishes articles from the British and Irish Association of Mission Studies).

Apart from very few non-Westerners who have managed to break the ceiling into Western missiological conversations, the key voices in mission are almost always European and North American, accompanied by a few Australians and New Zealanders. In most cases these thought leaders in mission and missiology are white and, naturally, they write from a white and Western perspective. If there are any non-Western scholars involved they will most likely be located in the study of world Christianity (and not mission or missiology). As a result our missiological discourse remains deprived of the rich missiological resources that God has given to the worldwide body of followers of Christ. Missiology is, to a great extent, a closed Western conversation.[5]

This closed nature of Western missiological dialogue has two further implications for us. First, most of the people involved in it have strong interests in the work of mission. They are missionaries at heart. Many of them are returned missionaries. As such they believe they – and fellow Western Christians – have a justified calling to go to other parts of the world to evangelize the heathens. As the anthropologist Kenelm Burridge suggests, missionaries share in what he refers to as 'the metacultural mandate' to extend the love of God.[6] Many believe they have a divine mandate to evangelize others in the conviction that, outside of Christ, humanity is lost, and to build a global Christian community as a witness to Christ's work. This is still the case in the twenty-first century. They are more often than not *insiders* – with an unshakable confidence that it is their duty and right to save the nations. Many mission scholars have vested interests in promoting mission to their congregations, denominations and students. Essentially, they study and write their missiology to keep mission going – they want more people to sign up and go (to the uttermost parts of the earth). Writing with these commitments to mission, their missionary biographies often read like hagiography. Local agency is usually diminished and mistakes made on the mission field are generally swept under the carpet. When they critique mission it is usually in the hope that the enterprise will become more effective. They have to be selective lest they bring the enterprise into disrepute. When they and other missionaries are critiqued, they often become defensive of themselves, of the idea and enterprise of mission as a whole and indeed of *their* work in the mission field.

Second, because of the closed nature of the conversation, people writing on mission tend to ignore critical voices from other disciplines, even those that are friendly and complementary to missiology. For example, historians have pointed out for many decades the colonial connotations of mission – how the missionaries often made way for the colonial agents by pacifying the people with the gospel of a peaceful Christ before the violence of colonialism was unleashed upon them, how they tend to disrupt and destroy indigenous cultures and languages around the world, and how they lord over local communities and create an elite society that goes on to dominate and colonize its own communities once the missionaries have moved on.[7] In addition, many non-Westerners have for many decades raised concerns about the connection between mission and colonialism. Yet, of course, such critique is usually dismissed as incorrect or malicious by those who feel they have the need to defend the Western missionary enterprise. If the critique comes from a black or brown person the defence is often verbally violent. For example, when an Ethiopian woman, Mekdes Haddis, dared to critique the imperial power differentials that are characteristic of US missions around the world in her 2022 book *A Just Mission*,[8] several white Evangelical missiologists rose to defend their enterprise. One of them, a prominent US missiologist, Brad Vaughn (using an Asian pseudonym, Jackson Wu), responded with the ugliest meanness by publishing a scathing rebuttal of Haddis' book, calling it 'The most dangerous book in mission in a generation', accusing it of 'bringing socialist Black Lives Matter ideologies to mission'.[9] Unfortunately for Vaughn, his rude takedown of *A Just Mission* effectively made the book more popular. Nevertheless the public nature of his rebuttal was a clear warning to anyone who dares to critique Western mission, especially if it is a black woman making the critique; they must be prepared for violence. Only those who have positive things to say about Western mission will be tolerated.

What happens on the mission field stays on the mission field

The need to silence voices that disclose the shortcomings of Western missionary movements is driven by the desire to protect stories that Western Christians have told themselves of their missionary work in the world for centuries. Right from the start, from Pope Nicholas V's *Dum Diversas* in 1452, Europeans have constantly convinced themselves that the world is theirs to save – and that they alone can do the job. Indeed, many Westerners believe that black and brown people cannot be involved in mission in the world; that Westerners know best what the work of making disciples for Christ in the nations looks like. In the centuries following *Dum Diversas* they have perfected the art of saving souls. In some cases they have narrowed down the gospel to a number of spiritual laws that can, in a flash, convince people to give their lives to Jesus. They even have scales of how far from or near to 'receiving Christ as their personal Lord and Saviour' a potential convert is. For many centuries they have believed that *the end* of their work – the salvation of souls – justifies *the means*, which has often included violence against people and their cultures. They have told themselves that to be good Christians, wherever in the world, people must believe and behave like

Westerners; where they do not they must be forced to conform or else they are to be considered outsiders.

Unmasking white Evangelicalism's superiority complex

Holly Berkley Fletcher, an American historian who identifies herself as a third-culture kid as she grew up in Kenya where her parents served as missionaries, has written a book, *The Missionary Kids: Unmasking the Myths of White Evangelicalism* (forthcoming 2025). In it she discusses some aspects of what she saw among the many missionaries who worked in Kenya at the time she lived there.[10] She also collects a large amount of data from other US missionary kids from various countries in the world through interviews and several other means.[11] The book discusses the perspective of many 'missionary kids' – children of missionaries, not child missionaries – on their upbringing and how growing up on the mission field has impacted their lives. In gathering the missionary kids' narratives, Fletcher uncovers a phenomenon that has to a large extent remained hidden from public discourse for ages – a superiority complex and lack of accountability among missionaries, both on the mission field and at home.

On the surface she is concerned about the negative impact the missionary life has on children – the trauma of continual separations from friends and family, the grief coming out of all these separations that takes a long time to be processed and, of course, the abuse that some missionary kids experience at school or at the hands of 'uncles' and 'aunties' on the mission field. (She starts her book with a story about one charismatic missionary uncle who was a murderer and a hero.) Throughout her argument she is in agreement with many other US missionary kids who have shared their stories over the years, some of which can be seen on MK Safety Net website.[12] She is also in agreement with some returned missionaries who continue to raise concerns about what happened wherever they served.

Beneath the surface, though, Fletcher's book is an exposé of the colonial attitudes that shape much of the Western missionary movement. She allows readers to see the white saviourism as well as the superiority complex that characterizes most Western missionary life. In addition she begins to tear down the myriad lies required to sustain the great Western facade of successful missionary work in the world. She shows that while there exist many great missionaries who go overseas to evangelize, much of the Western missionary enterprise serves the needs of Western Christians: the need to tick the boxes that show they are engaged in mission; the need to feel as if they are doing something about the conditions of needy people on the other side of the world; or indeed the need to be needed. I have heard a European mission agency say, 'Someone needs help in Kenya. Only we can rescue that person. We are good people chosen for this work at this time. So let us pack our bags and go.'

Many engage in mission because *they* need something – an outlet of some kind, recognition, an opportunity to self-actualize in ways that would be difficult back home, or just an opportunity to see life on the other side of the planet. This does not mean all who engage in mission have some ulterior motives other than evangelizing others. There are also many people who might lay down their lives, both figuratively and literally, to see the gospel shared with others around the world. Nevertheless many people do charity work such as mission for myriad personal reasons. In the early 2020s one British mission agency decided to end their premium 'short-term mission trips' project they were known for (which for a long time had given thousands of young middle-class British boys and girls an opportunity to serve in mission and experience life overseas). The director of the organization explained to me that they had done a thorough assessment of their short-term mission project before making the decision to pull the plug. They had been involved in numerous extended conversations with their partners who received the young British people and, through these, they had learned that the partners did not really benefit much from the short-term mission trips. They only tolerated them because they knew their British friends valued them so much.[13] 'Apart from the money they bring, we will not miss anything of their presence here. Everything they do when they come, we can do faster. Our real benefit is that our young people get to see that Europeans are still engaging in mission, but that does not need short-termers.' Without delay the mission agency decided that stopping short-term mission trips was the right decision. To their shock, the middle-class congregations that provided financial support to the agency vehemently pushed back against the decision. 'Where will our young ones get the international exposure they need as they grow up?' Ironically, of course, this was the reason the programme was cancelled. It served the needs of white middle-class Evangelicals in Britain and had minimal impact wherever those short-termers went.

That said, the greatest takeaway for me from Holly Berkley Fletcher's book is this: the attitudes of many Western Christians, Evangelical or not, on issues to do with mission and evangelism in other parts of the world are shaped by superiority and entitlement. She mostly reflects on the experiences of children of Evangelical missionaries who spent considerable time on the mission field – she works with raw data from her interviews with many missionary kids. She is clear that many of the missionary kids she interviewed believe their parents had exhibited behaviours that betrayed their sense of superiority complex among the people they worked with, whether in Africa, Asia or Latin America. To make her point, Fletcher engages the works of several Christian psychologists, including Dave Verhaagen, who confirm that US Evangelical mission is to some extent driven by narcissism:

> White evangelicals add a theological layer that supercharges a sense of importance, goodness, and, via a theology of certainty, rightness. American evangelicals are heavily, cosmically, existentially invested in being right, being special, and following a divine plan to save the world. They, of course, don't see things that way. They whole-heartedly believe they are right, and if they don't assert their rightness, if they don't 'share the love of Christ' with others, those folks will burn in hell for eternity. This is absolutely a sincere belief, I don't think secular people fully grasp that. But a hallmark of narcissism is the inability to really see oneself and a lack of critical thought about one's beliefs and behavior.[14]

It is this inability to *really see oneself* and the *lack of critical thought about one's beliefs and behaviour* that is of particular concern to this chapter. I do understand the tunnel vision that may be required for missionaries to do some of the work they are called to. Dave Verhaagen goes a step further: US Evangelicalism suffers from a problem of collective narcissism:

> The larger American culture is full of narcissism, which has permeated the church, while the church and other Christian ministries make prominent targets for those with narcissistic personality disorder to set up shop and consolidate power ... 'I continued to be surprised that in some contexts, narcissistic tendencies are renarrated as gifts for the church – that bullies are excused as "confident," that manipulators are excused as "good strategists," that a chameleon-like personality is seen as "adaptable."' The church has proven to be a haven for narcissists. Once inside, they can behave as they wish with little fear of repercussion, especially if they are talented or charismatic individuals. They do as they please, often to the detriment of the community and to the church.[15]

This narcissistic personality disorder is foundational to a great deal of Western Evangelical missionary work in the world. Many missionaries carry their narcissistic personality disorder to the mission field, where they tend to want to be heroes in the most difficult places, to have the most arduous stories to tell. Fletcher talks about the impact of the thrill of danger on missionary kids. Some missionary families would compete on who experienced the most danger with the understanding that the more danger one endured, the tougher they were, which of course meant the better (or higher) missionary they were. She says:

> We tried to outcompete each other with the most harrowing stories (I had a parasite dug out of my big toe by a safety-pin-wielding teenager, but that was nothing compared to my friend's years-long battle with bilharzia). Africa was where it was at – a missions obsession an MK from southeast Asia that I interviewed called 'Africa porn.' When kids growing up in American churches aspire to be missionaries, they invariably imagine going to *the deepest, darkest Africa*, where the people were the poorest, the most different (let's be clear: they were Black), and presumably the most 'heathen.'[16]

Not only does the Western missionary enterprise have a narcissistic personality disorder problem. Many individual missionaries – *not* all but *many* – believe they know best what the people they serve need, and think that they alone can fix them. More important for us is not necessarily the narcissistic tendencies of individual missionaries – though of course that is detrimental to mission – but the collective narcissism that makes missionaries stick together to order their relations with the local people they profess to serve (which is more often than many would want to admit). As a group, Western missionaries often tend to share key characteristics that put them together against everyone else; many of them believe they are *more* special than the Christians back home who do not support their work, or local Christians who desire independence and autonomy, or the people they work among overseas who often either put them on a pedestal, detest them or choose to remain indifferent to their presence because they are suspicious of their motives, or the historians who critique their work, and many others who for one reason or another feel the need to highlight the inconsistencies of the story of mission. Many missionaries do not even take the time to listen to the local agendas that would emerge if communities discerned for themselves how the good news of Christ can transform their societies. Still today much of mission is the work of white saviours, whose main job is to rescue the world from problems (many of which are a result of

Western political and economic activities in the world).[17] The mission to civilize the nations continues, especially in the age of non-governmental organizations and international development agencies.[18]

This attitude of superiority not only allows missionaries to behave badly on the mission field, it allows them to do so with impunity. Many missionaries are not accountable on the mission field. Most missionaries do not submit to local leadership. When they do it is usually a selective kind of submission – 'I can follow your lead in any area of local ministry. For everything else, I report to the mission board back in Europe or America.' Back home, especially in contemporary times of 'cancel culture', mission field scandals are often swept under the carpet. Thus, many missionaries are not held to proper account back home. I have heard it said many times, 'Whatever happens on the mission field stays on the mission field.' To see the manifestation of this sense of superiority, one simply needs to hear the real conversations Western missionaries have about the people they serve – the things missionaries can never say loudly about their mission field. They are often careful enough not to use the word 'savages'. Even the word 'heathen' is now often frowned upon. Yet they will complain about corruption, syncretism, poor leadership, low standards of education and how needy the people are. They speak condescendingly to those who, they believe, are below them.

The challenge for all of us as followers of Christ in the world is to put into practice the words of Paul that we are one in Christ – that in him there is neither Greek nor Jew, neither male nor female and neither free nor slave. Our baptism into the Body of Christ makes us all equal, and that is the most important thing. But the call is not only to treat those of our faith as equals, as if it gives us a warrant to treat those outside the faith as less than us. All humanity is God's humanity, made in God's image. It is God who made us different *and* equal, and I am certain that God did not mean the differences to negate the equality. White supremacy is a lie invented by humans. It has benefited many white people for generations going back 600 years when it has been ferociously enforced in parts of the world. It has created a world order in which to be white is normal and everyone else is a person of colour. This black skin is God's work, God's gift to the world through me. Unfortunately it is not a gift that is easily received – it covers me in a colour that many find unacceptable. If anyone really believes that their skin colour makes them individually better or superior (without the privileges that come with being white and living in a world shaped by white people for other white people), they have to encounter Christ again. God's Spirit will not let the sin of racism in all its forms – white supremacy, black supremacy and every colour in between – go unrevealed.

Decolonizing mission talk

Essentially, when some Western mission scholars and practitioners speak about their work in the world it is usually the voice of whiteness that comes out. Their postures and attitudes are those of people who believe themselves to be better and to know more than those they serve. They deflect, deny or dismiss any criticism that comes their way. Even when they mean well their empathy falls short because they have no idea what being without power feels like. The Jesus they preach cares more about saving people's souls to get them to heaven than to transform their lives to help make God's kingdom visible and tangible here on earth. He cares more about preventing women's access to abortion and upholding people's rights to own guns than he does about racist police brutality that terrorizes black and brown people in their neighbourhoods, or racialized education systems designed to keep parts of the population poor, and economic policies that enrich the rich while keeping poor people in poverty. Theirs is the Jesus of the Crusades who picks up arms against religious and imperial enemies. Without a doubt such missionaries are the Christian soldiers of our day. They are the citizens of the Christian empire of modern-day Rome. They march with all the imperial backing anyone could ever wish for behind them, believing that only they can fix the world: they have all the know-how and can answer all the world's questions; they have the money and, with it, they can smother all the problems of the world; finally, they have the military might, the nations will bow down before them. They are incapable of listening to others, especially those who are not white.

Without engaging the rest of the world a great deal of our Western missiological discourse happens in an echo chamber in which many of us love to hear our own words remixed and parroted back to us. This is quite evident in mission studies, where a great deal is written by Westerners for other Westerners. When Westerners talk about mission taking place in other parts of the world, their language is always telling. They reflect the ideals of Pope Nicholas V's *Dum Diversas*, 'dominate and occupy', or Ignatius of Loyola's 'conquer' or, indeed, William Carey's use of 'means' to evangelize the 'pagans and Mohammadans'. Since the inception of this way of talking about 'mission' and the 'missionary', the missionary enterprise has always involved Westerners *doing things* to people in the non-Western world. Many cannot imagine mission being different.

Even in the world today, where Africa has more Christians than Europe (and many of these African Christians are quite active in their faith – they go to church most days of the week, they are intentional about reading their Bibles as much as possible and their lives are usually dependent on God answering their prayers), Westerners will always have reasons to send missionaries to various Christian countries in the continent. Many Westerners behave as if the now-debunked theory that African Christianity is a mile wide and one inch deep is true. They believe that African Christians need them or their money or indeed their theology to be good followers of Christ. Today, when African Christians are holding the Christian faith up in many cities in Europe – if we were to rapture all black Christians away from London, church attendance would drop so low it would seem there are no Christians in parts of the city – yet we still work hard to send missionaries to Africa. The missionaries who go to teach English in English-speaking countries in Africa – for example, Kenya, Uganda, Malawi, Zimbabwe – are the most interesting. Many of them are not even trained educators but they end up displacing a local teacher who could do the job just as well, and in the process they reinforce the stereotypical colonial 'Western is always better' ideology. Increasingly I am fascinated by those who come to Africa to teach theology. They will almost invariably teach Western theology with minimal attention to the contextual issues their students wrestle with. Even when attempting to contextualize, many of them tend to seek ways to make their Western theology speak to African Christians and fail to pay sufficient attention to local *contextual* issues of theological concern. For many Evangelicals, Catholic theologians tend to overcontextualize, even though that journey is often led by African theologians embedded in their communities, seeking an authentic African Christianity. Evangelicals tend to suspicion of contextualization and contextual theologies and often try to persuade African Christians to believe and behave like Western Evangelicals.

If we pay attention to Western missiological discourse it becomes pretty evident very quickly that many Westerners still believe that mission and evangelism happen in the non-Western world, not in the West. This is more common in Europe but it is also true that US Christians do not generally consider their country a mission field. As it has been in history, mission is something that Western Christians do in other parts of the world. Many European Christians are not ready to accept that most of the migrants who have come to their cities are actually their fellow followers of Christ, co-labourers with them in God's vineyard and, most importantly, descendants of the people converted through the work of their own European ancestors who went around the world as missionaries. Many are not ready to receive the gifts of the global Church already living in their midst – gifts that God has sent them – simply because they are migrants. There is a famous quote from Walter Hollenweger who said in 1992 that 'Christians in Britain prayed for many years for revival, and when it came, they did not recognize it because it was black.'[19] This is just as true today as it was when he wrote those words.

All this is happening when Europe needs a fresh evangelization. The religious landscape of Europe has, since the 1950s, been dominated by rising secularism. European Christendom, just like the Christian heartland that Europe was for many centuries, is a thing of the past. Christianity has lost its privileged place at the centre of Europe's society. In many places in the European public sphere, Christianity seems marginalized like an old cultural heritage that served us many decades ago but now that we have progressed, we can leave it behind. Of course, when one engages scholars of religion in Europe it becomes evident that Europeans have leaned towards secularism[20] (even at a time when the rest of the world is becoming furiously religious[21]). The British sociologist of religion Grace Davie came to a conclusion long ago that in choosing to secularize while others around the world are embracing religion, Europe became the exceptional case.[22] With regard to religious enthusiasm around the world, the secularization theories of the 1960s and 1970s have been proved wrong.[23] In Europe the culture does not Christianize and disciple people any more. In some European countries church attendance has plummeted to levels never seen before. To put it in very direct terms, the *heathen* is in Europe now. Yet listening to strategy board meetings in mission agencies in Europe one would be forgiven for thinking that all is well in European Christianity. The model we have does not translate well to our current reality where Europe herself needs missionaries sent to her. In the end we send missionaries to countries that are more Christian than ours. For instance, both Kenya and Ghana, two African countries that get the most attention from the US missions community, have much larger and more vibrant and engaged Evangelical communities. They should be able to send missionaries to some Western countries. However, as Gina Zurlo once lamented, countries with the most Christians receive the largest numbers of missionaries.[24]

Decolonizing the 'use of means'

William Carey published his famous essay, *An Enquiry into the Obligations of Christians to Use Means for the Conversion of the Heathens*, in 1792. It was a groundbreaking essay that changed mission significantly. After its publication mission was never the same. In the essay Carey argued that Christians should use 'means' to evangelize the *heathens* in the unevangelized parts of the world. One such means was the formation of an association of interested individuals to send and support missionaries to other parts of the world. This suggestion started a revolution where numerous parachurch mission societies and associations could be involved in mission by sending people from Christendom to 'heathendom'.[25] In making that argument he essentially detached mission from the institution of the Church as it had historically been, especially in Britain. An association of Christians could send missionaries without the need to wait for the Church to do this. If a person wanted to go overseas as a missionary, all that was needed was to gather a few willing friends who could support them financially and in prayer. Once this was in place they could go. Carey's essay includes statistical data of the distribution of Christians around the world. Of course, most of it would be considered guesswork today but he had a fair understanding of the religious landscape of the time. He knew that a tiny percentage of all Christians in the world lived outside Europe and North America. Mission for him would be something that Christian Westerners were obliged to do, and it involved the movement of Christians and missionaries from Europe and North America to what he identified as *unevangelized lands*, and these included Latin America, Africa and Asia. Carey himself started the Baptist Missionary Society in 1792 and became its first missionary to India in 1793.

His global influence rightly earns him the title of the father of modern mission. The essay has without a doubt shaped Western Protestant and Evangelical missionary work around the world for the past two centuries. In the decade following the publication of the essay in Europe alone, more than a dozen missionary societies were formed. Several other mission agencies were also formed in North America in the early decades of the 1800s. Consequently, in the nineteenth century alone, thousands of European and North American missionaries – and for various economic reasons millions of European Christians – migrated from their home continents to the Americas, Africa and parts of Asia. By the end of the nineteenth century the missionary movement had thousands of workers scattered around the world.

William Carey's model of mission is still in use today, with much recognition worldwide. Western mission agencies continue to dominate our imagination of what taking the gospel to other parts of the world means. If asked what they know about mission, most Christians will talk about being sent by some mission agency to work in a foreign land. Many will most likely have in mind images or stories of white Westerners sent to save the heathens in the jungles of Africa or the Amazon – of course, the word 'jungle' was once part of the popular definition of 'mission'. An African or an Indian does not fit the description. Rightly so. In Carey's model, missionaries are those who are sent from the West to the rest of the world. That is why it has been referred to as the 'West to the Rest' model. It is easy to articulate and imagine. In their 2022 book, *Africa to the Rest: From Mission Field to Mission Force (Again)*,[26] my friends Yaw Perbi and Sam Ngugi are imagining the same model being used today, with the only difference being Africa at the centre. It is now Africa's time. 'Africa to the Rest', they say. Their subtitle further imagines Africa as a *mission force* – supposedly of Christian soldiers – deployed to the rest of the world. In reality it is mostly African migrants we see who, having migrated for various reasons, set up congregations for other African migrants and struggle to evangelize beyond the communities of their fellow nationals in the diaspora. Even if the militaristic term 'mission force' was appropriate, the missionary work of the African Christian diaspora does not amount to any force *yet*. Maybe in a generation or two something akin to a force will emerge but that too is highly unlikely. The era of the African missionary movement will be radically different from what we have seen in the past two centuries. Even the word 'mission' may disappear.

In the current religio-social landscape of the world, William Carey's model needs a rethink. Of course, this is not to take away from any of his great works. He is indeed the father of modern mission (not by virtue of being the first but because of his essay). He did great things for his time by making it possible for the masses, so to speak, to pick up the mantle of mission to evangelize the nations and, with the help of a few supporters, to travel to Africa, Asia or Latin America to share the good news of Jesus. However, truth be told Carey's model was not only grounded in a white-saviour complex, it was also shaped by white supremacy (as mission had been since *Dum Diversas* and *Regimini Militantis Ecclesiae*). It worked particularly well in the 1800s – the great century of European imperialism, marked by the great migration that saw more than a fifth of Europe's population emigrate, massive slave trade especially in the settler economies of the Americas, accelerated industrialization, and Christian awakenings. The language of Carey's essay is, even by the standards of his day, often insensitive and offensive. This should not be surprising, as he wrote the essay from the centre of England when England was the centre of the world. He wrote with the confidence of a white man who had the attention of his audience. His proposals, helpful as they were, could be easily translated into action by people of his social location – mostly fellow white European men of his calibre. It took him a significant amount of resolve and fortitude to keep going for 41 difficult years, in which time he lost two wives and was survived by the third. If mission is about heroism, William Carey is one of the best examples we have.[27]

William Carey's conception of mission was fundamentally unidirectional, grounded in a world view that divided humanity into two distinct and geographically separated realms: Christendom and heathendom. Within this framework, mission entailed sending Christians from the Christian West to evangelize non-Christian peoples elsewhere. Such a model reflected the colonial assumptions of the time, presuming that Christian truth and agency resided predominantly in the West. Contemporary missiology, however, recognizes the global and multidirectional nature of mission. In a world where the majority of Christians now live in the Global South, missionaries are as likely to be sent from Nigeria to Europe as from Britain to India. The old dichotomy no longer holds: secularism and spiritual need are increasingly evident in traditionally 'Christian' regions, including Europe itself. If the work of mission is viewed as the preserve of affluent churches alone, the global majority – often economically marginalized – would be unjustly sidelined from participation. Yet the Great Commission is not contingent upon wealth, education or geopolitical power. It is a universal mandate. To suggest otherwise would be to imply that Jesus erred in commissioning the poor, unlettered Galilean disciples. On the contrary, the history of mission testifies that the gospel has always been carried forward not only by the powerful but by the faithful – often the poor, the overlooked and the under-resourced.

Decolonizing the three Cs

David Livingstone's missiology of three Cs – 'Civilization, Commerce and Christianity' – popularized the concept of civilization as a purpose of mission in the 1850s and 60s. He believed that a new form of commerce needed to emerge in Africa for Christianity to gain traction. Yet that new trade would also be the foundation upon which the civilization of Africa would be built. Ultimately all three of them together – civilization, commerce and Christianity – were all part of one agenda. And they had to work together for transformation to happen in Africa. Since 1855, when Livingstone found his way to East Africa, following the Zambezi River from Zimbabwe and Zambia down to Mozambique, and saw the dreadful devastation caused by the Portuguese and Arabic slave trade, he had dedicated a great deal of his energy to the eradication of slavery. He understood that centuries of slave trade had left many Africans invested and dependent on it for their livelihood and security.[28] Bringing an end to slave trade would require a new form of commerce – possibly agriculture. African cotton could be useful to Europeans.

African minerals were yet to be discovered. Timber and rubber in the Congo would become big business in the 1890s. So in the 1850s and 60s it was agriculture that promised to be the bedrock of the new commerce. Yet that commerce would depend on the civilization and the Christianization of the Africans. The three Cs had to be pursued together. It appears what Livingstone had in mind was what we now call integral mission or as some call it, holistic mission. On the surface it makes sense. If you were a European looking to have a long-lasting impact in a Christianized Africa, commerce and civilization had to be part of the package. If anything, a civilized Africa would be a great home to the many Europeans migrating to the continent two decades later.

A new form of commerce was, for Livingstone, the way to evangelize the continent. Livingstone and many of his friends carried out a massive campaign in England. Bishop Samuel Wilberforce, the son of the famous abolitionist William Wilberforce, was one of Livingstone's key evangelists on the subject of commerce in Africa. Henry Rowley compiled a collection of Samuel's speeches and the theme of the significance of commerce for mission runs through them all. At a USPG event in Leeds in May 1860, Wilberforce explained:

> What is the connection between the Gospel and commerce? There is a great connection between them. In the first place, there is little hope of promoting commerce in Africa, unless Christianity is planted in it; and, in the next place, there is very little ground for hoping that Christianity will be able to make its proper way unless we can establish a lawful commerce in the country, because there is at this moment an unlawful commerce which checks the spread of Christianity. An unlawful commerce has got possession of the land, the immediate result of which is, that it supplies the necessities of the leading men of that country.[29]

Wilberforce had definitely been impressed by Livingstone, with whom he was in constant communication. He was persuaded that colonial commerce in Africa would eventually take off. He wanted Christianity to be part of that rise:

> As regards Africa, we should seek to impregnate our commerce with Christianity, and to prevent it from becoming an instrument of evil, that in times past commerce with Africa has, as you all know, been a special minister of evil.[30]

In the end Wilberforce makes a theological argument that England had no choice. It had to civilize and bring commerce to the heathendom or else it would be robbed of its place of power and influence:

> If we as a nation are not doing the work for which our commerce and our civilisation has fitted us, how can we expect but that we shall be put down from the place of power, and that those who will do the work of God will be put into our places.[31]

He had good reasons for his argument:

> We are about, God helping us, to send England in England's character, England's industry, England's commerce, England's religion, to be a nucleus around which, as we hope, God will gather a multitude of men of the other blood, that that nucleus, so gathered round, may become itself a mass, instinct with Christian life, to spread its life-giving influences amongst all the heathendom around it.[32]

For Livingstone, the three Cs were to serve a purpose – to eradicate slave trade and stabilize African communities in new forms of commerce (away from the trading of fellow Africans to be enslaved by the Europeans or the Arabs). Christianity would be the glue that held everything together. This made sense in the highly charged political context of the mid-nineteenth century. The transatlantic slave trade had intensified as it was coming to an end. As a matter of fact, the United States was at this time wrestling with the question of slavery (which had direct implications for both Europe and Africa). The first half of the 1860s would see the USA entangled in a civil war around slavery. To the east of Africa, the Arabic slave trade (which had gone on for more than a millennium) was still in full flow – they sought to get the most slaves they could before the Europeans stopped it. Britain had emerged as a global power with 'great things – ships, commerce, and colonies',[33] and used its force to get other countries to agree to end slavery. They knew if the changes were to remain, they had to be in charge. As a result the British Raj in India was declared in 1858. Europeans were poised to take advantage of the African continent that was in the process of being explored, with David Livingstone being the most celebrated of the explorers. More importantly, it was an era of European emigration to the colonies in the Americas, Australia and New Zealand. It was only a matter of time before Livingstone and others realized that the only way to manage the situation in Africa was to colonize the continent as well. Bishop Wilberforce celebrates the British empire again:

Almighty God has given us that, and, at the same time, in giving us an arm of strength, giving us ships which multiply our presence in every part of the earth, giving us colonies which enable us to reproduce our race and our Church wherever the sun rises and sets, He has intended, if we rise fully to the dignity of our birthright, to make the English branch of His Church, spread now throughout America, spreading now throughout Australia, seated in New Zealand, carried out in South Africa, blended with the blood of Africa in the West Indies, entering from Sierra Leone into the northern parts of Africa that with this apparatus for spreading it, and this gift of God's truth to spread, His purpose for England is that she shall be the regenerator of our race and the maintainer of the purity of Christendom.[34]

This is the challenge of the three Cs. During the nineteenth century it was impossible to execute them without colonizing people. Livingstone knew this and he hoped for benevolent colonialism. He pleaded with his British audience – the Monarchy, the Church and indeed everyone who would listen – for the 'English' (by which he meant the British) to have a colony in Central Africa. Europeans had to come and control the commerce and do the work of civilizing the people while Christianizing them. The three Cs made colonialism an express mission strategy. That which was started by Pope Nicholas V became the outright operational doctrine of European imperial missiology.

Decolonizing 'unreached people groups' and other such terms

Most of the ideas shaping our ways of understanding God's work among the nations today were formed in the first half of the twentieth century when European imperialism was at its peak. One would only need to look at the Commissions of the World Missionary Conference of Edinburgh 1910 to see a colonial missiology at play. The year 1910 is critical because on the one hand, Europe's colonial project was at its peak and on the other, it was also the high watermark for the Western missionary movement.[35] In the years following the Scramble for Africa the confidence of a colonial civilizing mission was at its highest. The momentum of the delegates at the Edinburgh Conference was so great that they believed they could evangelize the entire world in their generation. Indeed, the motto of their movement was 'To Evangelise the World in Our Generation'.[36] However, quite a few interesting things happened at Edinburgh that reflect the Eurocentric nature of both the conference and the entire missionary adventure of the time. For instance, the fact that there were only 18 delegates from the non-Western world (out of the 1,255) – and they all came from Asia – means that the deliberations that took place were very Western (and white) in nature. Indeed, black Africans were not invited because, as it was understood back then, they were not mature enough to belong.[37] Brian Stanley notes:

> If African churches were deemed to be insufficiently 'advanced' to merit their own representatives, it was not simply because these churches were young in years, but also because their members were thought to be starting from much further back in the process of human development than were Christian converts in Asia. The inhabitants of Africa were still in 1910 regarded as *primitive, childlike*, and *at the bottom of the evolutionary hierarchy, relatively unimportant for the future of the world church*.[38]

By the 1950s (after two devastating world wars that had been started by European Christian nations), the confidence of the missionary movement had been shaken. The colonies had started gaining independence from European nations. India and Pakistan gained their independence in August 1947. China had expelled Western missionaries in 1950. The language of mission itself shifted. The concept of *missio Dei* – meaning the mission of God and stating that mission belongs to God, not to humans (read Westerners), and certainly not to the Church – became a key descriptor of what God is about in the world, reflecting some humility in the missionaries' self-understanding. Before long the geography of mission would also change. Mission would no longer be from the West to the rest of the world. The distinction between Christendom and heathendom became blurred. Mission could happen from any continent to any other continent.

This is true of our sense of mission today. Yet for many of us the missiological language of the colonial era remains. We may not say 'heathens', 'pagans' or 'barbarians' but we still divide the world between evangelized and unevangelized lands. Crusades are generally speaking a thing of the past (unless you are in Africa, where the legacy of Reinhard Bonnke lives on). Now we use such terms as 'unreached people groups', 'the 10/40 Window', 'the 5/50 World' and many others to describe peoples and parts of the world that Westerners have not evangelized (read *civilized*) yet. A great deal of this language of 'unreached people groups' is attributed to Ralph Winter (1924–2015).[39] Winter and his generation of mission scholars and leaders were the bridge that connected stories of the missionary heroes of the nineteenth and early twentieth century to late-twentieth-century missionaries who picked up the baton in the changed postcolonial world of the second half of the twentieth century.

They wrote their missiology during the critical times when European governments were losing their colonies in Africa and Asia, and at the same time the United States was rising as a global superpower and, to borrow the words of Perbi and Ngugi, a mission force. Their commentary ushered in a new era of mission that would be shaped by North American leadership. Indeed, their missiology had to reflect the confidence and concerns of the new American Christian Empire. European empires had had their time to lead in global mission but that was beginning to come to an end. It was now time for the United States to remake mission in its own image.[40] The USA did not need to have colonies in Africa to support its missionary work. Of course, imperial support would be available when needed but physical colonies in the continent were not necessary. All they needed was to make Africans believe that whatever came from the USA was the truth.[41] Even today, many US leaders are shaping African Christianity without ever needing to set foot on the continent. Many of the books that African Christians are reading today were written by North American preachers, mostly popular on television and social media, who have never set foot on the continent of Africa.

With the resurgence of the USA in mission, a fresh sense of imperial confidence emerged and, alongside it, a return to the old colonial missionary mindset – *the greater evangelizes the lesser*. Essentially, mission continued to be framed as it had been during the era of European colonialism. Mission was the noble duty of enlightened and well-resourced American Christians, who should obey the Great Commission to evangelize the nations of the world. Within a few short decades a near-total commercialization of mission occurred and a multi-billion-dollar industry complex came into existence around it. The souls of the heathens became a commodity that could raise money for mission. A fresh wave of mission agencies emerged. They required new mission departments, schools and seminaries to come into existence in North America to train and equip the numerous men and women they would send around the world as missionaries.[42] Before long many more US Christians enlisted to go overseas for mission, to share the US version of the good news of Christ, just as the Europeans had done before them. For decades following the 1950s and 1960s, mission was still something that Westerners did in Africa, Asia and Latin America. Across those continents the 'younger churches' (as they called them) were beginning to emerge and expand, many of which were shaped in the image of the US missionary movement, were informed by US missionary theological resources and were to a great extent led by US missionary personnel. Naturally many of these desired to be independent to make their expressions of Christianity reflect their own cultures. Yet they needed to depend on the West not only for their theological formation but also for their financial well-being. In the end they had no choice but to follow the ways of their US leaders.

Decolonizing Evangelical mission

The 1970s saw a resurgence in Evangelical zeal for mission. The common words used to describe the effort were 'evangelization' and 'evangelism', and the goal was to make an immense effort for every person in the world to have a chance to hear the good news of Jesus (as some would add, at least once). This was yet another movement to evangelize the world as soon as possible – to hasten the much-desired second coming of Christ (which was believed by many to be delayed because there were still some people groups in the world who had not heard the good news – the general criteria for this being the availability of either the New Testament or the Jesus Film in their languages). A good part of this renewal of Evangelical zeal for mission was a reaction to the ecumenism of the World Council of Churches (WCC), which seemed too liberal to many conservative Christians to properly advance the evangelization of the nations and uphold the lordship of Jesus and the inerrancy of the Bible.[43] In addition to the World Evangelical Alliance (WEA, which had been in existence for more than a hundred years and had been central to the missionary movement of the nineteenth century), there arose a new movement, the Lausanne Movement, to help mobilize many for the evangelization of the world.[44]

Following two key conferences in 1966 (one in Wheaton and the other in Berlin), where Billy Graham shared his concerns about 'modern theology and humanistic interpretations of the Gospel', he hosted the First International Congress on World Evangelization (also known as Lausanne 74) in Lausanne in Switzerland in 1974.[45] More than 2,700 Evangelical Christian leaders from nearly 150 countries took part in the conference, making it one of the most important landmarks in Evangelical missionary work in the world. *TIME* magazine referred to Lausanne 74 as 'a formidable forum, possibly the widest-ranging meeting of Christians ever held'.[46] The conference had as its theme 'Let the Earth Hear His Voice'.[47] This was intended to be a call to action to all Christian leaders to respond to the opportunities and challenges of the work of world evangelization in the twentieth century. At the end of the conference the participants adopted the Lausanne Covenant as the guiding statement that would shape their evangelistic work in the world. After paragraphs on (1) the purpose of God, (2) the authority and power of the Bible, and (3) the uniqueness and universality of Christ, the Covenant turned to the nature of evangelism:

> To evangelize is to spread the good news that Jesus Christ died for our sins and was raised from the dead according to the Scriptures, and that, as the reigning Lord, he now offers the forgiveness of sins and the liberating gifts of the Spirit to all who repent and believe. Our Christian presence in the world is indispensable to evangelism, and so is that kind of dialogue whose purpose is to listen sensitively in order to understand. But evangelism itself is the proclamation of the historical, biblical Christ as Saviour and Lord, with a view to persuading people to come to him personally and so be reconciled to God.[48]

This movement would renew the focus on mission from the West to unevangelized peoples of the world at a time when in the ecumenical circles of the WCC, there was talk about a moratorium on mission.[49] Ralph Winter was one of the key speakers. He made a strong statement arguing for the evangelization of some 1,600 hidden 'unreached' nations (or people groups) around the world.[50]

In the end both the WEA and the Lausanne Movement focused on the evangelization of the nations, to lead as many people to a personal relationship with Jesus as possible. The WEA has its Mission Commission, which seems to do the same work that the Lausanne Movement does, only on a larger scale. There is a wide intersection between the two – some of the key leaders in world mission are active in both. At the beginning of the twenty-first century the Lausanne Movement seemed to be more active than the WEA and quite influential in shaping mission theology around the world.

The missiology of this Evangelical movement forms the foundation upon which most of our current missionary work is built. In the years since Lausanne 74 three other conferences have taken place: Manila (1989), Cape Town (2010) and Seoul (2024), with each of these producing a statement or a commitment to bind the movement together and help it focus on some key aspects of the Evangelical faith and its sense of mission among the nations. In addition, the Lausanne Movement has hosted many consultations on various topics in mission, each of them producing resources for the work of evangelism and discipleship around the world.[51]

Within the Evangelical movements, Western theological leadership makes most mission discourse follow the issues that concern Western

Christians. Even though the Evangelical movement is global its centres of power are predominantly located in the West – we find both its centres of theological formation and its financial resources in Western cities such as Frankfurt, London, Minneapolis and Dallas. Furthermore the movement's thought leadership – the Evangelical voice worth listening to – is certainly based in Western countries. In this case, those who have money determine what everybody else in the movement prioritizes in the discussion. Matters of US concern – for instance, abortion and gun rights – often find their way to many parts of the non-Western world. In addition, Western missiological institutions have over the decades produced trained non-Western scholars who, because of having been educated by Western professors using Western resources, sound like Westerners.

More often than not it is these Western-sounding non-Westerners who get invited into Western missiological conversations. They are a safe choice as they do not bring authentic outsider voices. The contextual concerns of other theologians, especially of Latin America and Asia (and to some extent South Africa) for holistic or integral mission are embraced with caution.[52] One would simply have to attend a theological conference in Africa, Asia or Latin America to see how far Western theology has gone. For many of us it is incredibly confusing to hear black and brown scholars, especially those located in the non-Western world, speaking like white Western Evangelical Christians from Europe or North America. Over the past years I have seen many non-Western mission agencies behave as if they are a Western agency in Europe or North America. An African mission agency I know – located in East Africa – talks about the people it serves as if it is a US organization based in some city where people know very little about black people in Africa. Mission, for them, as for most of their Western friends, is charity (or philanthropy), and the people they serve are the ultimate charity basket. Their works of charity have one goal – to save souls and put them on a train to heaven. The souls they save must also begin to assume their Western cultural identity.

While writing this book I attended a black mission conference in Europe that had *nothing* black about it. If you listened to its proceedings without seeing who was speaking or read a transcript of every word that was said, you would most certainly not think it was Africans speaking. Its entire posture towards the nations is not different from that of the West. It is aggressively concerned about the Arabic *unreached people groups* in North Africa. Its mission strategies are a carbon copy of those of Western agencies even though they have no money.

Herein lies the challenge with Evangelicalism – its self-confidence. The kind of Christianity that comes out of its work tends to lean towards uniformity. Evangelical Christians in all parts of the world have to believe and behave the same. There is very little room for diversity of thought because in fact many Western Evangelicals believe their interpretation of the Scriptures is the only correct one and that it must universally apply to all Christians throughout the world. To achieve this uniformity, Evangelicalism does not contextualize well. It does not need to. It spreads its influence by assimilating local Christians around the world into the orbits of its theology and self-understanding, causing them to think, believe and theologize like Westerners. Evangelical statements of faith seek to prescribe what a faithful follower of Christ will look like, whether in urban USA, rural Malawi or any other place in the world. Behaving like a religious empire, or indeed being the religious arm of Western imperialism – I read John Dominic Crossan say the USA is the new Rome[53] – it often ignores and demonizes local contextual realities of Christian communities around the world. If it provides a theological answer it will depend almost exclusively on those Western Evangelical theologians it trusts. For decades it was said that European missionaries sought to make their African converts European by teaching them European languages, giving them European names and forcing them to abandon their Africanness and live in Christian villages where everything African was unwelcome. Western Evangelicalism does something similar, without moving people to Christian villages or changing their names. It simply teaches them to trust all things Western (and indeed distrust and question their own resources). It has powerful gatekeepers who decide which persons can belong and which cannot. Those who fail to meet the standards for one reason or another are exiled from the Evangelical fold as syncretists and heretics.[54]

The Evangelical obsession with uniformity – for the purposes of standardizing and controlling people's belief systems – was again put on full display in November 2024 when US Evangelicals overwhelmingly voted a man who demonstrates no evangelical faith into power for the second time simply because he promised them power:

> I will tell you, Christianity is under tremendous siege, whether we want to talk about it or we don't want to talk about it ... And yet we don't exert the power that we should have ... Christianity will have power ... *If I'm there, you're going to have plenty of power, you don't need anybody else.* You're going to have somebody representing you very, very well. Remember that.[55]

The love of power and the felt need to shape broader US culture according to Evangelical belief betray the old need for Christians to dominate everyone else around them. We could invoke Pope Nicholas V again here, but at this point the tendency to want to enforce our preferred versions of acceptable Christian behaviour on others, even those who do not believe, is a normative part of the story. This faith tends to pander to the rich and powerful. It requires conformity from those it can control and will turn away when the people misbehaving are powerful. This Christianity justified slavery and colonialism. It was more concerned about the Christian obedience of the enslaved and the colonized while overlooking or justifying the atrocities of those who enslave and colonize them.

Furthermore Evangelical missiology struggles to make sense of sharing the gospel and discipling those in our societies who are experiencing poverty. This is usually because it is concerned with the *saving of souls* in order to get them to heaven and pays little attention to the material needs of those it converts. As long as people have received Christ in their hearts, and they are on their way to heaven, their social struggles and material needs are often ignored. In many cases Evangelical Christians preach the good news of Christ to the poor without challenging the unjust powers that keep some societies oppressed. Many of them are usually comfortable participating in and benefiting from systems that oppress and exploit others, fellow Christians included. In the end it becomes evident that a great deal of Evangelical Christianity – together with its missiology – is so wedded to capitalism that its main message is unlimited upward mobility. To be a good Christian, even here in the West, is to be a good middle-class citizen. Poor converts are often encouraged and pressured to polish up and 'leave the estates to join the rest of us in the suburbs'. The fact that a debate continues on whether issues of social justice belong in mission shows the problem of whiteness in Evangelicalism. Many black and brown people from Africa, Asia and Latin America instinctively understand that you cannot evangelize someone and leave the principalities and systems that keep them oppressed in place. The abundant life that Jesus offers is good news to the poor, breaks the chains of captivity and restores sight to the blind.

It is for this same reason that Evangelical missiology does not pay sufficient attention to the problem of racism in the Body of Christ. Indeed, the world of mission agencies is an extremely white one – an African missionary friend working in Germany says it is *white as snow*. It is quite a challenge to talk to mission agencies about cultural diversity. It feels as if they are the last bastion of segregation in the global Body of Christ. There is still an unconscious belief that mission is something white people do in other parts of the world. The idea that black and brown people can be involved in mission is still too far from their reality. If black and brown Christians engage in mission, it is in such exotic things as *dias-*

pora mission or *reverse mission* that they can participate, not the *real mission* that is the domain of white people. Of course, many Westerners realize that the landscape of Christianity has shifted, and that through migration the world has come to their neighbourhoods. Yet they fail to respond in ways that may include these many Christians from around the world in their work. They will often just say, 'We cannot find the right people.' This is generally simply an excuse. They are not looking. They are not really interested in changing because, 'You don't fix something that is not broken.' If they really look with the intention of finding good candidates they will notice many well-experienced, extremely educated and highly qualified people who can join their organizations, either as support staff in their headquarters in the West or as missionaries on the mission field. The challenge is that having these good people from around the world in Western mission agencies disrupts the 'West to the Rest' narrative of mission. If Western organizations start employing, supporting and sending non-Western missionaries, the whole idea of mission will have to change.

In the end Western Evangelicalism continues to be a white hegemony in which racial segregation is a normal part of the Christian life. As far as I can tell it is a Western expression of the Christian faith; it makes use of exclusively Western theological resources to shape its convictions, identity and practice, and then exports these to Africa, Asia and Latin America. Over the decades this decidedly Western faith has been spread around the world, presenting itself as the best possible expression of Christianity – the standard against which all other expressions of the faith are to be measured. It is simply the religion of the empire of our age, our New Rome. Many of its defenders have spent a great amount of energy, time and ink trying to justify the Evangelical domination of Christianity worldwide, which makes it difficult for multicultural worship communities and mission to happen. It does not know how to belong together with other followers of Christ who think and behave differently from itself. It certainly has not learned to listen to non-Western theological voices yet, apart from those who have assimilated into its culture. Its theology, the social locations of its people, church growth principles and practices, and many other factors explain away the problem of segregation among Christians. Yet the problem is simply the demand for uniformity. Christian leaders and their congregations may belong together in large bodies such as the Evangelical Alliances around the world, but Sunday morning remains the most segregated hour in their communities. The segregated church that is characteristic of the Western Christian landscape deprives the Body of Christ of the gifts God has already given to its members throughout the world.

Decolonizing the missional Church

In the past five decades there has been another conversation in missiological scholarship in the West, this one centred on the growing concerns of the emerging mission field of Europe and the wider Western world – Western Europe, North America, Australia and New Zealand. The most important voice in this conversation is that of the British missionary and theologian Lesslie Newbigin, who came back from 30 years of serving in India to the shock of finding that the Christian Britain that had sent him to the Asian mission field had become secular.[56] Later he said that the situation he met back in Britain was more difficult to evangelize than the one he saw in India: 'It is much harder than anything I met in India. There is a cold contempt for the Gospel [here], which is harder to face than opposition.'[57] He would later observe, 'England is a pagan society, and the development of a truly missionary encounter with this very tough form of paganism is the greatest and practical task facing the church.'[58] Though public institutions and popular culture in Britain, like those of Europe and North America, no longer made people culturally Christian, the British Church still ran its ministries assuming that a stream of traditionally moral people who looked favourably upon Christianity would simply show up in services, eager to join and belong. Evangelization and mission were still thought of as activities that churches engage in in far-off unevangelized lands overseas. Newbigin realized that the Church in the West had not adapted to the secular reality of its context. As such he argued that the Western Church had to become completely missionary in its own context if it were to be engaged with the non-Christian society surrounding it. It needed to develop a missiology for the Western postmodern culture just as it had done for other unevangelized cultures.

The secular England that he returned to in 1974 forced Newbigin out of his retirement. He would devote the ensuing 24 years of his life to articulating a contextually relevant missionary theology for the West that would start a ripple in theological conversations around the world and redirect missiological scholarship for the decades that followed. His books *Foolishness to the Greeks* and *The Gospel in a Pluralistic Society*[59] received a warm acceptance among many scholars worldwide and thereby extended the influence of his theology of mission. His exegesis of Western culture was astonishingly accurate. He did not shy away from criticizing the influence of the Enlightenment and modernity on Western Christianity.[60] The themes in his theology of mission have drawn interest from many other mission scholars. In the early 1980s Newbigin had been involved with a British Council of Churches programme, The Gospel and Our Culture, which laid the foundation for his book *The Other Side of 1984*. Following this the missiological conversation was picked up by a budding group of theologians and missiologists from North America who had been following Newbigin's writings from the early 1980s. They subsequently formed the Gospel and Our Culture Network (GOCN) in North America, which later changed its name to the Gospel and Culture Network. This network is the force behind the 1998 publication of *Missional Church*,[61] a book that came out in the year that Newbigin died. Newbigin's theological writings will certainly continue to inform missional theology worldwide deep into the twenty-first century.

The missional conversations currently happening in Germany may be a few years ahead of those we are having in the UK, and these will be a few years ahead of those taking place in the United States. This is due to the nature of the religious context of the West – secularization has impacted Western countries differently – but we know we are all going in the same direction. The sources that inform our Western missiological discourse are one and the same. The convictions that shape our missiology are similar. In the end the diagnoses always align.[62]

The missional church conversation needs decolonizing on several levels. The most obvious one is that it needs its mind stretched through some intentional engagement with non-Western scholars. It has to allow some strangers in its midst to help it make sense of the world in which it lives. Indeed, at the centre of the missional church movement is the voice of one stranger, Lesslie Newbigin. Certainly he was a stranger in India but he was also a stranger in Britain after his return. The critical distance that had come out of his 30 years in India enabled him to see Britain in a different light. Realizing that foreign Christians could possibly understand the missionary needs of Western culture, he said of non-Western Christians:

> We need their witness to correct ours, as indeed they need ours to correct theirs. At this moment our need is greater, for they have been far more aware of the danger of syncretism, of an illegitimate alliance with the false elements in their culture, than we have been. But ... we imperatively need one another if we are to be faithful witnesses to Christ.[63]

Another area in which the missional church conversation needs decolonizing is its theology of the Spirit, especially when it comes to the work of the Spirit in mission. In its arguments about what it would take to evangelize fellow Westerners, its imagination is often limited to such things as church marketing – so that people have more and better information about what congregations do – and a better social image and relationships with the people who need to be evangelized. Occasionally some imagine helping their congregations become missional by hiring a better preacher, having a more powerful choir or even providing better-quality coffee to their congregants before and after the service. All these ways of attempting to become missional are valid and they may yield some fruit in some places. Yet they fail to take seriously the fact that mission is first and foremost a work of the Spirit. Above all else it is a pneumatological adventure. All these things would yield more results if they were anointed by the power of the Spirit. They cannot be a substitute for the Spirit and they cannot make up for a lack of anointing. This is what the words 'Christ' and 'Messiah' mean – the Anointed One. The mission of God in the world needs the anointing of the Spirit. He ordered his disciples not to leave Jerusalem but to wait there for the promise of the Father, saying, 'you will receive power when the Holy Spirit has come upon you; and you will be my witnesses in Jerusalem, in all Judea and Samaria, and to the ends of the earth' (Acts 1.8). At the beginning of his own ministry, Jesus said:

> The Spirit of the Lord is upon me,
>   because he has anointed me
>   to bring good news to the poor.
> He has sent me to proclaim release to the captives
>   and recovery of sight to the blind,
>   to let the oppressed go free,
> to proclaim the year of the Lord's favour. (Luke 4.16–19)

A missional spirituality that understands the power of God that breaks yokes and sets captives free is critical, especially in the West, where people usually find Spirit-talk rather confusing, difficult and sometimes weird. The ministry of the missional Church needs a holistic spirituality that covers all of life. It must attempt to overcome the dualism that is foundational to modernity (that separates the spiritual from the material if it believes that spirits exist at all).[64] It will take a great deal of decolonizing to change people's minds – and theologies – about this. Yet it is foundational to the ministry of the missional Church. Part of the challenge I see in this conversation is that missional leaders usually want to evangelize people without taking them on the uncomfortable journey of widening their world views to help them understand that it is through the work of the Spirit that we are followers of Jesus. Inviting people to walk with Jesus is also an invitation for them to walk in the Spirit (Gal. 5.13). This reality requires a response. The almighty Spirit of God lives in us in this universe where there are myriad other spirit-beings. Our missional spirituality has to trust the Spirit of God enough to give up the need to control everything – the need for comfort and certainty. The Spirit is full of surprises that oftentimes make sense long after they have happened. The Spirit of God also empowers us to withstand the temptations of the evil one as he seeks to lure us into disobedience. A missional spirituality will understand that prayer is the lever that moves the spirits. Without prayer all missional conversation will remain only a conversation. Prayer is a double-edged sword. It reaches God and changes us and the situation around us. Prayer helps us become aware of our sins and guides us towards repentance. In the end the Spirit does not need the dramatic antics of the Pentecostals, the Charismatics or the prophetic – not that these are bad, but they are not what I am talking about here. Decolonizing the missional Church's theology of the Spirit will help churches, whatever their theological tradition, to embrace a spirituality that helps them engage the Spirit of God and their neighbours better. Having worked among Westerners for more than two decades, it never ceases to amaze me how little many of my Western friends pray. Many of them do not even expect God to answer their prayers.

Western missiology is too small for World Christianity

Over the years of working with Andrew Walls I heard him say more than a handful of times that 'Western theology is too small to answer the questions of all world Christianity.' Indeed, Walls thought that the future of the Christian faith, its shape in the twenty-first and twenty-second centuries, is being decided by events that are now, or will be in the near future, taking place in Africa, Asia and Latin America, adding that, 'New agendas for theology will appear in Africa.'[65] While these events continue to unfold and non-Western Christianity continues to explode, there is still an unjustifiable theological hegemony by the West over the world. Timothy Tennent once lamented, 'We cannot afford to ignore the theological implications inherent in the demographic reality that Christianity is currently in a precipitous decline in the West and that the vast majority of Christians now live outside the West.'[66] Indeed, the theological (and missiological) implications of the worldwide spread of Christianity in the twentieth century deserve a great deal of attention.[67] In the circumstances of the twenty-first century it is important that Christian theology becomes a field where Western and non-Western theologians can engage one another in mutually critiquing and edifying conversations that enrich each other. This requires Westerners to listen to others about what God is doing around the world.

To summarize everything said in this chapter so far, much of the missiological discourse in the West is written by Westerners for other Westerners and is usually designed to address issues of Western concern. Due to the Western nature of the entire enterprise and its impact around the world, a great deal of missiological discourses in Africa, Asia and Latin America also reflect Western interests. Many non-Western missionaries will speak of their own cultures in the same manner as the Westerners. For example, Western missiological thought on traditional religions of the world still shapes how many non-Western Christians think about their own religious heritages. Case in point: African Christians tend to echo Westerners when they speak of African indigenous religious heritage. Many still describe it as animism and believe they have been called to bring it to an end. Of course, the word 'animism' is used pejoratively – 'Africans are so primitive, they believe that all natural objects and phenomena have a soul.'[68]

Shall we talk about animism?

Edward B. Tylor (1832–1917), widely celebrated as the father of the discipline of anthropology, published his book *Primitive Culture* in 1871, in which he claimed to have carried out a 'systematic study of the religions of the lower races' (by which he meant black Africans and many other peoples outside Europe, including Arabs and Jews).[69] In Tylor's words, 'Animism investigates the deep-lying doctrine of spiritual beings, which embodies the very essence of spiritualistic as opposed to materialistic philosophy.'[70] Animists are understood to be persons who hold to 'extreme spiritualistic views' or 'the general belief in spiritual beings' that can intervene in the lives of human beings and in the natural world.[71] Later he adds, 'Animism characterizes tribes very low in the scale of humanity, and thence ascends, deeply modified in its transmission, but from first to last preserving an unbroken continuity, into the midst of high modern culture.'[72] Essentially, animism was the religion of the *savages* that continued to evolve up until the age of 'civilized men'.[73] Among his informers were such men as Charles Darwin and Samuel Baker, who from 1869 to 1873 served as the Governor General of the Equatorial Nile Basin (Southern Sudan and Northern Uganda today) and had written in 1867 of the people of the Sudan: 'Without any exception, they are without a belief in a Supreme-Being, neither have they any form of worship or idolatry, nor is the darkness of their minds enlightened by even a ray of superstition.'[74] Of course, Tylor believed that animism touched 'all men who believe in active spiritual beings ... [therefore], in some form or another it is the religion of mankind, from the rude savage of the Australian bush or the Brazilian forest, up to *the most enlightened Christian*.'[75] In this generalized sense European Christians were also animists. However, it is the negative meaning of the word – animism as the religion of the uncivilized savages – that stayed to define what the Westerners found in Africa. It has been used over the decades primarily to demean Africa's religious heritage.[76]

The deliberations of the 1910 Edinburgh World Missionary Conference on Africa were highly condescending. Overall the word 'animism' was almost exclusively used in connection with Africa and other black populations in the Oceania and Latin America because what existed in Africa back then was thought to be not a religion at all, for 'nothing deserves the name of religion which is false and unethical'.[77] Participants were reminded that 'two and a half times as many people await the Gospel in China as make up the entire population of Africa'.[78] Chapters on China and Japan have their names mentioned in their titles, 'Chinese Religions' and 'The Religions of Japan' respectively. Chapters on Islam and Hinduism are simply entitled 'Islam' and 'Hinduism'. Africa, however, appears to have been synonymous with animism. This emphasis on animism was to encourage more missionaries to go to Africa. They believed that Africa would be an easy mission field – animistic societies could not sustain resistance against Christianity. However, both Christianity and Islam were noted to be the two forces contending for the soul of Africa.[79] The conference deliberations suggest that it was believed that Islam was 'in many respects the more aggressive' of the two as 'the absorption of native races into Islam is proceeding rapidly and continuously in practically all parts of the continent'.[80] Overall it was concluded that 'if things continue as they are now tending, Africa may become a Mohammedan continent'.[81] Of course, Islam had existed in North Africa since the seventh century CE and had been making inroads in West Africa (along the Sahel, from Senegal to Sudan and beyond) and, from the ninth century CE, in East Africa (around what has now become Somalia, Kenya and Tanzania for almost a millennium). At the time of the Edinburgh conference, Islam seemed to be expanding more in Africa, along the Sahel as well as in the interior of Tanzania. In East Africa, Arabic Muslim slave traders, for example the famous Tippu Tib,[82] took advantage of improved transportation and commercial opportunities that were being created by colonialism and that *jihads* could not have accomplished. Thus, it seemed Islam had more prospects. Muslims had been in Africa for a long time and they had shaped aspects of African culture in parts of the continent. In 1910, when Africa had about nine million Christians, there were 34.5 million Muslims in the continent, and Islam was expanding. There was little hope Christianity could catch up. The combined threat of Islam and 'animism' seemed insurmountable.

Up until the 1960s, when most African countries gained independence from the European colonial governments, many missionaries who worked in Africa held negative views of African religious systems, dismissing them as evil and animist.[83] The word 'animism' was used to describe the religion of the Africans, defining it as the ascribing of personal agency to inanimate objects and using spirits, souls or gods to explain phenomena within the world. William Willoughby used the term in this manner in his book of 1928, *The Soul of the Bantu*, in which he declares, 'Bantu religion consists of animism and ancestor-worship.'[84] Teresia Hinga, a Kenyan theologian, explains that the missionaries were rather ruthless in their destruction of the African way of life. As she says, 'Behaving like a bull in a China Shop, they [the missionaries] dismissed African culture as primitive, and their spirituality as so much as superstition, fetishism, and animism.'[85] There was little regard for the possibility of the presence of God in the cultures before the arrival of the missionaries. African theological scholarship is often critical of those missionaries who disrespected African culture. Several African scholars and sympathetic Westerners have directly addressed the derogatory colonial and racist connotations such attitudes often precipitate. For instance, John Mbiti is quite clear in his indictment: 'Animism is not an adequate description of [African] religions, and it is better that the term be abandoned once and for all.'[86]

For this reason it is always shocking to find non-Western institutions offering courses on 'Animism' in the twenty-first century. In a 2022 study that I carried out with Professor Johannes (Klippies) Kritzinger, we found courses entitled 'How to Deal with Animism' being offered at several institutions in southern Africa.[87] (Later I found two other courses on 'responding to animism' at two British institutions.) In addition we noticed that many mission courses in Africa are a carbon copy of what is taught in the West. In most cases African institutions are using materials that shaped mission studies in the West in the 1970s and 80s, when Western Evangelical missionary confidence was high. As such, among many African Christians, attitudes towards aspects of indigenous cultures are often shaped by old colonial thought systems that sought to destroy whatever did not line up with Western definitions of Christianity and civilization.

Notes

1 It was E. B. Tylor who gave the most used definition of culture in his book *Primitive Cultures*: 'Culture, or civilization, taken in its broad, ethnographic sense, is that complex whole which includes knowledge, belief, art, morals, law, custom, and any other capabilities and habits acquired by man as a member of society.' Edward Burnett Tylor, *Primitive Culture: Researches into the Development of Mythology, Philosophy, Religion, Art, and Custom*, 3rd edn, vol. 1 (London: John Murray, 1891), p. 1. Also see Thomas Hylland Eriksen and Finn Sivert Nielsen, *A History of Anthropology* (London: Pluto Press, 2013).

2 By 'palefaces', he meant Westerners. Andrew F. Walls, 'Structural Problems in Mission Studies', *International Bulletin of Missionary Research* 15, no. 4 (1991), p. 152.

3 Andrew F. Walls, 'Christian Scholarship in Africa in the Twenty-First Century', *Transformation* 19, no. 4 (2002), p. 221.

4 Craig Ott and Harold A. Netland, *Globalizing Theology: Belief and Practice in an Era of World Christianity* (Grand Rapids, MI: Baker, 2006), p. 46.

5 It is true that there have emerged some non-Western scholars of mission and missiology. I argue here in line with Andrew Walls' statement quoted earlier that in the twenty-first century, when almost 70 per cent of Christians in the world live in Africa, Asia and Latin America, there ought to be many more missiological and theological voices from these parts of the world speaking to the global Body of Christ, beyond their own local communities. I am also concerned that many of these non-Western scholars are either translating and contextualizing Western missiology for their own localities and, in the process, fail to contribute their own original missiology, which I suggest is their unique contribution to the world. I cannot mention names, but a collection of missiology textbooks published in parts of Africa, Asia and Latin America often sound like simple paraphrased versions of Western books.

6 Kenelm Burridge, *In the Way: A Study of Christian Missionary Endeavours* (Vancouver, British Columbia: University of British Columbia Press, 2011), p. 72. Also see Johannes van den Berg, *Constrained by Jesus' Love: An Inquiry into the Motives of the Missionary Awakening in Great Britain in the Period between 1698 and 1815* (Kampen: Kok, 1956).

7 Edward Andrews, *Native Apostles: Black and Indian Missionaries in the British Atlantic World* (London: Harvard University Press, 2013).

8 Mekdes A. Haddis, *A Just Mission: Laying Down Power and Embracing Mutuality* (Downers Grove, IL: InterVarsity Press, 2022).

9 After a long discussion with InterVarsity Press, Brad Vaughn was forced to take his rebuttal down and make a public apology to Haddis. Vaughn complied, but the statement had been made – *whosoever dares to suggest that Western mission has a white supremacy problem will be silenced*. Here in the UK, Chris Sugden, with the help of Vinay Samuel and Kiprotich Chelashaw, sought to discredit my work in 2021 when Sugden published in the *Church Times* and on his own blog a rebuttal of my essay, 'Mission after George Floyd', in which I argued that mission in the twenty-first century must reflect the global nature of the Body of Christ. Their defence strategy was wrongly to say that the only way I could make this argument as an African was if I was shaped by African-American thought. Of course, that argument does not hold water, but the purpose of the

rebuttal was not to make a coherent argument but to warn anyone, especially from the non-Western world, that any critique of Western mission is unwarranted and that Westerners have many black and brown people who will jump up to defend them.

10 Holly Berkley Fletcher, *The Missionary Kids: Unmasking the Myths of White Evangelicalism* (Minneapolis, MN: Augsburg Fortress, forthcoming 2025). I am deeply grateful to Holly for giving me pre-publication access to the manuscript.

11 Her bibliography is quite extensive. It includes an impressive number of books, articles, podcasts and interviews. The issues she raises in the book are sensitive, so she needed to be thorough with her research and she achieved this.

12 Lauren Wells, *Unstacking Your Grief Tower: For Adult Third Culture Kids* (Fort Mill, SC: Independently published, 2021). Also see Lauren Wells, *The Grief Tower: A Practical Guide to Processing Grief with Third Culture Kids* (Fort Mill, SC: Independently published, 2021).

13 While processing this story I called some friends in Malawi to hear what they thought about short-term missions. Their answer was unanimous: 'We tolerate them because we know that the Americans [sic] need them.' They told me about the buildings they tear down every time short-term Westerners came to create some job for them. They should be able to take some pictures to show that they 'built a house in Malawi' when they return.

14 Fletcher, *The Missionary Kids*.

15 Dave Verhaagen, *How White Evangelicals Think: The Psychology of White Conservative Christians* (Eugene, OR: Wipf & Stock, 2022).

16 Fletcher, *The Missionary Kids* (my emphasis).

17 Several key overarching problems in the world – I can speak confidently about the poverty and civil political conflict in Africa – can be attributed to Western interference. For instance, the genocidal mess in the Democratic Republic of Congo, where foreign multinationals will do anything to access precious minerals, does not go back only to the days of Leopold's or Belgium's colonization of the country. More significant to the current situation in the Congo is the assassination of Patrice Lumumba by the US and Belgian governments in 1961. Yet, of course, the Western missionary movement has very little to say about this to their governments. I am not sure I have read anywhere of Western mission organizations lobbying their governments to stop exporting weapons for the sake of world peace. Mission agencies were moved to prayer and action when Russia invaded Ukraine. I know this because I was involved in organizing prayer meetings in the UK for the war to come to a quick end. When Israel invaded Gaza, the mission agencies were quiet; I did not hear of any prayer meeting for the people of Gaza, even from mission agencies working in the Middle East. The people who pray for world peace failed to advocate against the destruction of Gaza's peoples.

18 Dambisa Moyo has eloquently argued that Western aid keeps African countries poor – both the IMF and the World Bank were put in place to continue siphoning resources from Africa and other parts of the world. See Dambisa Moyo, *Dead Aid: Why Aid is Not Working and How There is a Better Way for Africa* (New York: Farrar, Straus & Giroux, 2009).

19 Walter Hollenweger, in his Foreword to Roswith Gerloff, *A Plea for British Black Theologies: The Black Church Movement in Britain in its Transatlantic Cultural and Theological Interaction with Special References to the Pentecostal*

Oneness (Apostolic) and Sabbatarian Movements, Studien zur interkulturellen Geschichte des Christentums (Frankfurt am Main: P. Lang, 1992). I am confident that the fact that the migrant Christians were black played a significant role in their invisibility or rejection, but I also think that part of the challenge was that they were mostly of Pentecostal inclinations. Nigel Rooms, a priest friend of mine, tells of an acquaintance of his who refuses to go to a Pentecostal church because he cannot stand singing 30 minutes of love songs to Jesus as if Jesus is his boyfriend. Of course, this is hyperbole but the point is clear. Many Europeans have not warmed up to world Christians among them because their Christianity is different. For instance, see Joseph Bosco Bangura, 'African Pentecostalism and Mediatised Self-branding in Catholic (Flanders) Belgium', *Stichproben: Vienna Journal of African Studies* 35 (2018).

20 Grace Davie, *Religion in Modern Europe: A Memory Mutates*, European Societies (Oxford: Oxford University Press, 2000), p. 11.

21 Peter L. Berger, *The Desecularization of the World: Resurgent Religion and World Politics* (Grand Rapids, MI: W.B. Eerdmans, 1999), p. 2.

22 See Grace Davie, *Europe – The Exceptional Case: Parameters of Faith in the Modern World* (London: Darton, Longman & Todd, 2002).

23 Davie, *Religion in Modern Europe*. Also see Grace Davie and Lucian N. Leustean (eds), *The Oxford Handbook of Religion and Europe* (Oxford: Oxford University Press, 2021), especially ch. 32.

24 Gina A. Zurlo, Todd M. Johnson and Peter F. Crossing, 'World Christianity and Mission 2020: Ongoing Shift to the Global South', *International Bulletin of Mission Research* 44, no. 1 (2020), p. 12.

25 Carey left England for India where he worked – without returning home – until his death in 1834. 'Heathendom' was understood to be those unevangelized parts of the world where Christianity had not yet been planted. Just as the word 'Christendom' generally meant Europe and North America, 'heathendom' had geographical connotations, generally meaning all other continents.

26 Yaw Perbi and Sam Ngugi, *Africa to the Rest: From Mission Field to Mission Force (Again)* (Maitland, FL: Xulon Press, 2022).

27 In the summer of 2023, I attended a conference where a seminar was offered on 'God's Missionary Generals'. I was curious to hear who the heroes were and what they had done. It all turned out to be three hours of the most extravagant hero-worshipping I have ever seen.

28 For example, one of Africa's female leaders of repute is Queen Nzingha (1583–1663), who ruled in the Ndongo Kingdom in the Congo-Angola area in the 1600s. She was a great leader who led her people in multiple wars against the Portuguese. But, of course, she was also involved in slave trade and sold numerous Africans directly to the ships, cutting out the Portuguese middlemen. See Linda M. Heywood, *Njinga of Angola: Africa's Warrior Queen* (London: Harvard University Press, 2017).

29 Henry Rowley (ed.), *Speeches on Missions by the Right Reverend Samuel Wilberforce* (London: William Wells Gardner, 1874), p. 213.

30 Rowley, *Speeches on Missions*, p. 177.

31 Rowley, *Speeches on Missions*, p. 56.

32 Rowley, *Speeches on Missions*, p. 199.

33 Rowley, *Speeches on Missions*, p. 218.

34 Rowley, *Speeches on Missions*, p. 143.

35 Four years after the conference, European nations that had been Christians for centuries sparked the First World War and dragged their colonies around Africa and Asia to take sides and engage in the fight.

36 John R. Mott, *The Evangelization of the World in this Generation* (New York: Student Volunteer Movement for Foreign Missions, 1900).

37 Chapter 2 of Commission IV of the conference (coming after a brief general 'Introduction' that made its Chapter 1) was dedicated to discussing the African problem of 'Animistic Religions'. World Missionary Conference 1910, *Report on Commission IV: The Missionary Message in Relation to Non-Christian Religions* (Edinburgh: Anderson & Ferrier Oliphant, 1910).

38 Brian Stanley, *The World Missionary Conference, Edinburgh 1910* (Grand Rapids, MI: Eerdmans, 2009), p. 13 (my emphasis). However, Stanley also observes that there was none present at Edinburgh 'from the Christian communities of the Pacific Islands or the Caribbean, or any representative of the North American missionary presence in Latin America, or from the tribal peoples of the Southeast Asia, some of whom already had significant and rapidly growing Christian communities'.

39 Harold Fickett, *The Ralph D. Winter Story: How One Man Dared to Shake Up World Missions* (Littleton, CO: William Carey Publishing, 2013).

40 The commercialization of mission was about to be maximized – in a few short years, mission would become big business. The imperialism of the United States was more ideological than physical and thus radically different from that of the Europeans.

41 Five hundred years of violent white supremacy in the form of slavery and colonialism makes this an easy task.

42 For example, Fuller Theological Seminary was established in 1947 to train evangelists and missionaries.

43 Time, 'Religion: A Challenge from Evangelicals', *Time*, 5 August 1974, https://time.com/archive/6817127/religion-a-challenge-from-evangelicals/, accessed 25.03.2025.

44 See Lars Dahle, Margunn Serigstad Dahle and Knud Jørgensen (eds), *The Lausanne Movement: A Range of Perspectives*, vol. 22 (Oxford: Regnum, 2014).

45 Robert A. Hunt, 'The History of the Lausanne Movement, 1974–2010', *International Bulletin of Missionary Research* 35, no. 2 (2011), p. 82.

46 Time, 'Religion: A Challenge from Evangelicals'.

47 James Dixon Douglas (ed.), *Let the Earth Hear His Voice: International Congress on World Evangelization, Lausanne, Switzerland [16–25 July 1974]. Official Reference Volume, Papers and Responses* (Minneapolis, MN: World Wide Publications, 1975).

48 Lausanne Movement, 'The Lausanne Covenant', accessible at https://lausanne.org/statement/lausanne-covenant, accessed 23.04.2025.

49 John Gatu had pushed the subject of the moratorium on mission into the limelight in 1971.

50 https://lausanne.org/global-analysis/lausanne-74, accessed 23.04.2025.

51 In 2024, 50 years after the first International Congress of Lausanne, the fourth Lausanne Conference took place in Seoul, South Korea, with more than 5,000 delegates in attendance.

52 For example, see the work of the International Fellowship for Mission as Transformation (INFEMIT), https://infemit.org/, accessed 23.04.2025.

53 John Dominic Crossan, *God and Empire: Jesus against Rome, Then and Now* (San Francisco, CA: Harper Collins, 2007), p. 3.

54 The father of African Evangelicalism, Byang Kato, made his name by attacking fellow African theologians, calling them universalist syncretists. His book *Theological Pitfalls in Africa* (which came out of his doctoral studies) is, above all else, a brutal takedown of Bolaji Idowu and John Mbiti (largely for their appreciative position on African religious heritage). With a Foreword written by Billy Graham, it had the ultimate Evangelical rubber stamp. See Byang H. Kato, *Theological Pitfalls in Africa* (Kisumu, Kenya: Evangel, 1975).

55 Elizabeth Dias, 'Christianity Will Have Power', *The New York Times*, 13 August 2020, https://www.nytimes.com/2020/08/09/us/evangelicals-trump-christianity.html, accessed 23.04.2025 (my emphasis).

56 Donald Leroy Stults, *Grasping Truth and Reality: Lesslie Newbigin's Theology of Mission to the Western World* (Cambridge: James Clarke, 2009), pp. 35–6. It is worth noting, however, that the realization of a post-Christian Europe goes far back into the twentieth century to 1943 when Henri Godin and Yvan Daniel published *La France, Pays de Mission?* This book was the first serious study to destroy the geographical myth of mission, describing Europe as a pagan milieu. Godin and Daniel shocked the Christian world by their radical pronouncement that France had become a mission field, a country of neo-pagans in the grip of atheism, secularism, unbelief and superstition. See Henri Godin and Yvan Daniel, *La France, Pays de Mission?*, Rencontres (Lyon: Éditions de l'Abeille, 1943). Also see David J. Bosch, *Transforming Mission: Paradigm Shifts in Theology of Mission*, American Society of Missiology Series (Maryknoll, NY: Orbis Books, 1991), pp. 3, 10.

57 Lesslie Newbigin, *Unfinished Agenda: An Autobiography* (Geneva: WCC Publications, 1985), p. 249.

58 Newbigin, *Unfinished Agenda*, p. 249.

59 Lesslie Newbigin, *Foolishness to the Greeks: The Gospel and Western Culture* (Grand Rapids, MI: Eerdmans, 1986); Lesslie Newbigin, *The Gospel in a Pluralist Society* (Grand Rapids, MI: Eerdmans, 1989).

60 See Lesslie Newbigin, *The Other Side of 1984: Questions for the Churches* (Geneva: World Council of Churches, 1983).

61 Darrell L. Guder (ed.), *Missional Church: A Vision for the Sending of the Church in North America* (Grand Rapids, MI: Eerdmans, 1998).

62 For people interested in exploring the concept of *missio Dei* and the missional church conversation, the same key names shape most of their discourse, whether in Europe or North America – Karl Barth, Darrell Guder, Craig van Gelder, Chris Wright and many others. Another group that would be interesting to discuss focuses on church growth and church revitalization in the West (particularly a big issue in North America) and is led by the works of Donald McGavran, C. Peter Wagner and to some extent Lyle Schaller. This group focuses on what churches and their leaders need to do to grow their membership numerically. It seeks to stem the ongoing exodus of numerous people from the Church primarily through better strategies for church marketing.

63 Newbigin, *Foolishness to the Greeks*, p. 147.

64 The most interesting conversations I have heard about this involved European Christians who want to talk about spirituality but do not really believe that spirits exist.

65 Andrew F. Walls, *The Cross-cultural Process in Christian History: Studies in the Transmission and Appropriation of Faith* (Maryknoll, NY: Orbis Books, 2002), pp. 85–6.

66 Timothy C. Tennent, *Theology in the Context of World Christianity: How the Global Church is Influencing the Way We Think About and Discuss Theology* (Grand Rapids, MI: Zondervan, 2007), p. 17.

67 For a fuller argument on how globalization and theology relate, see Joerg Rieger, *Globalization and Theology*, Horizons in Theology (Nashville, TN: Abingdon, 2010). Also see Philip Jenkins, *The Next Christendom: The Coming of Global Christianity*, 3rd edn (New York: Oxford University Press, 2011). Some readers may also love to see Soong-Chan Rah, *The Next Evangelicalism: Releasing the Church from Western Cultural Captivity* (Downers Grove, IL: IVP Books, 2009).

68 The word 'animism' comes from the Latin *anima*, which means 'soul'. See Tylor, *Primitive Culture*, pp. 1, 426. In a footnote Tylor explained: 'The term has been especially used to denote the doctrine of [Georg Ernst] Stahl, the promulgator also of the phlogiston-theory. The animism of Stahl is a revival and development in modern scientific shape of the classic theory identifying vital principle and soul.' For more on Georg Stahl, see Georg Ernst Stahl, *Theoria Medica Vera* (Orphanotropheus, 1737). For more on animism, see Janheinz Jahn, *Muntu: An Outline of Neo-African Culture* (London: Faber & Faber, 1961).

69 Tylor, *Primitive Culture*. Chapter 11 of the first volume is entitled 'Animism' and discusses in great detail his cultural evolutionary theory. A summary version of his argument appears as an excerpt in Michael Lambek, *A Reader in the Anthropology of Religion*, and that shorter essay, written by Tylor himself, informs this paragraph. See Lambek, *A Reader in the Anthropology of Religion*, 2nd edn (Malden, MA: Blackwell Publishers, 2008).

70 Lambek, *A Reader in the Anthropology of Religion*, p. 25.

71 Lambek, *A Reader in the Anthropology of Religion*, p. 26.

72 Lambek, *A Reader in the Anthropology of Religion*, p. 26.

73 Lambek, *A Reader in the Anthropology of Religion*, p. 26.

74 Samuel Baker, 'The Races of the Nile Basin', in *Transactions of the Ethnological Society of London* (London: John Murray, 1867), p. 231.

75 Edward Burnett Tylor, 'On the Survival of Savage Thought in Modern Civilization', *Notes on the Proceedings at the Meetings of the Royal Institute* 5 (1869), p. 523 (my emphasis).

76 Graham Harvey, *The Handbook of Contemporary Animism* (London: Routledge, 2014), p. 18.

77 World Missionary Conference 1910, *Report on Commission IV*, p. 6.

78 World Missionary Conference 1910, *Report on Commission 1: Carrying the Gospel to All the Non-Christian World* (Edinburgh: Oliphant, Anderson & Ferrier, 1910), pp. 84, 204.

79 World Missionary Conference 1910, *Report on Commission 1*, p. 20.

80 World Missionary Conference 1910, *Report on Commission 1*, p. 21.

81 World Missionary Conference 1910, *Report on Commission 1*, p. 21.

82 Tippu Tib was a ruthless slave trader who, for a season, worked with Henry Morton Stanley on his voyage from Zanzibar to the mouth of the Congo River.

83 William Charles Willoughby, *The Soul of the Bantu: A Sympathetic Study*

of the Magico-religious Practices and Beliefs of the Bantu Tribes of Africa (Garden City, NY: Doubleday, 1928), pp. 9–10.

84 Willoughby, *The Soul of the Bantu*, p. 1.

85 Teresia Mbari Hinga, 'Inculturation and the Otherness of Africa and Africans: Some Reflections', in Frans J. S. Wijsen and Peter Turkson (eds), *Inculturation: Abide by the Otherness of Africa and the Africans* (Kampen: Kok, 1994).

86 John S. Mbiti, *African Religions and Philosophy* (London: Heinemann, 1969), p. 10. Many African theologians have argued that the term 'animism' is too pejorative and colonial and that it should not be used in our world today. That said, the word has experienced a resurgence of some kind in the first quarter of the twenty-first century. Some Africans have reclaimed the word to describe the spirit-centred Christianity they want. A key proponent of this argument is the Jesuit theologian Agbon Orobator, who chooses to proudly own the term and argue that Christianity that is contextualized for the African peoples must be animist. See Agbon E. Orobator, *Religion and Faith in Africa: Confessions of an Animist* (Maryknoll, NY: Orbis Books, 2018). His upbringing in African religion exposed him to faith practices that can only work in the context of a spiritually charged world. He understands Christianity to have room for such expressions and wants to claim it for himself and others so inclined. He wants to be an animistic Christian. Of course, he is right. A properly contextualized Christianity in Africa must attend to the cultural sensibilities of Africans, and these are without a doubt grounded in a spirit-centred world view.

87 Johannes N. J. Kritzinger and Harvey Kwiyani, 'The Place of Missiology as a Theological Discipline in Africa', in Johannes Knoetze (ed.), *Mission: The Labour Room of Theology* (Wellington, RSA: CLF Publishers, 2022).

8

Mission According to the Colonized

There is too much failure among all Europeans in Nyasaland. The Three Combined Bodies: Missionaries, Government and Companies or Gainers of money do form the same rule to look upon a Native with mockery eyes. It sometimes startles us to see that the Three Combined Bodies are from Europe, and along with them there is a title 'CHRISTNDOM.' And to compare or make a comparison between the MASTER of the title and His Servants, it pushes any African away from believing the Master of the title. If we had power enough to communicate ourselves to Europe, we would advise them not to call themselves 'CHRISTNDOM' but 'Europeandom' ... Therefore the life of The Three Combined Bodies is altogether too cheaty, too thefty, too mockery. Instead of 'Give,' they say 'Take away from'.[1]

In this chapter, I intend to discuss some of the critical ways non-Westerners look at the missionary enterprise of the past 200 years. I am not seeking to deconstruct the act of sharing the gospel itself (as some have done).[2] Christ called us to make disciples for him in all nations. However, it is how this sharing of the gospel was done – in addition to the language that was used – that is the focus of this chapter. Primarily this chapter intends to burst the *echo chamber* that is home to our Western missiological discourse. Since the late 1800s many Christians worldwide have been critical of the marriage between mission and colonialism. Africans have certainly been vocal about the detrimental effect of colonial mission among their people. Most of the Africans who wrote about the presence of Western missionaries in Africa towards the end of the colonial era – when the number of Western-educated Africans reached a critical mass that could publish fictional and academic books on the African – were critical of the enterprise.

Can you hear us?

A Kenyan philosopher, Ali Mazrui, once said, 'Americans are brilliant communicators but bad listeners.'[3] He might as well have generalized this to include all Westerners. It would still be true, though of course to be a brilliant communicator one must be a good listener too. Generally speaking, when interacting with people from Africa, Asia and Latin America, Westerners expect to be listened to – they need to be the ones speaking, teaching and directing; non-Westerners exist to be spoken to, taught and directed. This is even more evident in Christian communities where the attitude of Western supremacist ideas still shapes the ways world Christians relate to one another. The almighty West is always right. In theology, for example, there is a longstanding tendency to treat Western theology as always correct. It is often taken to be context-free and universal. It is therefore expected to speak to all Christians worldwide without regard to where they are and what contextual and cultural issues shape their existence. Despite being products of particular European contexts centuries ago, the writings of Thomas Aquinas, John Calvin and Martin Luther continue to be treated as universally normative for all Christians. This tendency not only marginalizes but often devalues theological voices emerging from other parts of the world, reinforcing a Eurocentric hierarchy within global Christianity. The burden placed upon Western theology to do this, and upon those employed to enforce compliance, is too ambitious to be tenable. Yet this is how it goes. Many African, Asian and Latin American students of Christian theology are expected to internalize the works of European and North American theologians without attending deeply to the theological issues bothering their own peoples back home.[4]

It was John Mbiti who once lamented to Western theologians, 'We have eaten your theology, can you eat ours with us?'

> We have eaten theology with you; we have drunk theology with you; we have dreamed theology with you. But it has all been one-sided, it has all been, in a sense, your theology. We know you theologically. The question is, do you know us theologically? Would you like to know us theologically? Can you know us theologically? ... It is utterly scandalous for so many Christian scholars in older Christendom to know so much about heretical movements in the second and third centuries when so few of them know anything about Christian movements in areas of the younger churches.[5]

I am confident that one of the challenges that face us in mission today is simply communication, especially because a great deal of it goes in one direction. Westerners talk while everyone else must listen and obey. Many believe that this is what they are called to do. As long as they have proclaimed the gospel, it matters less whether the communication has really happened or not; they have done their work. While some of this is rooted in white/Western supremacy – what can the Africans teach us? – a great deal is simply lack of patience and vulnerability. Slowing down to listen to people requires certain human attributes that are scarce in many Western cultures. But to listen to people is to *see* them as people, to engage them in their vulnerabilities, which always requires that we stay vulnerable with one another. Many Westerners cannot do this, especially with people from other cultures and ethnicities. So following John Mbiti, I wonder: Can you eat our missiology with us? Not only that. The more pressing question for me to my Western missions community is this: Can you hear us in your bubbles? I am sure if you heard us you would know that a lot of what you do and call mission does not work.

'Mission' in twentieth-century African novels

Fiction writers such as Alan Paton, Chinua Achebe and Ngũgĩ wa Thiong'o told stories deeply critical of the missionaries. Alan Paton's novel, *Cry, the Beloved Country*[6] (published just months before apartheid became law in South Africa in 1948), is a heartbreaking story of how the missionaries – and white people in general – justified white supremacy and racism to oppress South Africans. Chinua Achebe's book, *Things Fall Apart*[7] (published in 1958), is an eloquent telling of how British missionaries disrupted the Igbo way of life and prepared the people of Umuofia of Nigeria for colonization. Ngũgĩ wa Thiong'o's novel, *The River Between*[8] (published in 1961), is a scathing critique of how the missionaries divided and conquered an otherwise united and strong community to take over their land and destroy their culture.

Critiquing colonialism and Christian mission in Africa seems to have been the main purpose of the African Writers' Series that was housed at Makerere University in Uganda (which, during the 1950s and 1960s, was serving the entire region as a college of the University of East Africa), providing ideological tools for the mental emancipation of Africa. Makerere provided the vibrant literary culture that produced some of the most celebrated postcolonial African writers of the twentieth century.[9] It was the literary powerhouse where a young academic faculty gathered around an even younger student body to wrestle with the issues that would dismantle colonialism's cultural legacy and shape the continent's liberated minds as its countries became independent.[10] It hosted the first African Writers' Conference in 1962. In attendance were such renowned writers as Chinua Achebe, Wole Soyinka, Obi Wali, Gabriel Okara,

Bernard Fonlon, Frances Ademola, Cameron Duodu, Kofi Awoonor, Ezekiel Mphahlele, Bloke Modisane, Lewis Nkosi, Arthur Maimane, Ngũgĩ wa Thiong'o, Robert Serumaga, Rajat Neogy, Okot p'Bitek, Pio Zirimu, Grace Ogot, Rebecca Njau, David Rubadiri, Jonathan Kariara and Langston Hughes. Each one of these names is a celebrated writer – between them, readers have access to the early discourse of postcolonial theory in East Africa. It was the Mecca where young Africans learned to claim their identity and dignity and to unmask the many lies of the Europeans who sought to keep the continent colonized, at least intellectually. Makerere was for some time an educational home to many of Africa's prominent writers of the 1960s, including Okot p'Bitek, Ali Mazrui, David Rubadiri, Okello Oculi, Ngũgĩ wa Thiong'o, John Ruganda, Paul Theroux, V. S. Naipaul and Peter Nazareth. In a nutshell, Makerere was central to the growing sense of nationalism that provided ideological foundations for the struggle for independence and decolonization of African thought. Its critique could not be complete without wrestling with the role of the missionaries in the colonial project.

Consequently, African fiction from the 1950s and 1960s is filled with narratives that expose the harmful impacts of both missionary activity and colonial rule – realities that for many Africans were inseparable and experienced as two sides of the same oppressive system. Just as the missionary enterprise was closely associated with the imperial expansion of the West, in African literature the word 'missionary' was also attached to this expansion effort and, as writers like Mongo Beti suggest, was often taken to imply 'the earliest foot-soldiers of colonial empires' or 'colonial administrators'.[11] Indeed, we could pick up almost any book from that era to find a scathing critique not only of European colonialism in Africa but also the missionaries. For instance, we could look at Ferdinand Oyono's 1956 French novel, *Une Vie de Boy* (translated to English in 1966), which offers a strong critique of both colonialism and Christianity.[12]

It is Mongo Beti's critique of Roman Catholic missionary work in Cameroon in *The Poor Christ of Bomba* – first published in French under as *Le Pauvre Christ de Bomba* in 1956 and translated into English in 1971 – that I find the most telling. Beti tells of the work of one Father Drumont, a Catholic missionary who served at Bomba. The book describes life and ministry as a missionary from the eyes of Father Drumont's servant, Dennis. Characteristic of many missionaries of his era, Drumont did the best he could to convert Africans and persuade them away from polygamy, but he also made some grave mistakes in the process, such as unleashing physical violence on his subjects when he lost his temper. However, it is Drumont's refusal to help the French colonists overrun Bomba that makes him stand out. When he reached the end of his 20 years of missionary work in Cameroon, after constant colonial upheaval in his region, Father Drumont told Monsieur Vidal, a newly arrived colonial administrator:

> I can stay in this country along with you, associated with you, and thus *assist you to colonize it, with dreadful consequences; softening up the country ahead of you*, and *protecting your rear* – for that is how you envisage [my role]. Or else, I can truly Christianize the country; in which case I'd better keep out of the way, as long as you are still here.[13]

With this, Father Drumont retired and returned to Europe, leaving the French to run wild in Cameroon. Such misunderstandings and confrontations were common between missionaries and colonialists. Some missionaries would cave in to the demands of the colonialists. Others would fight against them, while many like Father Drumont ended up leaving the mission field. However, in the eyes of most Africans, this association of the missionaries with the colonialists would permanently taint the identity of the missionary.

'Mission' in mid-twentieth-century African theological discourse

In African academic theological literature from the twentieth century, the critique of mission and colonialism can be seen in the discourse around African identity within the Christian faith. African theology begins to emerge in the 1940s and 1950s with people like Bolaji Idowu and John Mbiti writing about African religion. Admittedly, African theologians were only a handful compared to the many writers focused on general fiction. In addition, almost all African theologians were under Western tutelage until the 1960s, and Western missionary leadership in African Christianity stayed on until the 1970s. As African scholars they sought ways to decolonize both their identities and their Christianity. One of the most-asked questions of that era was: 'How can one be a Christian and an African at the same time?' To help Africans answer this question, they studied African religious heritage (which for centuries had been either denied, dismissed or demonized by the missionaries). The African is notoriously religious, declared Mbiti in his book, *African Religions and Philosophy*.[14] With that one statement, Mbiti – who was an Anglican priest – erased centuries of colonial and missionary misunderstanding of African peoples and their cultures.

The study of African religious heritage was for these African theologians a way of decolonizing their identity and Christianity. Courses in African traditional religion were first offered at the University of Ibadan in Nigeria in the late 1940s by a British Methodist missionary, Geoffrey Parrinder, who established and led the programme in African traditional religion at Ibadan until 1958.[15] Bolaji Idowu (1913–93), a Nigerian Methodist minister whose doctoral thesis Parrinder had supervised at the University of London in 1955, took over in 1958 and led the programme until 1976. Both Parrinder and Idowu focused most of their work on the religious heritage of the Yoruba people of south-west Nigeria. Parrinder's outstanding works, among many, include *West African Religion*[16] and *African Traditional Religions*,[17] published in 1949 and 1954 respectively. Idowu is a legendary figure in Nigerian scholarship on African religion. His published works include *Olodumare: God in Yoruba Belief* (1962)[18] and *African Traditional Religion* (1973).[19]

The collapse of the colonial empires in the 1960s showed that Africans could lead themselves politically. If Africans could lead nations, they should be able to lead their churches. Not long after, African church leaders began to agitate for their own ecclesial independence. Dana Robert observes, 'The process of decolonisation and independence began severing the connection between Christianity and European colonialism. The repudiation of missionary paternalism, combined with expanding indigenous initiatives, freed Christianity to be more at home in local situations.'[20] The contextualization of Christianity on the continent, as well as its rejection of European leadership, produced a type of Christianity radically different from the one that was brought by the missionaries. Daniel Jeyaraj observes:

> The process of decolonization facilitated the growth of non-Western Christianity. Non-Western Christian leaders were no longer restrained by their Western colonial masters, who for economic gains, have overtly been supporting the interests of non-Christian counterparts. Finally, these non-Western leaders were free to bear witness ... By critically reclaiming their pre-Christian heritages embodied in primal religions, they initiated a new kind of Christian indigenization that continues unabated, for example, in countless AICs and in the Pentecostal and Charismatic movements.[21]

The decolonization of the African Church took much longer than that of the political colonies. The missionaries did not trust that Africans – called the 'younger churches' – were mature enough to stand on their own feet. By the time the political decolonization of Africa reached its peak in the

1960s, native sentiments towards missionaries in Africa had generally also become antagonistic. The missionaries had usually collaborated with the colonial agents, and the atrocities of the colonial governments were often associated with the missionaries. Adrian Hastings said that by 1970 it had become clear that the foreign missionary was essentially irrelevant in Africa; the Western missionary enterprise had become more marginal to African Christianity than ever before.[22] 'The supreme concern of the foreign missionary must be to help get the local church firmly on its own two feet as quickly, as ruthlessly as is possible: to bring to a rapid end both the appearance and the reality of ecclesiastical colonialism.'[23] Many foreign missionary leaders returned to Europe and North America, feeling rejected by the very people they had discipled. Others remained, clinging to power under the belief that Africans were not yet ready for leadership. In time, African leaders were compelled to wrest control of their own churches from missionary oversight. Thus, the future of African Christianity was placed firmly in the hands of African leadership. E. Bolaji Idowu explained: 'The inherent urge to freedom and self-expression which resides in a man will bring about rebellion against any form of bondage.'[24] Phil Jenkins correctly observed that 'It was precisely as Western colonialism ended that Christianity began a period of explosive growth that still continues unchecked in Africa.'[25] John Mbiti, quoted in 1971 in a *New York Times* article, stated 'The days are over when we will be carbon copies of European Christians. Europe and America westernized Christianity. The Orthodox easternized it. Now it's our turn to Africanize it.'[26]

John Gatu and the moratorium

In October 1971 the General Secretary of the Presbyterian Church of East Africa, John Gatu of Kenya, shocked the missions world when he suggested that no missionaries or money should be sent to Africa for at least five years – later he said for good – at a missions festival in Milwaukee.[27] The main thrust of the moratorium was that the European and North American churches should stop sending missionaries and money to Africa and other non-Western churches, 'so that the short man could learn to hang his knapsack within reach'.[28] He went on to suggest a withdrawal of all Western missionaries from Africa:

> The time has come for the withdrawal of the foreign missionaries from many parts of the Third World, that the churches of the Third World must be allowed to find their own identity and that the continuation

of the present missionary movement is a hindrance to this selfhood of the church.[29]

He continued:

> We cannot build the church in Africa on alms given by overseas churches. Nor are we serving the cause of the Kingdom by turning all bishops, general secretaries, moderators, presidents, and general superintendents into good enthusiastic beggars, always singing the tune of poverty in the churches of the third world.[30]

Later on he added: 'We must ask missionaries to leave ... I started by saying that the missionaries should be withdrawn from the Third World for a period of at least five years. I will go further and say that the missionaries should be withdrawn, period.'[31]

These ideas about a moratorium had been in circulation for quite a while before Gatu brought them to Milwaukee. Adrian Hastings says that the concept of the moratorium had initially been suggested by Walter Freytag in 1958 and had been discussed on several platforms since then.[32] The Philippine missionary theologian Emerito Nacpil spoke about the 'death of mission' in 1971 when he made a famous speech in Kuala Lumpur, declaring that 'The present structure of modern mission is dead. ... The first thing we ought to do is eulogize it and then bury it. ... The most *missionary* service that a missionary under the present system can do today to Asia is to go home!'[33] He further stated:

> I have asked many young people what they see when they see a missionary. They tell me that when they see a missionary, they see green – the color of the mighty dollar. They see white, the color of Western imperialism and racism. They see an expert, the symbol of Western technology and gadgetry. They see the face of a master, the mirror of their own servitude. They do not see the face of a suffering Christ but a benevolent monster which must be tamed because it can become useful for their own convenience. In some instances, they do not even see a man but a CIA agent who must be crushed. The young people in my own country have a name for missionaries and ecclesiastics. They call them 'clerico-fascists.'[34]

In addition to Emerito Nacpil, Gerald Anderson adds two other voices calling for the moratorium in the early 1970s. The first one is Father Paul Verghese, a former associate general secretary of the World Council of Churches and principal of an Orthodox theological seminary in India, who said:

> Today, it is economic imperialism or neocolonialism that is the pattern of missions. Relief agencies and mission boards control the younger churches through purse strings. Foreign finances, ideas and personnel still dominate the younger churches and stifle their spontaneous growth ... So now I say, the mission of the church is the greatest enemy of the gospel.[35]

The second one is José Miguez-Bonino, who was at the time the dean of Union Theological Seminary in Buenos Aires, Argentina. He had this to say:

> We in the younger churches have to learn the discipline of freedom to accept and to refuse, to place resources at the service of mission rather than to have mission patterned by resources ... We cannot, for the love of our brethren or for the love of God, let anybody or anything stand in the way of our taking on our own shoulders our responsibility. If, in order to do that, we must say to you, our friends, 'Stay home,' we will do so because before God we have this grave responsibility of our integrity.[36]

The moratorium debate lasted more than five years. Gatu met resistance from all directions, both on theological and humanitarian grounds. Westerners misunderstood him, thinking he was calling for the separation of African Christian communities from those of the West, and telling Western mission agencies that Africa did not need them any more. Wade Coggins concluded that 'This moratorium call proved very attractive to some large denominational missions that are already in trouble because lay revolt against their radical political adventures has dried up a large part of their missionary resources.'[37] In addition, Peter Wagner likened the moratorium to 'the proverbial bulldog with rubber teeth', because the All Africa Conference of Churches (AACC) received 80 per cent of its budget from overseas.[38] Fellow Africans argued that they needed interdependence, not independence. For instance, Pius Wakatama's book *Independence for the Third World Church*, published in 1976, explores the moratorium to a great depth. First, he calls Gatu's call a 'selective moratorium'.[39] Later, he added that Odunaike, then president of the Association of Evangelicals of Africa and Madagascar, rejected the moratorium outright, stating: 'We completely resist the idea of a moratorium on missionaries in Africa. How can we talk like this when our governments are actively soliciting economic, technical, and educational aid from overseas?'[40] Another African leader, Mutombo Mpanya, rejected the moratorium, saying:

the solution is not independence as it may be possible to think, but interdependence. The choice is between the relation of domination and a Christian brotherhood or sisterhood. Interdependence means that Christian churches in central Africa need 'partners not patrons, brothers not benefactors.' It means a relationship that should allow an authentic African Christianity to develop and reflect African life and thought without being mothered by its western influence.[41]

In the end the decolonization of African Christianity was never really realized. Even today, in the twenty-first century, African Christianity remains too dependent on foreign help. It cannot be realized while the theology that shapes us was written by Westerners – especially from North America – for other Westerners. Nevertheless the moratorium made possible conversations, especially among Majority World Christians, encouraging them to engage in mission. There were loud discussions on whether cross-cultural mission is biblically mandated for white people only. Non-Western Christians began to wonder if the missionary nature of the Church was imparted to them as well. Were the Christians from the 'younger churches' also mandated to be missionaries, both in their own world and in the West? Gatu himself argued:

> How much longer can we continue to ask our friends to come to evangelise our northern frontier? Is it not time that we should be thinking of organising ourselves – with our own money and personnel, to reach the frontiers of Europe and America, where church membership is declining?[42]

As a result, part of the outcome of the moratorium debate was the emergence of missionary movements among the nations. The moratorium generated the reverse-flow concept, grounded its rationale and determined its characteristics.[43] Later, at the AACC in Lusaka in 1974, under the leadership of Burgess Carr, it was stated:

> To enable the African Church to achieve the power of being a true instrument of liberating and reconciling the African people, as well as finding solutions to economic and social dependency, our option as a matter of policy has to be a moratorium on external assistance in money and personnel. We recommend this option as the only potent means of becoming truly and authentically ourselves while remaining a respected and responsible part of the Universal Church.[44]

Third World churches began to gain confidence that they also had the mandate to do missionary work, both among themselves and in the West.

Indeed, most of the non-Western missionaries are serving in the non-Western world. However, thousands of non-Western Christians are now living and serving God in the West as well. Most of them are serving their own communities in the diaspora. For instance, John Gatu's congregation sent missionaries to London at the end of the 1970s. The Lutheran World Federation sent five pastors from Tanzania to work in Europe in 1982. Kalu reports that these missionaries 'were received politely and patronised',[45] a reality experienced by many African Christians in Europe until today.

Evangelical mission and the African Church

Looking back at the past seven decades it is rather evident that as the European Christian leaders were returning to Europe, North American Christians stepped in to influence African Christianity. A great deal of that influence came through the North American Evangelical movement. Of course, there were thousands of missionaries from the United States and Canada operating in different parts of Africa from the 1800s, but they often took a back seat to the work of the European missionaries whose colonial governments were in charge. Many more American missionaries came to Africa in the wake of the Pentecostal revival that connected the developments that took place at Azusa Street in 1906 to the rising of spirit-empowered African independent churches in Ghana, Nigeria, Congo and South Africa. To some extent, during the era of 80 years of European colonialism in Africa, American missionary activity was limited. With European colonial governments in charge, American missionaries usually followed the work of their European counterparts. Even in Liberia, which was never colonized by any European country, British missionaries were present and highly admired.[46]

Starting in the 1970s, largely through the work of Byang Kato, American Evangelicalism gained ground in Africa. In the broader context of the Christian faith in the continent, Christianity was at that point flourishing in two primary expressions. The first was missionary-established and missionary-led churches, divided along the lines of Western denominationalism. In this group were mainline churches such as Methodists, Anglicans, Presbyterians, Seventh-Day Adventists and many others. Most of these were European in origin. Some of those who came from North America had strong European heritage too. For example, the Methodist Episcopal Church, which was quite active in Congo, had its origin in North America but was shaped by the English theological sensibilities of John Wesley.

In the other camp was a type of church pejoratively called African Independent Churches, which were deemed to be rogue and unorthodox for refusing white leadership and Western theology. African Independent Churches were mostly founded by charismatic leaders wanting to make connections between Christianity and the African religious cultural heritage. For many of them, religion only made sense if it helped them access the spiritual world, and missionary Christianity did not do this for them.[47] There were millions of Christians in these churches but for the entire 80 years of European colonization of Africa their numbers were never certain as they were not easily accessible to the missionaries and the colonial agents.[48] Their explosion was hidden; it took place away from the Western gaze. As soon as the colonial empires crumbled, many of these churches came out to become members of the Christian mainstream, joining the Pentecostal and Charismatic movements – because of their spirit-centred communal ecclesiology – and adding their numbers to the Christian population that was already exploding under African leadership. Some, generally a minority, remained in Zionist and Ethiopian types of African independent churches where they continue to *Africanize* Christianity.[49] That said, many African independent churches simply joined the Pentecostal and Charismatic movement and transformed themselves to become just like any other church in that tradition. A good example of such a church is the Redeemed Christian Church of God, the largest Pentecostal Church in Africa (its presence reaches at least 197 countries in the world today). It started out as an African independent church.

In the 1960s and 70s, when European leadership of the Church in colonial Africa was brought to an abrupt end, there was a chance for North American Evangelicals to step in to take over the discipleship of the continent. Without caring about the contextual realities of the Africans, many North American Evangelicals taught what they know to be (Reformed) evangelical theology and, in doing so, they formed much of African Christian identity in their own image. They found African leaders who would champion the cause for them, blurring the line between Pentecostals and Evangelicals, in most cases making the former adopt the latter's identity without really knowing its implications. (The identity of an African Evangelical often looks so much like that of a Western Christian that it begs the question of whether it is indeed possible to be an African and an Evangelical Christian at the same time.)

North American Evangelicals taught their ways of sharing the gospel and calling people to 'ask Christ into their hearts to become their Lord and Saviour'. Their evangelism strategies were made for a Western context where culture is generally shaped by individualism and people need to hear a logical explanation of the gospel to convert. Africans took those strategies, contextualized them for a spirit-orientated communal culture (by adding prayer and fasting to them, for instance), and for oral communities that largely communicate through stories and proverbs, and used them to evangelize their own communities with great success. They did not call this 'mission', neither did they identify themselves as 'missionaries'. Both those terms are usually reserved for Westerners who come to work in Africa. For many Africans, most of what we call 'mission' is simply evangelism and pastoral ministry. African missionaries are, generally speaking, pastors and evangelists.

Often when Africans engage in *mission* (actually using the word 'mission'), they try to do everything they see their Western counterparts do – *and they consider this to be mission, totally different from their everyday work in evangelism and pastoral ministry*. What Westerners do – or have done in the past centuries – is what Africans call mission. As a result, when Africans engage in *mission* they try to make it look Western.[50] In many cases they will often be just as colonial, territorial and tribal as their Western counterparts. Kenyan mission agencies, if we can call them that, are different from Nigerian agencies as well as Ghanaian agencies, and they have minimal connections between them. Where they work in the same context they hardly collaborate because the colonial fault lines are still in place. Many African agencies will attempt to discredit other people's cultures in order to impose their own, just as Westerners did among them. They tend to believe that their type of Christianity is the best and should be normative and universal. They often find it difficult to accommodate fellow Africans in their churches and spend considerable energy trying to convince Westerners that aspects of their culture – like the pub in the UK – are evil. Finally, they also tend to use the militaristic language that shapes a great deal of Western missiology. Mission for them is still about conquering even though many of them have no idea what military might looks like. They know they cannot conquer other peoples militarily and so they focus on spiritual conquest.

Essentially, contemporary mission talk among African Christians began to take shape as North American Evangelical influence gained traction on the continent. While the All African Conference of Churches was taking place up in Lusaka in 1974, the Association of Evangelicals in Africa had just been established in Nairobi, with Byang Kato himself installed as its first General Secretary (while finishing his doctorate degree at Dallas Theological Seminary). He came to fame when he published his polemical book, *Theological Pitfalls in Africa*,[51] in which he sought to discredit other African theologians at the time – John Mbiti and Bolaji Idowu – for being too liberal and encouraging what he called syncretism. It came with the highest recommendations anyone in Evangelical circles could ever hope for. Its Foreword was written by Billy Graham. Kato was directly connected to the throne room of Evangelicalism and was on track to reshape African Christianity. As African Christianity came of age, with the missionaries dislodged from their powerful positions and African independent churches coming out into the open in droves and beginning to pentecostalize the faith throughout the continent, it all had to be *Evangelical*. Unfortunately, Kato died in 1975 at the young age of 39. His influence continues to shape African Christianity today and numerous people have worked hard over the decades to assume his mantle.

A Pentecostal missiology emerges

African Pentecostalism has always been torn between its own African identity and that of its Evangelical friends who provide a great deal of the theological resources that inform it, from the United States and Canada and their brothers and sisters in the ecumenical movement of the World Council of Churches. Come to think of it, many African Pentecostals and Charismatics tick both boxes: Evangelical and ecumenical. Not that this means anything big to them because in the end, it is their Pentecostal Christian experience that matters the most. Their missiology – and this is the missiology shaping a great deal of contemporary African Christianity – takes the best of the Evangelical and ecumenical worlds, mixes it with the contextual understanding of the African world, adapts it to make it communal and charismatic (as in spirit-centred) and then democratizes it so that everyone can participate. We have what could be called the *evangelisthood* of all believers in most African countries. When all is said and done you have a lay-led missionary movement that is grounded in an understanding that it is the work of the Spirit and takes place in a spiritually charged world (and is therefore soaked in prayer and fastings), which includes all believers reaching all of their neighbourhoods and communities. It understands what John V. Taylor articulated in his book, *The Go-Between God*, that 'the Holy Spirit is the *chief actor* in mission' and that the Spirit is 'the director of the whole [missionary] enterprise'.[52] This makes African missiology somewhat different from what we see in the West.

Notes

1 Charles Domingo's letter to Joseph Booth, dated 20 September 1911, Domingo Papers, University College Library, Zomba, cited in John McCracken, *Politics and Christianity in Malawi: The Impact of the Livingstonia Mission in the Northern Province*, Kachere Monographs (Zomba: Kachere Series, 2008), p. 216.

2 I have become increasingly aware in the past ten years or so of the dilemma that many of my Western friends face on whether to continue with mission or stop engaging because of its colonial legacy. In a sense this book attempts to resolve that dilemma by suggesting that the sharing of the gospel must continue, but we must let go of our colonial ways when we go about this business of our Father in heaven.

3 Ali Al'amin Mazrui, *Cultural Forces in World Politics* (London: J. Currey, 1990), p. 116.

4 I was once profoundly shocked when a potential doctoral student from Africa walked into my office to ask me to be his supervisor. He had studied in Africa all his life until this point. His resumé looked good. He had a Bachelor of Theology degree, a Master of Theology degree and a Master of Divinity, all of which he had obtained in Africa. When I asked which African theologian he thought was his closest conversational partner, he had none. He had never really read any African theologians. When I asked why he said, 'Our professors discouraged us from reading Africans.' Those professors were also African.

5 John S. Mbiti, 'Theological Impotence and the Universality of the Church', *Lutheran World* 21, no. 3 (1974), pp. 16–17.

6 Alan Paton, *Cry, the Beloved Country: A Story of Comfort in Desolation* (New York: Scribner, 1948).

7 Chinua Achebe, *Things Fall Apart* (London: Heinemann, 1958).

8 Ngũgĩ wa Thiong'o, *The River Between* (London: Heinemann, 1965).

9 The 1960s were a very important decade in African literature and higher education, not only for Makerere University itself but also for the entire continent.

10 Seventeen African countries had gained independence in 1960 alone (including the Democratic Republic of Congo, Madagascar and Côte d'Ivoire). Four more countries (Sierra Leone, Tanzania, Nigeria and Cameroon) became independent in 1961. Another four (Burundi, Rwanda, Algeria and Uganda) gained their independence in 1962. Kenya gained its independence in 1963. Malawi and Zambia gained theirs in 1964. Seventeen more countries would gain independence between 1965 and 1980.

11 Mongo Beti, *The Poor Christ of Bomba* (Long Grove, IL: Waveland, 1971), p. 153. Also see John H. Darch, *Missionary Imperialists? Missionaries, Government and the Growth of the British Empire in the Tropics, 1860–1885* (Colorado Springs, CO: Paternoster, 2009), p. 1.

12 Ferdinand Oyono, *Houseboy*, African Writers Series (Edinburgh: Heinemann, 1966).

13 Beti, *The Poor Christ of Bomba*, p. 153 (my emphasis).

14 John S. Mbiti, *African Religions and Philosophy* (London: Heinemann, 1969), p. 1.

15 Parrinder was appointed to the highly innovative religious studies department at University College of Ibadan, Nigeria, first as lecturer (1949–50) then as senior lecturer (1950–58), teaching many African students and making lasting

friendships. The University of Ibadan was founded in 1948 as a college of the University of London.

16 Geoffrey E. Parrinder, *West African Religion* (London: Epworth Press, 1949).

17 Geoffrey E. Parrinder, *African Traditional Religion* (London: Sheldon Press, 1954).

18 E. Bolaji Idowu, *Olodumare: God in Yoruba Belief* (London: Longman, 1962).

19 E. Bolaji Idowu, *African Traditional Religion: A Definition* (London: SCM Press, 1973).

20 Dana Lee Robert, 'Shifting Southward: Global Christianity since 1945', *International Bulletin of Missionary Research* 24, no. 2 (April 2002), p. 53.

21 Daniel Jeyaraj, 'The Re-emergence of Global Christianity', in Todd. M. Johnson and Kenneth R. Ross (eds), *Atlas of Global Christianity 1910–2010* (Edinburgh: Edinburgh University Press, 2009), p. 54.

22 Adrian Hastings, *A History of African Christianity, 1950–1975*, African Studies Series 26 (Cambridge: Cambridge University Press, 1979), p. 224.

23 Adrian Hastings, *Mission and Ministry* (London: Sheed & Ward, 1971), p. 4.

24 E. Bolaji Idowu, *Towards an Indigenous Church* (Oxford: Oxford University Press, 1965), p. 41.

25 Philip Jenkins, *The Next Christendom: The Coming of Global Christianity* (New York: Oxford University Press, 2011), p. 70.

26 Edward B. Fiske, 'African Christians are Developing their Own Distinctive Theologies', *The New York Times* (1971), https://www.nytimes.com/1971/03/12/archives/african-christians-are-developing-their-own-distinctive-theologies.html, accessed 25.03.2025.

27 He tells the story of the journey to making the argument for the moratorium in his book, John G. Gatu, *Joyfully Christian, Truly African* (Nairobi: Acton Publishers, 2006). The request for a moratorium was inspired by the process of political decolonization that swept through sub-Saharan Africa in the 1960s. See Robert Reese, 'John Gatu and the Moratorium on Missionaries', *Missiology* 42, no. 3 (2014). He also rehashes the argument in his autobiography, John G. Gatu, *Fan into Flame: An Autobiography* (Nairobi: Moran Publishers, 2020).

28 Ogbu Kalu, 'The Anatomy of Reverse Flow in African Christianity: Pentecostalism and Immigrant African Christianity', in Frieder Ludwig and J. Kwabena Asamoah-Gyadu (eds), *African Christian Presence in the West: New Immigrant Congregations and Transnational Networks in North America and Europe* (Trenton, NJ: Africa World Press, 2011), p. 35.

29 Cited in Bengt Sundkler and Christopher Steed, *A History of the Church in Africa*, Studia Missionalia Upsaliensia 74 (New York: Cambridge University Press, 2000), p. 1027. Also see R. Elliott Kendall, 'On the Sending of Missionaries: A Call for Restraint', *International Review of Mission* 64, no. 253 (1975).

30 Emele Mba Uka, *Missionaries Go Home? A Sociological Interpretation of an African Response to Christian Missions* (New York: Lang, 1989), p. 192.

31 Cited in R. Elliott Kendall, *The End of an Era: Africa and the Missionary* (London: SPCK, 1978), pp. 90–1.

32 Hastings, *A History of African Christianity, 1950–1975*, p. 225.

33 Emerito P. Nacpil, 'Mission But Not Missionaries', *International Review of Mission* 60, no. 239 (1971). Also published as Emerito P. Nacpil, 'Whom Does

the Missionary Serve and What Does He Do?', in *Missionary Service in Asia Today* (Hong Kong: Chinese Christian Literature Council, 1971, emphasis original).

34 Nacpil, 'Mission But Not Missionaries', p. 359. Also see David Jacobus Bosch, *Transforming Mission: Paradigm Shifts in Theology of Mission*, American Society of Missiology Series (Maryknoll, NY: Orbis Books, 1991), p. 2.

35 Gerald H. Anderson, 'A Moratorium on Missionaries', 1974, https://www.religion-online.org/article/a-moratorium-on-missionaries/, accessed 28.05.2025.

36 Anderson, 'A Moratorium on Missionaries'.

37 Wade Coggins, 'What's Behind the Idea of a Missionary Moratorium?', *Christianity Today*, 22 November 1974, p. 8.

38 C. Peter Wagner, 'Colour the Moratorium Grey', *International Review of Mission* 64, no. 254 (1975), p. 167.

39 Pius Wakatama, *Independence for the Third World Church: An African's Perspective on Missionary Work* (Downers Grove, IL: InterVarsity Press, 1976), p. 11.

40 Pius Wakatama, 'The Role of Africans in the World Mission of the Church', *Evangelical Missions Quarterly* 26, no. 2 (1990), p. 128.

41 Mutombo Mpanya, 'Problems of the Churches in Central Africa', in Charles R. Taber (ed.), *The Church in Africa* (Pasadena, CA: William Carey, 1977).

42 Reese, 'John Gatu and the Moratorium', p. 252.

43 Ludwig and Asamoah-Gyadu, *African Christian Presence*, p. 36.

44 Hastings, *A History of African Christianity, 1950–1975*, p. 225.

45 Ludwig and Asamoah-Gyadu, *African Christian Presence*, p. 36.

46 William Wade Harris, a charismatic leader and founder of the Harrist Church in Liberia, was jailed for raising the Union Jack to show his belief that British missionaries and, indeed, British colonialism were better for Liberia. The African Christian Biography Database, 'Harris, William Wade', https://dacb.org/stories/liberia/legacy-harris/, accessed 25.03.2025.

47 See my argument in Harvey C. Kwiyani, 'Independent, Enthusiastic, and African: Reframing the Story of African Christianity', in Nimi Wariboko and Adeshina Afolayan (eds), *African Pentecostalism and World Christianity: Essays in Honor of J. Kwabena Asamoah-Gyadu* (Eugene, OR: Wipf & Stock, 2020).

48 There are numerous Zionist and Ethiopian churches in southern Africa. One of the key examples of these is the Kimbanguist Church in the Democratic Republic of Congo. For more about these, see David B. Barrett, *Schism and Renewal in Africa: An Analysis of Six Thousand Contemporary Religious Movements* (Nairobi: Oxford University Press, 1968). Also see Allan Anderson, *African Reformation: African Initiated Christianity in the 20th Century* (Trenton, NJ: Africa World Press, 2001).

49 For more on this, see Anderson, *African Reformation*. You may also find Deji Ayegboyin's book, *African Indigenous Churches*, helpful. Deji Ayegboyin and S. Ademola Ishola, *African Indigenous Churches: An Historical Perspective* (Lagos: Lagos Greater Heights Publishing, 1997).

50 Mission leaders in countries like Ghana, Nigeria and Kenya use the language of 10/40 Window to refer to the northern part of Africa and beyond. They are now attempting to send missionaries to reach the north, using all the strategies of their Western counterparts.

51 Byang H. Kato, *Theological Pitfalls in Africa* (Kisumu, Kenya: Evangel, 1975).

52 John V. Taylor, *The Go-Between God: The Holy Spirit and the Christian Mission* (London: SCM Press, 1972), p. 3 (my emphasis).

9

We Need a New Missiology

In talking about decolonizing mission I intend to imagine the work of sharing the good news of Jesus around the world in the context of the twenty-first century. Central to the argument that shapes this book is the conviction that colonial ways of doing mission ought to be confined to history. We need to find or create new ways of talking about and understanding what bearing witness for Christ among the nations needs to look like in our day and age. The models of mission that have been prevalent in the past two to five centuries are becoming increasingly irrelevant in the current global context of postcoloniality and where Christianity has become a worldwide religion. There is an ongoing crisis in mission agencies and wider Christian communities in the West about how they can place themselves in the new global landscape of Christianity. White Western Christianity is still losing members – the missionary work they do in other parts of the world is increasingly needed in many Western countries. For instance, there is a clear need for a fresh missional encounter in Europe yet many European Christians still think of mission as something Europeans do elsewhere. Generally speaking, and for various reasons, Europeans do better in evangelizing other peoples around the world than they do in Europe.

There is also a cognitive dissonance among many Western Christians when talking about mission today. Many see Christianity in its current global expressions, some of which are radically different from the Christianity they know, and do not know how to relate to it. In many places, especially outside the Evangelical fold, world Christianity looks nothing like the Christianity brought by the missionaries. The easy response is almost always to treat it as an exotic other – interesting enough to look at but only from a distance. Even those who think and behave like Western Evangelicals do not find an easy welcome among Western Christians. Other factors such as race and culture continue to hold them at the margins.

Can we say 'mission'?

Over the past few years I have also become aware of the many Western Christians who understand the colonial legacy of mission and are not sure how to go about sharing the news of Jesus with their neighbours. How can they bear witness about Jesus while being fully aware that mission has for centuries been used to colonize people and destroy their cultures? They do not want to continue with this legacy but they still need to continue making disciples for Christ in the world. How can they do this without exporting their cultures? How can they let local peoples determine what following Jesus in their context looks like without teaching them to be disciples as if they are in the West? How will they know when discipleship has happened if those disciples believe and behave differently? Indeed, how do they account for the money they get from their donors if they cannot say with certainty how many people accepted Christ as their Lord and Saviour through their ministry? An American friend told me, 'If I tell my funders that I am going to Africa to learn from the people there (and not to teach), I will lose all my funding.' He has since turned around and become the very thing he despised, an American missionary who goes around the world teaching Christians how to be good followers of Christ.

In some Western missiological circles there is a debate currently going on about the use of the word 'mission'. In some places the word is not to be mentioned – it brings back too much colonial shame and guilt. In other places it is too dear to be dismissed and must therefore continue. As far as I can see, Germans are almost totally done with the term. They speak about intercultural theology as a way of encouraging a listening and learning posture among German Christians as they encounter non-Western Christians. In this discourse, at least on paper, there is an openness to learning from Christians in other parts of the world. Intercultural theological discourse is encouraged. Exciting connections happen when our theologies are shaped in hybridity – theological cross-pollination enriches the Body of Christ.[1]

The British tend to try to hold on to 'mission'. A great deal of their missionary work is still shaped for a world in which the British Empire is a powerful force. They have the legacy to prove their commitment to mission. The history of mission in the past two centuries is replete with UK names. Thousands of young British men and women were involved in mission in the nineteenth and twentieth centuries. However, many British Christians and mission agencies are not sure what to do in a world where many African countries are more Christian than the United Kingdom. They do not even know what to do when Christians from around the world show up in the UK. The British study and teach 'world Christianity' to help UK Christians understand what is happening in Christian communities globally. Some actually teach world Christianity in the context of Religious Studies. World Christianity is for them one of many religions in the world. One aspect of world Christianity courses in the UK is that students from around the world come here to learn about Christianity in their own countries. To some extent this is because the historical resources from those countries are to be found in Western archives. There are a handful of institutions teaching 'missions' but they often seek to train British Christians going to serve elsewhere. Some who teach students to engage in mission in Britain find it difficult to recruit students.

Many North Americans do not even understand why the debate is happening. My American friends are as confident as ever. Jesus said, 'Go into all the nations and make disciples', and that is what they do, in obedience to the Great Commission. Many are oblivious to the reality of the imperial nature of their country's role in the world. Their posture in world missions is just as colonial as that of the Europeans in the years following the Scramble for Africa, but many of them would not recognize it as such. For most US Christians it is 'mission all the way down', although, of course, there are some Christians in the USA who are just as concerned as the Germans. I find it interesting that Africans generally speaking are still invested in the term 'mission'. The general response among African Christians has been to question why Westerners are seeking to shift the language as Africans are beginning to join the effort. An African missionary in Germany lamented, 'We are ready to be involved in mission, and the Europeans are moving the goalposts!' To her and many like her, the change in the discourse feels like another colonial move.

This entire debate feels legitimate to me. The military context that shaped its origins makes it a difficult word to justify. The fact that those who colonized other parts of the world also evangelized those lands and used Christian mission to further their purposes makes it a suspicious word, especially outside Western Evangelical circles. The Messiah we serve came to liberate people from the heavy-handed military machinery of the Roman Empire. His work was anything but military. He was betrayed with a kiss; he needed no protection from imperial soldiers. The cornerstone of his work was peace.

Sharing the gospel without empire

My broader concerns in this discourse are largely focused on the general subject of witnessing for Christ in the context of global imperialism. If followers of Christ from other parts of the world will bear witness for Christ among the nations, they cannot do so in the same manner that Westerners have done for the past five centuries. They lack almost everything that made the Western missionary movement a success. Yet, of course, in their lack they are just like the Galileans who heard Jesus say, 'Go and make disciples of all nations.' Beyond this I have often wondered: 'How should followers of Christ carry themselves in the context of empire?' If mission depends on empires, the rest of the world has no hope of participating. As such we ought to share the good news without aligning ourselves to, or in support of, empires. While connecting mission and imperialism may make the sharing of the gospel easier for some, it essentially conflates the good news of Jesus and the 'good news of the empire'. This is critical in the world today where God calls the whole of the Body of Christ to bear witness for him to the whole of God's creation. Those outside the empire may not find it easy to engage, but they have to. Those who for one reason or another are on the wrong end of the empire's violence may also find it difficult to receive the good news of Jesus from people who seem to serve the empire. The people whom the empire dislikes also become enemies of the Church – those whom we do not know how to evangelize.

At the centre of my argument I wonder: 'Is the mission of God possible without the help of empires?' I am confident that the sharing of the good news is indeed not only possible without imperial help but it also works out better without colonialism. God does not need empires to push the mission forward. In this book I argue that Jesus of Nazareth did not need the help of the emperor in Rome, neither did the puppet king in Jerusalem or Galilee help kickstart his mission in the world. He spent his early years as a refugee in Egypt, fleeing the wrath of King Herod in Israel. When he returned to Israel as a young boy it was not to the powerful centres of commercial and political influence that he went, not to Jerusalem or any other major cities in his homeland. Instead he became a man in a little-known village of Nazareth, helping his father's business as a carpenter in a colonized land. He launched a world-changing movement of 'fishers of people' (and not a battalion of warriors for Christ) from the northern shore of the small lake of Galilee (of the nations) and not from the hills of Jerusalem, and certainly not from Rome, Alexandria or Antioch, the three major cities of the Roman Empire at the time. His 12 disciples had no political power whatsoever.

Their key leaders – John, James and Peter – were uneducated and uncultured Galileans who spoke with an accent that gave them away as men from the backyard of a colonized country.

The gospel Jesus preached was not about how to get power to become like the Romans but how to subvert the empire to live in the kingdom of God and invite others to do the same while still living under the mighty hand of Rome. He was a strange Messiah, one who did not need violence to establish himself, whose kingdom was spiritual and not physical. This kingdom of God is not like the Roman Empire. It is a kingdom of peace, love and compassion, not military might. It does not colonize like earthly empires but brings freedom and liberty in the Spirit. In the end the empire's representatives in Jerusalem killed Jesus not for starting an insurrection against Rome but for disturbing the religious structures of the Jews. For almost 300 years after this, followers of Christ were minorities in the empire, often living and dying in conditions of persecution by the empire. Yet his followers have increased in numbers globally throughout the history of the Church. For the first 300 years of the Church, within the Roman Empire, Christianity grew in spite of the empire. It grew elsewhere as well, beyond the empire. When it finally triumphed over the empire it adapted to its newly found position and often used its power to persecute others.

The Son of God who 'emptied himself, taking the form of a slave, being born in human likeness … being found in human form, [who] humbled himself and became obedient to the point of death – even death on a cross' does not send humans to colonize other humans (Phil. 2.7–8). Mission carried out with the help of – or rather under the guise of – colonialism should cause us to ask serious questions about God and God's relationship with humanity. Does God's mission in the world really need imperial support? Would the story of Jesus' life and ministry be different if he had had the backing of the empire in his mission on earth? What difference would it make if Mary and Joseph had raised Jesus among the rich and powerful in Jerusalem, Alexandria, Antioch or even Rome? Would his messiahship have been different? He would probably have spoken Greek, had a better means of travel and most likely high-level connections with those in the upper echelons of society – politicians and the religious leaders. Would that change the story?

Mission theology in a postcolonial world

From the Gospels we see that the work of bearing witness for Christ in the world ought to be rooted in love and compassion. For God so loved the world that Jesus laid down his life for God's creation. Often Jesus was moved by compassion to heal and to save. This grounding of mission in love has significant implications for us. Those sending missionaries to the other side of the world say they love the people out there. When 'those people' show up in Western cities they are often invisible. Where they are seen they are marginalized because we love people when they are out there and not when they become *migrants* in our cities. Anti-migration rhetoric rules in many Western countries, especially during times of political elections. The summer of 2024 gave us, 'The Haitians are eating the dogs and the cats of people of Springfield, Ohio.' Some people who send missionaries to Haiti hated the fact that Haitians living in the USA legally have been called up to address a labour shortage in the meat processing and poultry industries. It makes no sense to love the Haitians in Haiti and hate them in the USA.

Mission in the twenty-first century must embrace weakness and vulnerability as precious resources in the work of sharing the good news of Christ in the world. We learn this from Christ himself. He came to the world as a vulnerable child who had to be taken out of the country for protection. He lived with this vulnerability all his life. Eventually his own people got the empire to crucify him. In all this he could have stopped the process – he almost did when he prayed, 'if it is possible, let this cup pass from me' (Matt. 26.39) – but he never did. It is this vulnerability that in the end allowed him 'All authority in heaven and on earth' (Matt. 28.18). Our Messiah had no army. He could call down 12 legions of angels from heaven to fight on his behalf but he did not (Matt. 26.53). The power of the Christian message in the first 300 years was in the fact that it was a vulnerable and often persecuted religion. Its mission had to be humble. The gospel had to be carried around the empire primarily by Christian migrants moving up and down the empire for trade.

Pentecost is the first missional event that ever happened in the Christian Church. The world was not only represented in Jerusalem on that day. New Christians, by virtue of becoming followers of Jesus, were invited to take the gospel of Jesus to the ends of the earth. Such a missionary movement would have to be diverse and multicultural. This ought to be characteristic of mission in the twenty-first century. The whole Body of Christ ought to serve in mission together. The world has changed in ways that make twentieth-century missiology seem totally out of context. God calls Africans, Asians, Latin Americans, Westerners and everyone else following Jesus to share the good news wherever they are and wherever they go. A snapshot of twenty-first-century missionary movements has to look like global Christianity.

A great deal of what was said and published in missionary journals of the colonial era needs to be revisited, corrected or discarded. The paternalistic attitude with which many Western missionaries approached the rest of the world, the demeaning language that was used to enforce their own supremacy over the people they were trying to evangelize, and the dependence on Western colonialism to establish Christian rule need to be called out, named for what they are and repented of. It is high time we agreed that God's mission does not colonize. The connection between colonialism and mission was wrong. The missionaries did not bring God to the rest of the world – God was already at work in the world before the missionaries arrived. The superiority complex of the missionaries, both as white Westerners and as Christians – thus racial or ethnic and religious – hindered mission instead of aiding it. The missionaries refused to see anything good in African cultures, for instance, and could not learn anything from them. A careful reflection is necessary. We need to learn how to engage in God's mission among God's people in God's world, simply as God's co-labourers, servants and slaves – with no armies to make the way before us and no empires behind us.

Note

1 For instance, see Sadiri Joy Tiya and Juliet Lee Uytanlet, *A Hybrid World: Diaspora, Hybridity, and Missio Dei* (Littleton, CO: William Carey Publishing, 2020).

Bibliography

Achebe, Chinua, *Things Fall Apart*, London: Heinemann, 1958.
Anderson, Allan, *African Reformation: African Initiated Christianity in the 20th Century*, Trenton, NJ: Africa World Press, 2001.
Anderson, Gerald H., 'A Moratorium on Missionaries', 1974, http://www.religion-online.org/showarticle.asp?title=1574.
Anderson-Morshead, Anne E. M., *The History of the Universities' Mission to Central Africa, 1859–1896*, 2nd edn, London: Office of the Universities' Mission to Central Africa, 1899.
Andrews, Edward E., *Native Apostles: Black and Indian Missionaries in the British Atlantic World*, London: Harvard University Press, 2013.
Arnold, David, *The Age of Discovery, 1400–1600*, London: Routledge, 2013.
Aslan, Reza, *Zealot: The Life and Times of Jesus of Nazareth*, New York: Random House, 2013.
Ayegboyin, Deji and S. Ademola Ishola, *African Indigenous Churches: An Historical Perspective*, Lagos: Lagos Greater Heights Publishing, 1997.
Baines, Dudley, *Emigration from Europe, 1815–1930*, New Studies in Economic and Social History, New York: Cambridge University Press, 1995.
Bangura, Joseph Bosco, 'African Pentecostalism and Mediatised Self-Branding in Catholic (Flanders) Belgium', *Stichproben: Vienna Journal of African Studies* 35 (2018), pp. 1–23.
Barrett, David B., *Schism and Renewal in Africa: An Analysis of Six Thousand Contemporary Religious Movements*, Nairobi: Oxford University Press, 1968.
Baskerville, Geoffrey, *English Monks and the Suppression of the Monasteries*, New Haven, CT: Yale University Press, 1937.
Bellarmine, Robert, *On the Church Militant*, trans. Ryan Grant, Post Falls, ID: Mediatrix Press, 2016.
Berg, Johannes van den, *Constrained by Jesus' Love: An Inquiry into the Motives of the Missionary Awakening in Great Britain in the Period between 1698 and 1815*, Kampen: Kok, 1956.
Berger, Peter L., *The Desecularization of the World: Resurgent Religion and World Politics*, Grand Rapids, MI: Eerdmans, 1999.
Bernard, George W., 'The Dissolution of the Monasteries', *History* 96, no. 324 (2011), pp. 390–409.
Beti, Mongo, *The Poor Christ of Bomba*, Long Grove, IL: Waveland, 1971.
Betten, Francis S., 'The Milan Decree of A. D. 313: Translation and Comment', *The Catholic Historical Review* 8, no. 2 (1922), pp. 191–7.
Bierman, John, *Dark Safari: The Life Behind the Legend of Henry Morton Stanley*, London: Lume Books, 1990.
Bisaha, Nancy, *From Christians to Europeans: Pope Pius II and the Concept of the Modern Western Identity*, London: Routledge, 2023.

Booth, Joseph and Laura Perry (eds), *Africa for the African*, Zomba: Kachere Series, 2008.
Bosch, David J., *Transforming Mission: Paradigm Shifts in Theology of Mission*, American Society of Missiology Series, Maryknoll, NY: Orbis Books, 1991.
Bradley, Michael, *The Columbus Conspiracy: An Investigation into the Secret History of Christopher Columbus*, Willowdale, Ontario: Hounslow Press, 1991.
Brooks, Noah, *The Story of Marco Polo*, New York: Cosimo, 2008.
Brown, Robin, *Marco Polo: Journey to the End of the Earth*, Stroud: The History Press, 2011.
Burgtorf, Jochen, Shlomo Lotan and Enric Mallorquí-Ruscalleda, *The Templars: The Rise, Fall, and Legacy of a Military Religious Order*, London: Routledge, 2021.
Burridge, Kenelm, *In the Way: A Study of Christian Missionary Endeavours*, Vancouver, British Columbia: University of British Columbia Press, 2011.
Butler, Alfred Joshua, *The Arab Conquest of Egypt and the Last Thirty Years of the Roman Dominion*, Oxford: Oxford University Press, 1978.
Buxton, Meriel, *David Livingstone*, Basingstoke: Palgrave, 2001.
Carey, Hilary M., *God's Empire: Religion and Colonialism in the British World, c.1801–1908*, New York: Cambridge University Press, 2011.
Carey, William, *An Enquiry into the Obligations of Christians to Use Means for the Conversion of the Heathens in Which the Religious State of the Different Nations of the World, the Success of Former Undertakings, and the Practicability of Further Undertakings Are Considered*, London: Carey Kingsgate, 1961.
Catholicam, Unam Sanctum, 'Dum Diversas (English Translation)', *Defending the Goodness, Truth and Beauty of Catholicism*, 2011, https://unamsanctamcatholicam.blogspot.com/2011/02/dum-diversas-english-translation.html.
Chadwick, Owen, *Mackenzie's Grave*, London: Hodder & Stoughton, 1959.
Coggins, Wade, 'What's Behind the Idea of a Missionary Moratorium?' *Christianity Today*, 22 November 1974, pp. 7–9.
Columbus, Christopher, *The Journal of Christopher Columbus*, trans. Cecil Jane, New York: Bonanza Books, 1989.
Columbus, Christopher, *Letters*, trans. Richard H. Major, London: Hakluyt Society, 1847.
Columbus, Christopher, *Libro De Las Profecias*, trans. Delno C. West and August Kling, Gainesville, FL: University of Florida Press, 1991.
Comaroff, Jean and John Comaroff, *Of Revelation and Revolution: Christianity, Colonialism, and Consciousness in South Africa*, Vol. 1, Chicago, IL: University of Chicago Press, 1991.
Conklin, Alice, *A Mission to Civilize: The Republican Idea of Empire in France and West Africa, 1895–1930*, Stanford, CA: Stanford University Press, 2000.
Conrad, Joseph, *Heart of Darkness*, London: Legend Press, 2020.
Cox, George William, *The Life of John William Colenso, D.D., Bishop of Natal*, London: W. Ridgway, 1888.
Crossan, John Dominic, *God and Empire: Jesus against Rome, Then and Now*, San Francisco, CA: HarperCollins, 2007.
Da Gama, Vasco, *Em Nome De Deus: The Journal of the First Voyage of Vasco da Gama to India, 1497–1499*, ed. and trans. Glenn J. Ames, Leuven: Brill, 2009.
Dahle, Lars, Margunn Serigstad Dahle and Knud Jørgensen (eds), *The Lausanne Movement: A Range of Perspectives*, Vol. 22, Oxford: Regnum, 2014.
Davenport, Frances Gardiner, *European Treaties Bearing on the History of the United States and its Dependencies to 1684*, Washington DC: Carnegie Institution of Washington, 1917.

Davidson, Julie, *Looking for Mrs Livingstone*, Edinburgh: Saint Andrew Press, 2012.
Davie, Grace, *Europe – the Exceptional Case: Parameters of Faith in the Modern World*, London: Darton, Longman & Todd, 2002.
Davie, Grace, *Religion in Modern Europe: A Memory Mutates*, European Societies, Oxford: Oxford University Press, 2000.
Davie, Grace and Lucian N. Leustean (eds), *The Oxford Handbook of Religion and Europe*, Oxford: Oxford University Press, 2021.
Disney, Anthony R., *A History of Portugal and the Portuguese Empire: From Beginnings to 1807*, Vol. 2, Cambridge: Cambridge University Press, 2009.
Douglas, James Dixon (ed.), *Let the Earth Hear His Voice: International Congress on World Evangelization, Lausanne, Switzerland, [July 16–25, 1974]. Official Reference Volume, Papers and Responses*, Minneapolis, MN: World Wide Publications, 1975.
Drobena, Thomas John and Wilma Samuella Kucharek, *Heritage of the Slavs: The Christianization of the Slavs and the Great Moravian Empire: A History of Political and Religious Events AD 800–899*, Columbus, OH: Kosovo Publishing Company, 1979.
Duffy, Aoife, 'Legacies of British Colonial Violence: Viewing Kenyan Detention Camps through the Hanslope Disclosure', *Law and History Review* 33, no. 3 (2015), pp. 489–542.
Dunn, Edmond J., *Missionary Theology: Foundations in Development*, Washington DC: University Press of America, 1980.
Endean, Philip, 'Ignatius in Lutheran Light', *The Month* 24 (1991), pp. 271–8.
Erasmus, Desiderius, *Handbook of the Militant Christian*, trans. John P. Dolan, Notre Dame, IN: Fides Publishers, 1962.
Erichsen, Casper and David Olusoga, *The Kaiser's Holocaust: Germany's Forgotten Genocide and the Colonial Roots of Nazism*, London: Faber & Faber, 2010.
Eriksen, Thomas Hylland and Finn Sivert Nielsen, *A History of Anthropology*, London: Pluto Press, 2013.
Eusebius, *Life of Constantine*, trans. Averil Cameron and Stuart Hall, Oxford: Clarendon Press, 1999.
Fairbank, John King, *The Missionary Enterprise in China and America*, Harvard Studies in American–East Asian Relations, Cambridge, MA: Harvard University Press, 1974.
Falk, Peter, *The Growth of the Church in Africa*, Grand Rapids, MI: Zondervan, 1979.
Fickett, Harold, *The Ralph D. Winter Story: How One Man Dared to Shake Up World Missions*, Littleton, CO: William Carey Publishing, 2013.
Finkel, Caroline, *Osman's Dream: The History of the Ottoman Empire*, London: Hachette, 2007.
Fiske, Edward B., 'African Christians are Developing Their Own Distinctive Theologies', *The New York Times*, 12 March 1971, https://www.nytimes.com/1971/03/12/archives/african-christians-are-developing-their-own-distinctive-theologies.html.
Fletcher, Holly Berkley, *The Missionary Kids: Unmasking the Myths of White Evangelicalism*, Minneapolis, MN: Augsburg Fortress, forthcoming 2025.
Gappah, Petina, *Out of Darkness, Shining Light: A Novel*, New York: Simon & Schuster, 2019.
Gardner, Leigh, *Taxing Colonial Africa: The Political Economy of British Imperialism*, Oxford: Oxford University Press, 2012.

Gatu, John G., *Fan into Flame: An Autobiography*, Nairobi: Moran Publishers, 2020.
Gatu, John G., *Joyfully Christian, Truly African*, Nairobi: Acton Publishers, 2006.
George, Timothy, *Faithful Witness: The Life and Mission of William Carey*, Birmingham, AL: New Hope, 1991.
Gerloff, Roswith, *A Plea for British Black Theologies: The Black Church Movement in Britain in its Transatlantic Cultural and Theological Interaction with Special References to the Pentecostal Oneness (Apostolic) and Sabbatarian Movements*, Studien zur interkulturellen Geschichte des Christentums, Frankfurt am Main: P. Lang, 1992.
Godin, Henri and Yvan Daniel, *La France, Pays De Mission?* Rencontres, Lyon: Éditions de l'Abeille, 1943.
Goldsworthy, Adrian, *The Fall of Carthage: The Punic Wars 265–146 BC*, London: Weidenfeld & Nicolson, 2012.
Grant, George, *The Last Crusader*, Wheaton, IL: Crossway Books, 1992.
Guder, Darrell L. (ed.), *Missional Church: A Vision for the Sending of the Church in North America*, The Gospel and Our Culture Series, Grand Rapids, MI: Eerdmans, 1998.
Haddis, Mekdes A., *A Just Mission: Laying Down Power and Embracing Mutuality*, Downers Grove, IL: InterVarsity Press, 2022.
Hale, Edward Everett, *The Life of Christopher Columbus: From His Own Letters and Journals and Other Documents of His Time*, La Vergne, TN: True Sign Publishing House, 2023.
Hanciles, Jehu J., *Beyond Christendom: Globalization, African Migration, and the Transformation of the West*, Maryknoll, NY: Orbis Books, 2008.
Harvey, Graham, *The Handbook of Contemporary Animism*, London: Routledge, 2014.
Hastings, Adrian, *A History of African Christianity, 1950–1975*, African Studies Series 26, Cambridge: Cambridge University Press, 1979.
Hastings, Adrian, *Mission and Ministry*, London: Sheed & Ward, 1971.
Hegel, Georg Wilhelm Friedrich, *Lectures on the Philosophy of World History*, trans. H. B. Nisbett with an Introduction by Duncan Forbes, Cambridge: Cambridge University Press, 1984.
Hegel, Georg Wilhelm Friedrich, *The Philosophy of History*, trans. J. Sibree, Kitchener, Ontario: Batoche Books, 2001.
Hegel, Georg Wilhelm Friedrich, *Philosophy of Mind*, trans. W. Wallace and A. V. Miller, rev. edn with Introduction and Commentary by Michael Inwood, Oxford: Clarendon Press, 2007.
Heywood, Linda M., *Njinga of Angola: Africa's Warrior Queen*, London: Harvard University Press, 2017.
Hinga, Teresia Mbari, 'Inculturation and the Otherness of Africa and Africans: Some Reflections', in Frans J. S. Wijsen and Peter Turkson (eds), *Inculturation: Abide by the Otherness of Africa and the Africans*, Kampen: Kok, 1994, pp. 10–18.
Hitchens, Christopher, *Blood, Class and Empire: The Enduring Anglo-American Relationship*, New York: Bold Type Books, 2004.
Hobsbawm, Eric J., *The Age of Empire: 1875–1914*, New York: Vintage Books, 1989.
Hochschild, Adam, *King Leopold's Ghost: A Story of Greed, Terror, and Heroism in Colonial Africa*, 1st Mariner Books edn, Boston: Houghton Mifflin, 1999.
Hodges, Geoffrey W. T., 'African Manpower Statistics for the British Forces in

East Africa, 1914–1918', *The Journal of African History* 19, no. 1 (1978), pp. 101–16.
Horsford, Eben Norton, *The Landfall of Leif Erikson, AD 1000: And the Site of His Houses in Vineland*, Boston, MA: Damrell & Upham, 1892.
Hourani, Albert, *A History of the Arab Peoples*, London: Faber & Faber, 2013.
Housley, Norman (ed.), *The Crusade in the Fifteenth Century: Converging and Competing Cultures*, London: Routledge, 2016.
Housley, Norman (ed.), *Crusading and the Ottoman Threat, 1453–1505*, Oxford: Oxford University Press, 2013.
Hubbard, Ethel Daniels, *The Moffats*, New York: Missionary Education Movement of the United States and Canada, 1917.
Hume, David, *Essays: Moral, Political and Literary*, Oxford: Oxford University Press, 1963.
Hunt, Robert A., 'The History of the Lausanne Movement, 1974–2010' [in English], *International Bulletin of Missionary Research* 35, no. 2 (2011), pp. 81–4.
Huntington, Samuel P., *The Clash of Civilizations and the Remaking of World Order*, New York: Touchstone, 1997.
Hutchison, William R., *Errand to the World: American Protestant Thought and Foreign Missions*, Chicago, IL: University of Chicago Press, 1987.
Hutchison, William R. and Torben Christensen, *Missionary Ideologies in the Imperialist Era, 1880–1920*, Aarhus, Denmark: Aros, 1982.
Idowu, E. Bolaji, *Towards an Indigenous Church*, Oxford: Oxford University Press, 1965.
Jahn, Janheinz, *Muntu: An Outline of Neo-African Culture*, London: Faber & Faber, 1961.
Jeal, Tim, *Livingstone*, New Haven, CT: Yale University Press, 2013.
Jeal, Tim, *Livingstone*, New York: Dell, 1973.
Jenkins, Philip, *The Next Christendom: The Coming of Global Christianity*, 3rd edn, New York: Oxford University Press, 2011.
Jennings, Willie James, *The Christian Imagination: Theology and the Origins of Race*, New Haven, CT: Yale University Press, 2010.
Jerome of Stridon, 'Life of St. Paul the First Hermit', *The Australian Province of The Order of Saint Paul The First Hermit*, https://paulinefathers.org.au/about/st-paul/life-paulus-first-hermit/.
Jerónimo, Miguel Bandeira, *The 'Civilising Mission' of Portuguese Colonialism, 1870–1930*, trans. Stewart Lloyd-Jones, London: Springer, 2015.
Jeyaraj, Daniel, 'The Re-emergence of Global Christianity', in Todd. M. Johnson and Kenneth R. Ross (eds), *Atlas of Global Christianity 1910–2010*, Edinburgh: Edinburgh University Press, 2009, p. 54.
Johnson, Robert, *British Imperialism*, London: Springer, 2003.
Johnston, Anna, *Missionary Writing and Empire, 1800–1860*, Cambridge: Cambridge University Press, 2003.
Jones, Gwyn, *A History of the Vikings*, Oxford: Oxford University Press, 2001.
Josephus, *Jewish Antiquities, Books XVIII–XX*, trans. Louis H. Feldman, London: William Heinemann Ltd, 1965.
Kalu, Ogbu, 'The Anatomy of Reverse Flow in African Christianity: Pentecostalism and Immigrant African Christianity', in Frieder Ludwig and J. Kwabena Asamoah-Gyadu (eds), *African Christian Presence in the West: New Immigrant Congregations and Transnational Networks in North America and Europe*, Trenton, NJ: Africa World Press, 2011.

Kamen, Henry, *The Spanish Inquisition: A Historical Revision*, New Haven, CT: Yale University Press, 2014.

Kant, Immanuel, *Immanuel Kant: Observations on the Feeling of the Beautiful and Sublime and Other Writings*, ed. Patrick R. Frierson and Paul Guyer, Cambridge: Cambridge University Press, 2011.

Kant, Immanuel, *Lectures on Anthropology*, trans. Robert R. Clewis and G. Felicitas Munzel, ed. Allen W. Wood and Robert B. Louden, Cambridge: Cambridge University Press, 2012.

Karari, Peter, 'Modus Operandi of Oppressing the "Savages": The Kenyan British Colonial Experience', *Peace and Conflict Studies* 25, no. 1 (2018), p. 2.

Kato, Byang H., *Theological Pitfalls in Africa*, Kisumu, Kenya: Evangel, 1975.

Kendall, R. Elliott, *The End of an Era: Africa and the Missionary*, London: SPCK, 1978.

Kendall, R. Elliott, 'On the Sending of Missionaries: A Call for Restraint', *International Review of Mission* 64, no. 253 (1975), pp. 62–6.

Kennedy, Hugh, *The Great Arab Conquests: How the Spread of Islam Changed the World We Live In*, Philadelphia, PA: Da Capo Press, 2007.

Kritzinger, Johannes N. J. and Harvey Kwiyani, 'The Place of Missiology as a Theological Discipline in Africa', in Johannes Knoetze (ed.), *Mission: The Labour Room of Theology*, Wellington, RSA: CLF Publishers, 2022, ch. 8.

Kumm, Hermann Karl Wilhelm and Karl Kumm, *African Missionary Heroes and Heroines*, New York: The Macmillan Company, 1917.

Kwiyani, Harvey C., 'Independent, Enthusiastic, and African: Reframing the Story of African Christianity', in Nimi Wariboko and Adeshina Afolayan (eds), *African Pentecostalism and World Christianity: Essays in Honor of J. Kwabena Asamoah-Gyadu*, Eugene, OR: Wipf & Stock, 2020.

Lacouture, Jean, *Jesuits: A Multibiography*, trans. Jeremy Leggatt, Washington DC: Counterpoint, 1995.

Lambek, Michael, *A Reader in the Anthropology of Religion*, Blackwell Anthologies in Social and Cultural Anthropology, 2nd edn, Malden, MA: Blackwell Publishers, 2008.

Langworthy, Harry W., *'Africa for the African': The Life of Joseph of Booth*, Blantyre, Malawi: CLAIM, 1996.

Langworthy, Harry W., 'Joseph Booth, Prophet of Radical Change in Central and South Africa, 1891–1915', *Journal of Religion in Africa* 16, no. 1 (1986), pp. 22–43.

Larner, John, *Marco Polo and the Discovery of the World*, London: Yale University Press, 1999.

Latourette, Kenneth Scott, *A History of Expansion of Christianity, Volume 4: The Great Century, A.D. 1800–A.D. 1914, Europe and the United States of America*, London: Harper & Brothers, 1941.

Latourette, Kenneth Scott, *A History of the Expansion of Christianity*, Vol. 4, *The Great Century: Europe and the United States*, Grand Rapids, MI: Zondervan, 1970.

Lehtsalu, Liise, 'Rethinking Monastic Suppressions in Revolutionary and Napoleonic Italy: How Women Religious Negotiated for Their Communities', *Women's History Review* 25, no. 6 (2016), pp. 945–64.

Livingstone, David, *The Life and Explorations of Dr. David Livingstone: Comprising All His Extensive Travels and Discoveries: As Detailed in His Diary, Reports, and Letters, Including His Famous Last Journals*, Philadelphia, PA: John E. Potter & Company, 1857.

Livingstone, David, *Missionary Travels and Research in South Africa*, London: John Murray, 1857.
Livingstone, David and Charles Livingstone, *Narrative of an Expedition to the Zambesi and its Tributaries: And the Discovery of the Lakes Shirwa and Nyassa, 1858–1864*, New York: Harper & Brothers, 1865; Stroud: Nonsuch, 2005.
Loubser, Johannes Albertus, *The Apartheid Bible: A Critical Review of Racial Theology in South Africa*, Cape Town: Maskew Miller Longman, 1987.
Ludwig, Frieder and J. Kwabena Asamoah-Gyadu (eds), *African Christian Presence in the West: New Immigrant Congregations and Transnational Networks in North America and Europe*, Trenton, NJ: Africa World Press, 2011.
Maryks, Robert Aleksander, *A Companion to Ignatius of Loyola: Life, Writings, Spirituality, Influence*, Brill's Companions to the Christian Tradition, Leuven: Brill, 2014.
Maxwell, John Francis, *Slavery and the Catholic Church: The History of Catholic Teaching Concerning the Moral Legitimacy of the Institution of Slavery*, London: Barry Rose, 1975.
Mazrui, Ali Al'amin, *Cultural Forces in World Politics*, London: J. Currey, 1990.
Mbiti, John S., *African Religions and Philosophy*, London: Heinemann, 1969.
Mbiti, John S., 'Theological Impotence and the Universality of the Church', *Lutheran World* 21, no. 3 (1974), pp. 251–60.
McCabe, Joseph, *A Candid History of the Jesuits*, Louisville, KY: Bank of Wisdom, 1913.
McCracken, John, *Politics and Christianity in Malawi: The Impact of the Livingstonia Mission in the Northern Province*, Kachere Monographs, Zomba: Kachere Series, 2008.
McNeil, Kent, 'The Doctrine of Discovery Reconsidered: Reflecting on Discovering Indigenous Lands: The Doctrine of Discovery in the English Colonies', *Osgoode Hall Law Journal* 53, no. 2 (2016), pp. 699–728.
Milbrandt, Jay, *The Daring Heart of David Livingstone: Exile, African Slavery, and the Publicity Stunt that Saved Millions*, Nashville, TN: Nelson Books, 2014.
Miller, Robert J., Jacinta Ruru, Larissa Behrendt and Tracey Lindberg, *Discovering Indigenous Lands: The Doctrine of Discovery in the English Colonies*, Oxford: Oxford University Press, 2010.
Mott, John R., *The Evangelization of the World in This Generation*, New York: Student Volunteer Movement for Foreign Missions, 1900.
Moyo, Dambisa, *Dead Aid: Why Aid is Not Working and How There is a Better Way for Africa*, New York: Farrar, Straus & Giroux, 2009.
Moyo, Simbarashe, 'A Failed Land Reform Strategy in Zimbabwe. The Willing Buyer Willing Seller', *Public Policy and Administration Review* 2, no. 1 (2014), pp. 67–74.
Mpanya, Mutombo, 'Problems of the Churches in Central Africa', in Charles R. Taber (ed.), *The Church in Africa*, Pasadena, CA: William Carey, 1977.
Mukherjee, Janam, *Hungry Bengal: War, Famine and the End of Empire*, Oxford: Oxford University Press, 2015.
Mullett, Michael A., *The Catholic Reformation*, London: Routledge, 1999.
Mwase, George Simeon and Robert I. Rotberg, *Strike a Blow and Die: The Classic Story of the Chilembwe Rising*, Cambridge, MA: Harvard University Press, 1975.
Nacpil, Emerito P., 'Mission but Not Missionaries', *International Review of Mission* 60, no. 239 (1971), pp. 356–62.
Nacpil, Emerito P., 'Whom Does the Missionary Serve and What Does He Do?',

in *Missionary Service in Asia Today*, Hong Kong: Chinese Christian Literature Council, 1971, pp. 76–80.

Neill, Stephen, *Colonialism and Christian Missions* (New York: McGraw Hill, 1966).

Neill, Stephen and Owen Chadwick, *A History of Christian Missions*, The Pelican History of the Church, New York: Penguin Books, 1986.

Newbigin, Lesslie, *Foolishness to the Greeks: The Gospel and Western Culture*, Grand Rapids, MI: Eerdmans, 1986.

Newbigin, Lesslie, *The Gospel in a Pluralist Society*, Grand Rapids, MI: Eerdmans, 1989.

Newbigin, Lesslie, *Unfinished Agenda: An Autobiography*, Geneva: WCC Publications, 1985.

Ngũgĩ wa Thiong'o, *The River Between*, London: Heinemann, 1965.

O'Malley, John W., *The First Jesuits*, London: Harvard University Press, 1993.

O'Malley, John W., *The Jesuits: A History from Ignatius to the Present*, London: Rowman & Littlefield, 2014.

O'Malley, John W., *Saints or Devils Incarnate? Studies in Jesuit History*, Vol. 1, Leuven: Brill, 2013.

O'Reilly, Terence, 'Ignatius Loyola and the Counter-Reformation: The Hagiographic Tradition', *Heythrop Journal* 31, no. 4 (1990), pp. 439–70.

Orobator, Agbon E., *Religion and Faith in Africa: Confessions of an Animist*, Maryknoll, NY: Orbis Books, 2018.

Otieno, Nicholas and Hugh McCullum, *Journey of Hope: Towards a New Ecumenical Africa*, Geneva: WCC Publications, 2005.

Oyono, Ferdinand, *Houseboy*, African Writers Series, Edinburgh: Heinemann, 1966.

Pastor, Ludwig, *The History of the Popes: From the Close of the Middle Ages*, Vol. II, London: Kegan Paul, Trench, Trübner & Co., 1899.

Pastor, Ludwig, *The History of the Popes: From the Close of the Middle Ages*, Vol. III, London: Kegan Paul, Trench, Trübner & Co., 1923.

Pastor, Ludwig, *The History of the Popes: From the Close of the Middle Ages*, trans. Frederick Ignatius Antrobus, Vol. IV, London: Kegan Paul, Trench, Trübner & Co., 1900.

Paton, Alan, *Cry, the Beloved Country: A Story of Comfort in Desolation*, New York: Scribner, 1948.

Perbi, Yaw and Sam Ngugi, *Africa to the Rest: From Mission Field to Mission Force (Again)*, Maitland, FL: Xulon Press, 2022.

Polo, Marco, *The Travels of Marco Polo*, DigiCat, 2022.

Porter, Andrew N., *The Imperial Horizons of British Protestant Missions, 1880–1914*, Studies in the History of Christian Missions, Grand Rapids, MI: Eerdmans, 2003.

Priestley, Herbert Ingram, *France Overseas: A Study of Modern Imperialism*, London: Routledge, 2018.

Rah, Soong-Chan, *The Next Evangelicalism: Releasing the Church from Western Cultural Captivity*, Downers Grove, IL: IVP Books, 2009.

Rahman, Aziz, Mohsin Ali and Saad Kahn, 'The British Art of Colonialism in India: Subjugation and Division', *Peace and Conflict Studies* 25, no. 1 (2018), p. 5.

Ransford, Oliver, *David Livingstone: The Dark Interior*, London: John Murray, 1978.

Reese, Robert, 'John Gatu and the Moratorium on Missionaries', *Missiology* 42, no. 3 (2014), pp. 245–56.
Reese, Robert, 'Roland Allen and the Moratorium on Missionaries', *Southeast Regional* (2012).
Rieger, Joerg, *Globalization and Theology*, Horizons in Theology, Nashville, TN: Abingdon, 2010.
Robert, Dana Lee, *Converting Colonialism: Visions and Realities in Mission History, 1706–1914*, Studies in the History of Christian Missions, Grand Rapids, MI: Eerdmans, 2008.
Robertson, William, *The Martyrs of Blantyre: Henry Henderson, Dr. John Bowie [and] Robert Cleland: A Chapter from the Story of Missions in Central Africa*, London: James Nisbet & Co., 1892.
Rotberg, Robert I., *The Founder: Cecil Rhodes and the Pursuit of Power*, Oxford: Oxford University Press, 1988.
Rowley, Henry (ed.), *Speeches on Missions by the Right Reverend Samuel Wilberforce*, London: William Wells Gardner, 1874.
Rukuni, Rugare and Erna Oliver, 'Ethiopian Christianity: A Continuum of African Early Christian Polities', *Theological Studies* 75, no. 1 (2019), pp. 1–9.
Said, Edward W., *Culture and Imperialism*, New York: Vintage Books, 1994.
Saint Augustine, *Answer to Faustus, a Manichean*, trans. Roland Teske, The Works of Saint Augustine: A Translation for the 21st Century, Hyde Park, NY: New City Press, 2007.
Saint Ignatius of Loyola, *The Autobiography of St. Ignatius of Loyola*, trans. Joseph F. O'Callaghan, New York: Fordham University Press, 1992.
Saint Ignatius of Loyola, *The Constitutions of the Society of Jesus and Their Complementary Norms: A Complete English Translation of the Official Latin Texts*, trans. George E. Ganss SJ, St Louis, MO: Institute of Jesuit Sources, 1996.
Sanneh, Lamin O., 'Christian Missions and the Western Guilt Complex', *Christian Century* 104, no. 11 (April 1987), pp. 330–4.
Sanneh, Lamin O., *Translating the Message: The Missionary Impact on Culture*, American Society of Missiology Series, Maryknoll, NY: Orbis Books, 1989.
Sardar, Ziauddin and Merryl Wyn Davies, *The No-Nonsense Guide to Islam*, Oxford: New Internationalist, 2004.
Schirrmacher, Thomas, *William Carey: Theologian, Linguist, Social Reformer*, Eugene, OR: Wipf & Stock Publishers, 2018.
Setton, Kenneth M., *The Papacy and the Levant, 1204–1571: The Fifteenth Century*, Vol. II, Philadelphia, PA: American Philosophical Society, 1978.
Shepperson, George and Thomas Price, *Independent African: John Chilembwe and the Origins, Setting, and Significance of the Nyasaland Native Rising of 1915*, Edinburgh: Edinburgh University Press, 1958.
Silverberg, Robert, *The Realm of Prester John*, Athens, OH: Ohio University Press, 2020.
Slattery, Brian, 'Paper Empires: The Legal Dimensions of French and English Ventures in North America', in John McLaren, A. R. Buck and Nancy E. Wright (eds), *Despotic Dominion: Property Rights in British Settler Societies*, Vancouver, British Columbia: University of British Columbia Press, 2005, pp. 50–78.
Smith, A. Christopher, 'Carey, William', in Gerald H. Anderson (ed.), *Biographical Dictionary of Christian Missions*, New York: Macmillan Reference, 1998.
Smith, David, *Mission after Christendom*, London: Darton, Longman & Todd, 2003.

BIBLIOGRAPHY

Smith, Edwin W. (ed.), *African Ideas of God, a Symposium*, Edinburgh: Edinburgh University Press, 1950.

Stahl, Georg Ernst, *Theoria Medica Vera*, Orphanotropheus, 1737.

Stanley, Brian, *The Bible and the Flag: Protestant Missions and British Imperialism in the Nineteenth and Twentieth Centuries*, Leicester: Apollos, 1990.

Stanley, Brian, *Christian Missions and the Enlightenment*, Studies in the History of Christian Missions, Grand Rapids, MI: Eerdmans, 2001.

Stanley, Brian, *The World Missionary Conference, Edinburgh 1910*, Grand Rapids, MI: Eerdmans, 2009.

Stanley, Henry Morton, *In Darkest Africa: Or the Quest, Rescue, and Retreat of Emin Governor of Equatoria*, Vol. 1, London: Sampson Low, Marston, Searle & Rivington, 1890.

Stanley, Henry Morton, *In Darkest Africa: Or the Quest, Rescue, and Retreat of Emin Governor of Equatoria*, Vol. 2, London: Sampson Low, Marston, Searle & Rivington, 1890.

Stanley, Henry Morton, *Through the Dark Continent: Or, the Sources of the Nile around the Great Lakes of Equatorial Africa, and down the Livingstone River to the Atlantic Ocean*, 2 vols, New York: Harper, 1878.

Stoddard, Lothrop, *The Rising Tide of Color Against White World Supremacy*, Liberty Bell's Politically Incorrect Classics, York, SC: Liberty Bell, 2006.

Stults, Donald Leroy, *Grasping Truth and Reality: Lesslie Newbigin's Theology of Mission to the Western World*, Cambridge: James Clarke, 2009.

Sundkler, Bengt and Christopher Steed, *A History of the Church in Africa*, Studia Missionalia Upsaliensia 74, New York: Cambridge University Press, 2000.

Tacitus, *Agricola*, Vol. 1.

Taylor, John V., *The Go-between God: The Holy Spirit and the Christian Mission*, London: SCM Press, 1972.

Tengatenga, James, *The Umca in Malawi: A History of the Anglican Church 1861–2010*, Zomba, Malawi: Kachere Series, 2010.

Tennent, Timothy C., *Theology in the Context of World Christianity: How the Global Church is Influencing the Way We Think About and Discuss Theology*, Grand Rapids, MI: Zondervan, 2007.

Thomas, Antony, *Rhodes: Race for Africa*, New York: Martin's Press, 1997.

Thompson, Richard W., *The Footprints of the Jesuits*, Cincinnati, OH: Cranston & Curts, 1894.

Tiya, Sadiri Joy and Juliet Lee Uytanlet, *A Hybrid World: Diaspora, Hybridity, and Missio Dei*, Littleton, CO: William Carey Publishing, 2020.

Twells, Alison, *The Civilising Mission and the English Middle Class, 1792–1850: The 'Heathen' at Home and Overseas*, London: Palgrave Macmillan, 2009.

Tylor, Edward B., *Primitive Culture: Researches into the Development of Mythology, Philosophy, Religion, Language, Art, and Custom*, 4th edn, 2 vols, London: J. Murray, 1993.

Tylor, Edward Burnett, 'On the Survival of Savage Thought in Modern Civilization', *Notes on the Proceedings at the Meetings of the Royal Institute* 5 (1869), pp. 522–35.

Tylor, Edward Burnett, *Primitive Culture: Researches into the Development of Mythology, Philosophy, Religion, Art, and Custom*, 3rd edn, Vol. 1, London: John Murray, 1891.

Uka, Emele Mba, *Missionaries Go Home? A Sociological Interpretation of an African Response to Christian Missions*, New York: Lang, 1989.

Verhaagen, Dave, *How White Evangelicals Think: The Psychology of White Conservative Christians*, Eugene, OR: Wipf & Stock, 2022.

Vickery, Paul S., *Bartolomé De Las Casas: Great Prophet of the Americas*, Mahwah, NJ: Paulist Press, 2006.

von Ranke, Leopold, *History of the Popes: Their Church and State*, Vol. 3, New York: Colonial Press, 1901.

Wagner, C. Peter, 'Colour the Moratorium Grey', *International Review of Mission* 64, no. 254 (1975), pp. 165–76.

Wakatama, Pius, *Independence for the Third World Church: An African's Perspective on Missionary Work*, Downers Grove, IL: InterVarsity Press, 1976.

Wakatama, Pius, 'The Role of Africans in the World Mission of the Church', *Evangelical Missions Quarterly* 26, no. 2 (1990).

Waller, Horace, *The Last Journals of David Livingstone in Central Africa*, New York: Harper & Brothers, 1875.

Walls, Andrew F., *The Cross-Cultural Process in Christian History: Studies in the Transmission and Appropriation of Faith*, Maryknoll, NY: Orbis Books, 2002.

Walls, Andrew F., *The Missionary Movement in Christian History: Studies in the Transmission of Faith*, Maryknoll, NY: Orbis Books, 1996.

Wells, Lauren, *The Grief Tower: A Practical Guide to Processing Grief with Third Culture Kids*, Fort Mill, SC: Independently published, 2021.

Wells, Lauren, *Unstacking Your Grief Tower: For Adult Third Culture Kids*, Fort Mill, SC: Independently published, 2021.

Whaley, Joachim, *Germany and the Holy Roman Empire: Volume I: Maximilian I to the Peace of Westphalia, 1493–1648*, Vol. 1, Oxford: Oxford University Press, 2012.

White, Landeg, *Magomero: Portrait of an African Village*, New York: Cambridge University Press, 1987.

Wiest, Jean-Paul, 'Catholic Activities in Kwangtung Province and Chinese Responses, 1848–1885', PhD diss., University of Washington, 1977.

Willmott, Hugh, *The Dissolution of the Monasteries in England and Wales*, Sheffield: Equinox, 2020.

Willoughby, William Charles, *The Soul of the Bantu: A Sympathetic Study of the Magico-Religious Practices and Beliefs of the Bantu Tribes of Africa*, Garden City, NY: Doubleday, 1928.

Winroth, Anders, *The Conversion of Scandinavia: Vikings, Merchants and Missionaries in the Remaking of Northern Europe*, London: Yale University Press, 2012.

World Missionary Conference 1910, *Report on Commission I: Carrying the Gospel to All the Non-Christian World*, Edinburgh: Anderson & Ferrier Oliphant, 1910.

World Missionary Conference 1910, *Report on Commission IV: The Missionary Message in Relation to Non-Christian Religions*, Edinburgh: Anderson & Ferrier Oliphant, 1910.

Wright, Jonathan, *God's Soldiers: Adventure, Politics, Intrigue, and Power – A History of the Jesuits*, London: Image Books, 2005.

Wright, N. T. and Michael F. Bird, *Jesus and the Powers: Christian Political Witness in an Age of Totalitarian Terror and Dysfunctional Democracies*, London: SPCK, 2024.

Zurlo, Gina A., Todd M. Johnson and Peter F. Crossing, 'World Christianity and Mission 2020: Ongoing Shift to the Global South', *International Bulletin of Mission Research* 44, no. 1 (2020), pp. 8–19.

Index of Names and Subjects

Achebe, Chinua 186
'Africa for the African' (Joseph Booth) 32, 34–6
Alexander the Great 48, 66, 76
Alexander VI 85–6, 90, 120–1
Alexandria 4, 42–4, 58–9, 63, 66–7, 76, 78, 204–5
All Africa Conference of Churches (AACC) 192–3
Anderson, Gerald 191
animism 95, 174–6
Apartheid 16
Archelaus 43, 46–7, 49–50, 64
Aslan, Reza 56
Athanasius 74
Augustus 42–4, 46–7, 50, 53–4, 64, 77, 89
Azusa Street 194

Bahamas 81, 86
Baptist Missionary Society 133, 156
Benin 13, 36
Berlin Conference 99
Beti, Mongo 135, 187
Black Lives Matter movement 9, 137, 147
Blantyre, Malawi 26, 34
Booth, Joseph ('Africa for the African') 34–7
BRICS 138
British Raj 130–1, 160

Bruce, Alexander Livingstone 27, 128
bull (Papal) 84, 87, 90–1, 109, 119, 120, 124

Caesarea (Maritima) 70–2
Caesarea Philippi 49, 67
Cao, Diogo 81
Cape Town 60, 165
Carey, William xiii, 10, 123, 130, 133, 135
Chilembwe, John 2, 32–3, 37, 128
Chilembwe's Uprising (1915) 2, 33, 128
Chupanga 28
Christianity *see also* 'Three Cs'
  Africanize 190, 195
  and colonialism 12, 37, 131, 168, 187, 189
  decolonizing of 7, 188, 193
  and Europe 13, 37, 77, 79, 100, 117, 138, 155, 179n19
  growth, spread of xii, 3–7, 11, 31, 37, 62, 117, 129, 130–1, 134–5, 137, 143, 173, 205
  imperialize, imperialization 131
Church
  African independent 7, 32, 194, 195, 197
  Early Church 41, 68–9
  Ethiopian 75, 195, 200n48

expansion of 5, 12, 31
militant 115–17, 118, 121
missional church 170–3, 181n62
Roman Catholic 73, 84–6, 108, 109–10, 112–13, 121–2
zionist 195, 200n48
Church Missionary Society (CMS) 5, 133–4
Civilizing Mission 4, 8, 91–4, 136, 161
Clement XIV 123
Cleopatra 42, 50, 76–7, 89
Colenso, Bishop William 10, 35, 38
Cook, James 135
Columbus, Christopher 1, 79–83, 86, 90, 100, 104
Constantine xii, 3, 5, 62–3, 87–90, 118
Constantinople 3, 77, 80, 83–4, 86–7, 89–90, 104, 108–9, 118–21, 126, 143
Constitutions (of the Society of Jesus) 110, 113, 116
Council of Mantua 119
Council for World Mission 134
Critical Race Theory 9
crusade(s) 37, 87, 89, 111, 117–18, 121, 131, 153, 162

Dark Continent 99 *see also* Stanley, Henry Morton
Darwin, Charles 174
de las Casas, Bartolomé 10, 82
Desert Fathers and Mothers 73
Dias, Bartolomeu 81
diaspora 43, 60, 62, 66–70, 101, 157, 169, 194
diversity 9, 167, 168
Doctrine of Discovery 4, 87, 90
Drumont (Father) 187–8

Edict of Milan 88–9, 131
empire 15, 18, 36, 37, 80, 88–90, 134, 135, 137–8, 153, 167, 189, 195, 204–5, 207
  American, US xii, 11, 138, 163
  British 6, 30, 39n27, 130, 160, 202
  Byzantine xii, 76–8, 83, 90
  Carthaginian 77
  Ottoman 77, 79, 83, 87, 89, 90, 119–21
  Roman xii, 3–4, 15, 41–63, 69, 73, 75, 76–7, 80, 87–9, 117, 121, 131, 203, 204–5, 206
Erasmus, Desiderius 118
Eusebius 88
Evangelicalism 148, 150, 166–9, 181, 194, 197
expansionism xii, 4–5, 7, 15, 16, 80, 100, 130
Exposcit Debitum 109–10

Ferdinand (King of Castille) 82–3, 90
Festus 72
First World War 32–4, 136, 180
Fletcher, Holly Berkley (*The Missionary Kids*) 148–9
Formula of the Institute 109–11, 113–15
Fort Jesus 100

Galilee of the Gentiles/Nations 42–9, 51–2, 54, 59–62, 65, 67–8
Gatu, John 190–4
Graham, Billy 164, 197
Gibraltar, 79–80

Haddis, Mekdes (*A Just Mission*) 147, 177n9
Hasmonean Dynasty 41–2

INDEX OF NAMES AND SUBJECTS

Hannington, Bishop James 3
Hegel, Georg F. W. 95
Henry VIII 110
Herod I (the Great) 42–51, 54–6, 64, 66–7, 204
Herod Antipas 43, 45–7, 51, 60, 64
Hume, David 97–8
Huntington, Samuel 94, 138

Iberia 80, 138
Idowu, E, Bolaji 181, 188–90, 196
Ignatius of Loyola 100, 109, 111–12, 114, 116–18, 122
Spiritual Exercises 108–9, 116
imperialism xii, 5–6, 11, 15–16, 59, 63, 87, 94, 130, 157, 161, 167, 180, 191–2, 204
Inter Caetera 85–7, 90, 91
Isabella (Queen of Castille) 81–3, 86, 90
Islam 48, 77–9, 121, 136–7, 175–6

Jerusalem 41–52, 66–72, 204–6
Jesuits 74, 91, 99–100, 108–18, 121–3, 131, 183 *see also* Society of Jesus
vows 113–15, 123
John the Baptist 43, 45, 51
Julius Caesar 42, 44, 53, 89

Kant, Emmanuel 97–8
Kato, Byang 181, 194, 196–7
Kenyatta, Jomo 129
Kipling, Rudyard 92
Knights Templar 81, 103
Krapf, Ludwig 135
Kuruman 22–3

Lausanne Movement 164–5
Leopold II (King of Belgium) 36

Linyanti 23, 28
Livingstone
Agnes 27, 31
David (*Missionary Travels and Research in South Africa*) 2, 3, 18, 20–34, 37
William J. 2, 27, 32–3
Luther, Martin 108, 110–12, 117–18, 121, 185

Mackenzie, Charles 3, 26
Maghreb 78
Magomero 3, 26–7, 32, 34, 37, 128–9
Malawi 2, 3, 8, 20–1, 25, 26–8, 31–2, 33–6, 128–9, 154, 167, 178n13
Manila 165
Mark Antony 42, 50
Maxentius 87
Mazrui, Ali 184, 187
Mbiti, John 176, 181, 185–6, 188, 190, 196
Mehmed 84, 108, 120–1, 126
Messiah 2, 17, 32, 43, 47, 49, 55, 56, 61, 63, 64, 69, 137, 172, 203, 205, 206
military language xii, 108, 115, 116, 117, 123
Military Order of Christ 81
Missio Dei 162, 181n62
mission
diaspora 157, 169, 194
history of xii, 1, 2, 3, 6, 9–10, 12, 15, 108, 130, 134, 143, 158, 202
reverse 169
war and conquest xii, 81, 116, 137, 196
missionary kids 148, 150–1 *see also* Fletcher, Holly Berkley
Missionary Kids Safety Net 148

221

Moffat
  Mary 3
  Robert 3, 22–3
monks 74–5, 115, 122
moratorium 5, 165, 190–3

Nacpil, Emerito 191
Neill, Stephen (*Colonialism and Christian Mission*) 5–6, 130
Newbigin, Lesslie 170–1
Ngũgĩ wa Thiong'o 186–7
Nicholas V 84, 89–90, 100, 103, 118–19, 121, 131, 147, 153, 161, 168
  Dum Diversas 84, 87, 89–90, 118, 147, 153, 157
  Romanus Pontifex 84, 87, 90
Nyasa (Lake) 25–6, 28
Nyasaland 21, 26, 33, 39–40, 93, 184

Orwell, George (*Animal Farm*) 16
Oyono, Ferdinand 187

Park, Mungo 135
Parrinder 189, 198
Paton, Alan 186
Paul (Apostle) 69–74
Paul III 109, 110, 114, 117, 122
Pax Romana 50, 56, 69, 89
Pentecost 69
Pentecostal 133, 173, 189, 194–5, 197
Philo of Alexandria 67
Pilate, Pontius 43, 45, 47, 51, 53–4, 56, 58, 60, 65
Polo, Marco 79–80, 103
Pompey 41–3, 46, 50, 57
Prester John 80–1, 87
Prince Henry (the Navigator) 80, 85, 90

Rashidun Caliphate 78
Redeemed Christian Church of God (RCCG) 195
Reformation 74, 108–12, 121–2
Regimini Militantis Ecclesiae 109, 112–15, 117, 157
Rhodes, Cecil 36, 40, 93
Roman Counter-Reformation 110–13

Saint Anthony (the Great) 73–5
Saint Paul of Thebes 73, 75
Saint Robert 121
Sahel 175
Sanneh, Lamin (*Translating the Message*) 7
Saviourism, white 148
Scramble for Africa 31, 161, 203
Seoul 60, 165
Sixtus IV 86, 120
slave trade 13, 16, 24–31, 80, 95, 99
Slave Bible 7, 129
slavery 129, 140, 158, 160, 168
Society of Jesus *see also* Jesuits 100, 108–9, 112–14
soldier(s) xi, xii, 12, 43, 48, 49, 54, 58, 62–3, 76, 81, 87, 89, 90, 103n18, 108–23, 153, 157, 187, 203
Stanley, Brian (*The Flag and the Bible*) 5, 93, 143
Stanley, Henry Morton (*Through the Dark Continent*) 21, 99

Taylor, John V. 197
theology
  contextual 154
  intercultural 202
  mission 17, 165, 206
  missional 171

INDEX OF NAMES AND SUBJECTS

'Three Cs' 31, 158–61
Thirty Years War 116
Tiberius 43–5, 47, 50, 54, 62
Tylor, Edward B. 174–5

Universities' Mission to Central Africa (UMCA) 26
Unreached People Groups 101, 107, 161–2, 165–6
Ummayad Caliphate 78
Uthman (Caliph) 78

Victoria Falls 23, 25
Voyages of Discovery 83–4, 91

Walls, Andrew (*Globalizing Theology*) 93–4, 134, 136, 144, 173
White Supremacy 4, 17, 129, 152, 157, 186

Wilberforce, Bishop Samuel 159–60
Winter, Ralph 162, 165
Wittenberg 108, 110
World Council of Churches (WCC) 165–6
World Evangelical Alliance (WEA) 164 *see also* Lausanne Movement
World Missionary Conference 161, 175

Xavier, Francis 10

Zambezi River 20–1, 23–5, 28, 34, 158
Zanzibar 26
Zimbabwe 13, 23, 24, 25, 29, 36, 134, 154, 158
Zomba 32–4

www.ingramcontent.com/pod-product-compliance
Lightning Source LLC
LaVergne TN
LVHW090413310825
819854LV00003B/74